THE NEW
GRAND STRATEGY

THE NEW GRAND STRATEGY

RESTORING AMERICA'S PROSPERITY, SECURITY, AND SUSTAINABILITY IN THE 21ST CENTURY

MARK MYKLEBY, PATRICK DOHERTY, AND JOEL MAKOWER

St. Martin's Press
New York

THE NEW GRAND STRATEGY. Copyright © 2016 by Mark Mykleby, Patrick Doherty, and Joel Makower. All rights reserved. Printed in the United States of America. For information, address St. Martin's Press, 175 Fifth Avenue, New York, NY 10010.

www.stmartins.com

Design by Letra Libre, Inc.

Library of Congress Cataloging-in-Publication Data

Names: Mykleby, Mark G., author. | Doherty, Patrick C., author. | Makower, Joel, 1952– author.

Title: The new grand strategy : restoring America's prosperity, security, and sustainability in the 21st century / Mark Mykleby, Patrick Doherty, and Joel Makower.

Description: New York, N.Y. : St. Martin's Press, [2016] | Includes bibliographical references and index.

Identifiers: LCCN 2016000025| ISBN 9781250072306 (hardcover) | ISBN 9781466883895 (e-book)

Subjects: LCSH: United States—Economic policy—2009– | United States— Foreign relations—2009– | United States—Politics and government—2009–

Classification: LCC HC106.84 .M95 2016 | DDC 338.973—dc23

LC record available at http://lccn.loc.gov/2016000025

Our books may be purchased in bulk for promotional, educational, or business use. Please contact your local bookseller or the Macmillan Corporate and Premium Sales Department at 1-800-221-7945, extension 5442, or by e-mail at MacmillanSpecialMarkets@macmillan.com.

First Edition: June 2016

10 9 8 7 6 5 4 3 2 1

CONTENTS

PROLOGUE

HOW WE GOT HERE

THIS BOOK BEGINS IN THE PENTAGON. IN JULY 2009, TWO UNITED States military officers, a Marine colonel and a Navy captain, were sequestered in Room 2E928, on the second floor of the building's E-ring, the outermost of five concentric corridors, where the highest-profile work is done. There, just a few months into President Barack Obama's first term, Colonel Mark "Puck" Mykleby and Captain Wayne Porter were given an assignment by Admiral Mike Mullen: to create a grand strategy for America.

Not a military strategy. We already had one of those—several, in fact. Mullen was seeking a strategy for the next chapter of America's future.

At the time, Mullen was the seventeenth Chairman of the Joint Chiefs of Staff, the highest-ranking officer in the United States Armed Forces, nominated to the post in 2007 by President George W. Bush. He was no stranger to Washington or the Pentagon: in his previous role as Chief of Naval Operations, he already was a member of the Joint Chiefs. It was the culmination of a distinguished 40-year career, which also included assignments as Commander, U.S. Naval Forces Europe; Commander, Allied Joint Force Command Naples; and Vice Chief of Naval Operations.

As chairman, Mullen found himself frustrated. "I caught the Bush administration in the last 15 months, and they were beat to death," he recalled when we spoke with him in 2015. "Iraq hadn't gone well, and I wanted to know what Obama was going to do when he came in. What's the strategic approach?"

Up to that point, there was no strategy—at least, none that related to the twenty-first-century world Mullen and his troops were facing. America's Cold War strategic architecture remained largely intact, designed for a world that no longer existed. Our once-prosperous economic engine, built in the 1940s and '50s, had recently collapsed from too much debt—and the only way to keep the machine going was to feed it even more debt. Our foreign policy apparatus, devised to contain the tyranny of Soviet authoritarianism, was struggling just to preserve and defend the status quo in the face of far different challenges. By the summer of 2009, it was clear that the Cold War–era global institutions and capabilities, designed to control and coerce through military force and technology, were ill-suited to the current era. Our national security mind-set was reactive, able to manage crises as they arose but with no ability to envision, much less define, a new strategic era.

This was no idle concern. Our threat-centric worldview had very real consequences for the United States. We had spent the first decade of the twenty-first century focused on al-Qaeda, Iraq, and Afghanistan, running up trillions of dollars of debt fighting wars with little to show for it. Meanwhile, the rest of the world focused on the economic opportunity embedded in the resurgence of Asia, as well as the emerging threats from climate change and the opportunities for new technologies to help solve it. By early 2009, when Admiral Mullen met Barack Obama, his new commander in chief, America's post-9/11 worldview inspired little, if any, enthusiasm beyond our shores.

America was learning, sometimes painfully, that global dominance was not a sustainable strategy. Today's world is complex and dynamic, with constant change and uncertainty. Mullen wanted Porter and Mykleby to offer up a new, more relevant narrative of where America stood in the world and where it wanted to go—in effect, what the million and a half or so men and women of America's armed forces were fighting for.

"I had this constant need for a strategy and an inability to get interest from anybody—quite frankly, right up through the White House," Mullen recounted. "I wanted to know how I fit in. I had significant leadership responsibilities and I needed to know where to go. I needed something for the country."

He added, after a momentary pause, "Now, those are not words that come out of the Chairman of Joint Chief of Staff's mouth because that's what the president is supposed to do." But Mullen wasn't getting what he needed from the White House or anyone else.

He charged Colonel Mykleby and Captain Porter with the mission of creating a vision of the future. "First of all," he told them, "it's got to be different. And second, it's a lot bigger than just the military."

Those, in effect, were their marching orders.

FROM NARRATIVE TO STRATEGY

Mykleby and Porter set out to create the vision they believed Mullen was looking for. A month later, in August 2009, they emerged with a document titled *A National Strategic Narrative*. It outlined an approach "to achieve sustainable prosperity and security . . . through the application of credible influence and strength, the pursuit of fair competition, acknowledgment of interdependencies and converging interests, and adaptation to complex, dynamic systems—all bounded by our national values."

The *National Strategic Narrative* was intended to explain—both to the American people and to others around the world—the direction our nation would take in the twenty-first century. Porter and Mykleby felt that Americans were searching for a consistent, enduring path that not only addressed their interests of prosperity and security but also preserved and propagated their values and national purpose as delineated in the Preamble of our Constitution. They felt that America needed a clear, coherent, and compelling national design to carry us through the complexities we face today in order to lead us toward a better tomorrow.

Substantively, the *National Strategic Narrative* argued for a grand strategy that focuses foreign and domestic policies toward the common goal of building our national strength and credible influence. And in doing so, that strategy would allow us to adapt, compete, grow, and evolve in a manner commensurate with our values and sustain us over time.

In fact, the document cited sustainability as our number-one national strategic imperative for the twenty-first century.

Why should sustainability serve as the centerpiece of a new American grand strategy? The reason lies in its literal scientific definition. Sustainability describes the state in which biological systems are able to "remain diverse and productive over time." Porter and Mykleby believed this definition fit nicely into America's purpose: diversity fosters resilience, and productivity leads to growth—resilience and growth being two critical aspects of America's enduring national interests of security and prosperity. Equally important, "over time" reminds us that we must think and act in generational terms, not just in the here and now.

Porter and Mykleby saw the organizing logic of sustainability as key to rebuilding strength at home and informing our investments in education, training, the environment, energy, and America's crumbling infrastructure. By building this strength, the United States could once again lead by example and, through restored credibility and influence, shift global trend lines toward a more opportunities-based and positive future. In the simplest terms, by walking the talk here in America, our smart growth at home could become our smart power abroad. To support the transition to sustainability, the report called for a National Prosperity and Security Act, the modern-day equivalent of the National Security Act of 1947, which led to a major restructuring of the federal government's military and intelligence agencies following World War II.

Mykleby and Porter delivered their *Narrative* to Mullen in August 2009. Mullen liked what he saw but also recognized the political sensitivities of releasing the document, given what it said and that it was coming from the office of the military's most senior officer. As a result, Porter and Mykleby began seeking feedback from individuals within the executive branch and among Washington's many think tanks. Early on, they met Dr. Anne-Marie Slaughter, then Director of Policy Planning at the State Department. Slaughter rapidly became a key advocate for Porter and Mykleby and their *Narrative,* opening doors on their behalf within the Washington establishment.

Even though the *Narrative* reached the top levels of the Departments of State and Defense and the National Security Council, it was only a narrative, not a strategy, and did not lay out a prescriptive course of action. This was mostly because Porter and Mykleby, as uniformed military officers, could not and would not cross the established line of their professional responsibilities and prescribe domestic policy, which would have to be at the heart of any new grand strategy. That is the realm of civilian leadership.

As a result, even with Slaughter's help, the *National Strategic Narrative* languished in the Pentagon for almost two years. It wasn't until

2011 that the report was introduced to the public domain, when former California Congresswoman Jane Harman, in her capacity as the new head of the Woodrow Wilson International Center for Scholars, published the document and hosted a public debate on its merits, moderated by *New York Times* columnist Tom Friedman, who quickly became another key advocate for the *Narrative*.

Slaughter, by then a private citizen at Princeton University, wrote the foreword for the *Narrative* and argued forcefully on behalf of the paper during the Wilson Center debate, along with Friedman and Brent Scowcroft, National Security Advisor for both Gerald Ford and George H. W. Bush. Yet even with this support, the *Narrative* made little impact in Washington. In the end, the *National Strategic Narrative* was met with a big "So what?"

After a two-year push for an integrated strategic conversation, the situation became all too clear: Washington had allowed its strategic muscles to atrophy since the days of President Dwight D. Eisenhower, and there was, and remains, little will or capacity to actually do anything that resembles a grand strategy.

In 2011, after 28 years in uniform, Mykleby retired from the Marine Corps and joined the only civilian policy program in Washington that was working on grand strategy. Housed at the think tank New America, the program was founded by Patrick Doherty, a foreign policy and macroeconomics expert who had seen the need for such a strategy while working in conflict zones from the Balkans to the Middle East to sub-Saharan Africa.

Mykleby and Doherty worked out a simple framework for developing a grand strategy: identify the broad contours of a sustainable economic engine that could do the nation's heavy lifting and tailor the foreign policy to match. By the summer of 2012, they had a full outline. Wary of the vicissitudes of presidential campaign seasons, Mykleby and Doherty waited for the outcome of the general election in November.

President Barack Obama, of course, won reelection and immediately put out a call for big ideas to inform his second term. In the wake of Hurricane Sandy and with the government about to confront a "fiscal cliff," Mykleby and Doherty sensed the timing was perfect. In early November 2012, Doherty produced a white paper that described the "so what": a new grand strategy for the United States. By the end of that year, with the help of Lawrence Wilkerson, a long-time aide to former Secretary of State Colin Powell, and a handful of supporters in the Obama administration, their paper found its way to the Executive Office of the President.

The response from the administration was blunt: "Meets our ambitions, exceeds our expectations." The big ideas it was looking for turned out to be not so big after all—things like gun control, mapping the brain, and immigration reform. The administration was not expecting a full-on grand strategy. But something else in its response offered a glimmer of hope.

The administration challenged Mykleby and Doherty to produce three ingredients necessary for any administration to consider a new grand strategy: content, coalition, and an implementation plan. In other words, go deeper and broader on the concepts and create a political safe zone for politicians to come together in a bipartisan fashion so the country could begin to adopt a new grand strategy amid the hyperpartisan political environment. In 2014, certain that a Beltway-based effort was not possible, Mykleby and Doherty began that quest, launching the Strategic Innovation Lab at Case Western Reserve University in Cleveland, Ohio, in partnership with the change-management specialist Dr. David Cooperrider and, at the invitation of the university's chairman, Chuck Fowler.

Meanwhile, in 2013, Mykleby met Joel Makower, a celebrated writer and strategist in sustainable business and clean technology. His company, GreenBiz Group, is at the forefront of convening corporations, entrepreneurs, policy makers, and others to explore the technologies, business strategies, and new business models that align business objectives with sustainability and resilience. Makower signed on as a senior fellow at the Strategic Innovation Lab. Suddenly, the pieces fit together: a military strategist, a policy strategist, and a sustainable business strategist who arrived at a similar vision from different disciplines, perspectives, political leanings, even generations. That convergence led to this book.

This book is part of the years-long effort to take the *Narrative* to a deeper level. It tells the story of a grand strategy, born within the Pentagon, to recapture America's greatness at home and abroad by elevating sustainability as a strategic imperative. It aligns our enduring national interests of prosperity and security with a new framework that blurs the lines between domestic and foreign policy by addressing pressing economic, security, political, social, and environmental issues at home, and looking at how those issues impact and connect with the global community. It is an inspiring vision of what's possible when Americans hold an optimistic and opportunity-centric view of the future and come together to bring it to reality.

This book is divided into three parts: Part I provides the historical context—the role grand strategy has played in America's history to drive economic growth in a way that supports our national and global interests, and how we can use it again in the twenty-first century. Part II looks at the three pools of demand that represent a massive business opportunity, one that can provide the economic foundation America needs to be strong and resilient. Part III looks at what it will take to bring this scenario to life: the players, institutions, and financing mechanisms we'll need to deploy, and the role that Washington could—but need not—play.

This is no idealistic pipe dream or wonky policy prescription. The story that unfolds weaves together hardnosed economic analysis, a clear-eyed study of demographic and societal shifts, the implications of climate change and resource scarcity, a risk assessment of America's challenges and opportunities, and on-the-ground reporting of solutions that are already being implemented across the nation. By rediscovering the power and discipline of grand strategy—and taking responsibility for our future—we can reimagine the American dream and once again take on what Thomas Paine called "the cause of all mankind."

In many respects, the collaboration and ideas contained in this book represent the best of the America we intend to illuminate: a nation rooted in a deep and rich history, unbound in its vision, capable of turning seemingly insurmountable challenges into vast new opportunities, always seeking to be an example to the world.

THE NEW
GRAND STRATEGY

PART I

THE CHALLENGE OF A GENERATION

CHAPTER ONE

THE CAUSE OF ALL MANKIND?

WHAT DOES AMERICA STAND FOR?

At first blush, it's a silly question with an obvious answer. Of course, we stand for freedom. For democracy and free markets. For life, liberty, and the pursuit of happiness.

But what do we stand for beyond those worthy aspirations? What role do we want to play in the world? How do we want the world to view us? How do we want to view ourselves? These aren't easy questions to answer. There's no clear vision about what America stands for these days.

On the other hand, we've gotten pretty good over the past quarter century at saying what we're against: Terrorists and taxes. Big Brother and big government. Endless wars and election campaigns. High-priced gas. High-priced anything.

We're largely against change. We want to maintain the status quo at any cost, even if we're not completely satisfied with it (and regardless of whether maintaining it is even a realistic option). We have a painful nostalgia for the "good old days," even if they weren't all that good for a lot of people. Even those who look to the future do so along a fairly narrow path. We want the economy to "recover" to the way it was before 2008. We want to regain the sense of security we had before 9/11. And when we ask others—say, the Chinese or Iranians—to change, and they actually do it, we often don't like the result. It turns out we tend to like the *idea* of change more than change itself.

We also seem to be against competition. That is, we want America to be the best in every respect—*We're Number 1!*—but don't like it when others challenge us or, worse yet, outcompete us. When we do get bested by others, we seek to blame somebody, anybody—the president, liberals, conservatives, Congress, Wall Street, the media, immigrants—instead of looking in the mirror and taking stock of what we, as citizens, need to do to improve ourselves, our communities, and our country. We fail to remember that *competition* comes from the Latin word *competere*, which means "to strive together," usually for the attainment of some common goal. Instead, competition has become a zero-sum game, where we win only if others lose. That's fine for sports; not so much for economies and geopolitics.

We even seem to be against citizenship, at least as it relates to actively participating in a democracy. We've largely given up on our elected officials, and on elections themselves. Most of us don't bother to vote, or if we do, it's only every four years. We rarely show up for city council meetings or town halls, or otherwise speak out when we're dissatisfied or see injustice. At best, we'll grouse on social media in the hope that someone out there is listening.

Collectively, Americans have lost sight of any common vision or purpose that sets us apart. Yet politicians talk more than ever about American exceptionalism or crow that "we're the greatest nation in the history of the world!" We desperately want to believe that it's true, but it's not always clear that it is. We seem stuck between a nostalgically glorious past and a despairingly uncertain future. We know we can't turn back the clock, yet moving forward is proving difficult. There's a palpable sense of powerlessness among Americans—both leaders and the general populace—a feeling that the country has lost its compass, its mojo, and its way. We seem to have lost sight of the American dream itself—that by working hard and playing by the rules, anyone can create a better life for themselves, their family, and their country.

Most of us feel this despair in some way, even if we can't quite put our finger on it. Surveys since 2009 by Rasmussen Reports have found that only about three in ten Americans think the country is headed in the right direction and about half think America's best days are in the past. But we don't need pollsters to tell us what we already know. Every day, we see the evidence in our communities and our lives.

OUR NATIONAL PURPOSE

In these hyperpartisan times, one might think any assertion of national purpose would be controversial. On the contrary. The nation's founders believed a shared and enduring purpose was so important that they put it at the top of the Constitution:

> We the people of the United States, in order to form a more perfect union, establish justice, insure domestic tranquility, provide for the common defense, promote the general welfare, and secure the blessings of liberty to ourselves and our posterity, do ordain and establish this Constitution for the United States of America.

Those aren't just 52 well-crafted words. As Hubert Humphrey reminded us, they're a call to action and demand constant tending from all of us. The Preamble's six action words—*form, establish, insure, provide, promote,* and *secure*—are the great purposes of America's experiment in self-government. Each represents a thread that, woven together, creates the fabric of who we are and what we are supposed to do as citizens. They are the table of contents for America's user manual. As such, the Preamble gives the United States an irreplaceable endowment, a permanent keel to our ship of state. Through those six words, we know why we have a government. We have a test by which we can judge any given course of action. And in that light, these words not only express the promise *of* America, they also articulate our obligation *to* America.

Grand strategy is ultimately about creating the conditions at home and abroad in which we can live out that enduring purpose as a self-governing people. Eleven years before the Founders wrote the Constitution, Colonial America was more focused on one massive precondition for self-government. In 1776, Thomas Jefferson and the signers of the Declaration were focused on self-determination:

> We hold these truths to be self-evident, that all men are created equal, that they are endowed by their Creator with certain unalienable Rights, that among these are Life, Liberty, and the pursuit of Happiness. That to secure these rights, Governments are instituted among Men, deriving their just powers from the consent of the governed. That whenever any Form

of Government becomes destructive of these ends, it is the Right of the People to alter or to abolish it, and to institute new Government, laying its foundation on such principles and organizing its powers in such form, as to them shall seem most likely to effect their Safety and Happiness.

Jefferson, while acknowledging in his correspondence that he was "not an advocate for frequent changes in laws and Constitutions," noted that institutions must "change with the change of circumstances" and "keep pace with the times," adding, "We might as well require a man to wear still the coat which fitted him when a boy, as civilized society to remain ever under the regimen of their barbarous ancestors."

For some American generations, living up to the Declaration of Independence and the Preamble to the Constitution means going further than being educated on the issues, participating in civil society, and voting. Every so often, it falls to a particular generation to choose a new strategic direction and the governing institutions that support it. Every so often, we need a new approach to how we create the conditions at home and abroad in which we may live out that manifold purpose amid the unique set of challenges, opportunities, and knowledge that define the current era.

Over the past century, this was required in the midst of the Great Depression in 1933, at the advent of world war in 1941, and at the dawn of the Cold War in 1947–53. Not only did Americans respond to the challenges, internal and external, that threatened to derail our forward progress, we did so in a way that allowed us to continue advancing the Preamble's purpose.

This is one of those times. We, all of us alive today, are part of the next chosen generation.

IN SEARCH OF TODAY'S COMMON SENSE

"The cause of America is in a great measure the cause of all mankind," wrote Thomas Paine, a political activist, philosopher, and revolutionary, in *Common Sense*. His pamphlet, published in 1776 just before the signing of the Declaration of Independence, and 11 years before the Constitution, was a hard-hitting argument for independence. As we would say today, it went viral. It was sold and distributed widely and read aloud at taverns and meeting places. George Washington read it to his troops, who at the time had surrounded British troops in Boston.

Paine is credited with turning the tide of public opinion at a crucial juncture, making it "common sense" that fighting for independence was the only option to take, and it was an option that needed to be taken immediately. It was a call to arms that inspired British subjects in 13 of the 20 British colonial possessions in North America to seek independence from the Crown. Thomas Jefferson may have been the political philosopher, but Tom Paine was the campaigner, the master marketer who sold the "cause" of self-determination to enough fellow colonists to ensure the success of the revolution.

By so clearly asserting the right of self-determination as an unalienable human right, our Founding Fathers set in motion a wave that has leveled despotic regimes and empires throughout our history. The Civil War, the Great Depression, World War II, and the Cold War were clear-cut tests that challenged the very notion that a self-determined government of the people, by the people, and for the people could survive the realities of our world.

But survive we did. In the tests of slavery, depression, fascism, and communism, Americans understood that we faced threats so large that we rallied together as a nation to holistically redesign ourselves, to alter the form of our government, just as it's called for in the Declaration of Independence. It was in this way that we not only could meet and overcome the challenges of the day but in the process become stronger and more vibrant as a nation and as a people.

But since the end of the Cold War, the dynamics of the twenty-first-century world do not fit this twentieth-century template, no matter how hard we may try to force them into that mold. We've tried imposing a good-versus-evil, might-makes-right framework on the post-9/11 world. It has failed. We misdiagnosed the geopolitics of our perceived enemies and fomented a national obsession with threat and risk while America's economy foundered.

Is it that the authoritarian regimes have disappeared? Hardly. There are still billions of people living without the right to self-determination. Is it that there are no more threats to the United States? No again; there are plenty. But the global impact of these twentieth-century-like challenges are not nearly what they were at the height of the Cold War. In fact, these lingering twentieth-century challenges have been eclipsed by a far more complex and vexing global reality.

THE UNSUSTAINABLE NATURE OF THINGS

We can sum up the great challenge of our era in two words: "global unsustainability." We, as human beings, simply cannot continue on the economic, social, and environmental paths we've been on. And the cause we must embrace as a nation is to lead the world's transition to a more sustainable order. No one else is in a position to do this.

Global unsustainability is not an over-the-horizon danger. It is right here and now. It is causing Americans, and all humans, daily harm. In describing this challenge, we see four global dynamics—what we call "strategic antagonists"—that make the current U.S. and international order unsustainable. These intertwined and fused dynamics—or, more accurately, disruptions—make for an immense, wicked problem that is signaling that the global system is now in a process of disarray. Until the United States digests, processes, and addresses this wicked problem, the nation will face even more rapid degradation of domestic and global conditions.

In brief, these strategic antagonists are:

- **Economic Inclusion.** The great global project of the twenty-first century is no longer to stop communism, counter terrorists, or promote a superficial notion of freedom. Rather, the world must accommodate 3 billion additional middle-class aspirants in two short decades without provoking resource wars, insurgencies, and the collapse of our planet's ecosystems. Those 3 billion people are expected to increase their per-capita consumption by 300 percent, driving resource competition to the brink, with the potential for great power conflict over access to food, water, and other resources. That's on top of having to solve the growing issue of income equality here at home.
- **Ecosystem Depletion.** Climate change is outpacing scientific models while natural-capital stocks are being depleted below levels necessary for vital planetary systems to maintain essential ecosystem services. Climate change is the most pressing: Hurricane Sandy; droughts in California, India, China, and

Russia; accelerated polar melting; and record heat have become recurring headlines. With no further changes in policy, we could see warming of 6 degrees Celsius by the end of the century, with potentially ruinous impacts. Well before midcentury, we are likely to face widespread food insecurity, economic disruption, mass human migration, and regional conflicts as these critical systems degrade further. As of this writing, the ongoing situation in Syria, triggered in part by a three-year drought, seems to be showing us a taste of what is to come.

• **Contained Depression.** The extended crisis intervention by the Federal Reserve Bank and European Central Bank has failed to address the two factors suppressing aggregate demand: consumer deleveraging and a generational shift in lifestyle preferences. Central banks cannot generate the circumstances necessary to rescue us by reviving aggregate demand and restoring the economics of lending and equity investment. Congress can't either, as pumping more stimulus dollars into the old economic engine or fixing the federal debt won't, by themselves, do the trick. Consumer preferences have shifted such that pumping more money into the system, even directly into citizens' bank accounts, will have little lasting effect beyond propping up an unsustainable economy and adding to deficits.

• **Resilience Deficit.** The systems, supply chains, and infrastructure that connect our markets are fragile and prone to disruption. Today's corporate value chains are designed to increase efficiency but have little redundancy or resilience. During 2011 alone, Japan's tsunami curtailed production of auto parts used by all six major American and Japanese automakers, shutting down production plants across the United States and helping to drive up U.S. unemployment from 8.9 to 9.1 percent; flooding in Thailand led to global disruptions in U.S. computer manufacturing due to shortages in disk drives; and China temporarily shut off exports of rare-earth minerals—it possesses 95 percent of the global supply—leading to price spikes for such things as lightbulbs, wind turbines, and batteries. We no longer control our own destiny, and it's not limited to supply chains. Infrastructure arrears in the United States alone stand at $3.6 trillion to get the bridges, roads, railways, schools, ports, and airports that undergird the Cold War–era economic engine up to standard. Without rethinking and rebuilding these systems, we'll be forced to react to their breakdowns, some of them with tragic consequences.

Taken together, these four fused and interlocking challenges compose the global challenge of our time; it will require focused and determined leadership—and new forms of partnership—if we are to survive and thrive. To solve one requires solving the entire set. And for this we need to rethink the system.

THREE INTERNAL WEAKNESSES

Today, only America possesses the capacity, weight, and cultural wherewithal to lead change of that magnitude. To do that, we'll need to be honest about where we are at this time and place. We're not the best America we could be, and that is getting in the way of our taking on the heavy mantle of world leadership just when the world so desperately needs it.

Though it has become politically unpopular to say it, America's inability to adapt to these four strategic antagonists is weakening the foundations of America's security and prosperity and making the status quo untenable. Specifically, there are three internal flaws we must acknowledge and overcome.

1. OUR ECONOMIC ENGINE IS MISALIGNED WITH TODAY'S THREATS AND OPPORTUNITIES.

Today's economy evolved out of a different time and a different world order. It took shape during and after World War II and was designed explicitly to exploit postwar demand for suburban housing and consumer goods for Americans, and reconstruction materials for Europe and Japan. However, the conditions that allowed that design to succeed expired by the early 1970s, and its shelf life has been extended only by accommodative monetary policy and the accumulation of household, corporate, and government debt. Today, with rock-bottom Federal Reserve interest rates, Americans' debts exceeding their incomes, and extreme weather lashing U.S. cities, the country is nearing the end of the road.

A brief history is in order. World War II saw a massive move by Americans from the farms to the cities, where jobs abounded to produce war materiel. This was, in part, the Great Migration of African Americans who moved north seeking better economic and social climes. Most people stayed in cities after the war ended, at the same time that 15 million or so GIs came home to find work and start families. Suddenly, there was a shortage of urban housing, not to mention jobs, for all of the victorious soldiers, sailors, airmen, and Marines. The upshot: after a decade and a half of economic depression and war, there was a pent-up demand for housing and for life's essentials and luxuries.

Shaping this raw demand into a powerful economic engine required a little help from Washington, meaning demobilization was nearly as big an intervention as mobilization. The Servicemen's Readjustment Act of 1944, better known as the GI Bill, provided a range of benefits for returning veterans, including low-cost mortgages; low-interest loans to start a business; cash payments for tuition and living expenses to attend university, high school, or vocational education; and a full year of unemployment compensation. Suddenly, millions of Americans had the means to live out their version of the American dream: a house, a car, two kids, and all the furnishings and appliances you could imagine.

The result was an unprecedented housing boom, along with the birth of the suburbs. Beyond mortgage assistance, the suburbs were enabled in large part by massive government investments in infrastructure—streets, sewers, schools, and other underpinnings of modern communities—that enabled workers to live outside the city and commute "into town" for work. In short order would come the Interstate Highway System and a burgeoning car culture. Together they created mobility, both physical and economic, as Americans found themselves on the move outside of cities and into a new middle-class suburban lifestyle.

The Interstate Highway System would top out at 46,837 miles when completed in 1991. Total population increased nearly 60 percent between 1946 and 1979. Adjusted for inflation, disposable personal income would rise more than 400 percent over the same period. Between 1940 and 1980, home ownership increased by 20 percent. It was an unqualified boom period.

The massive pools of demand created by the combination of government policies and demographic shifts were buttressed by the reconstruction of Europe and Japan that took place after World War II. The investments were spurred by the $13 billion European Recovery Program, better known as the Marshall Plan, which funneled money to rebuild parts of Europe decimated during the war. The reconstruction that immediately followed World War II helped to absorb a lot of America's industrial capacity, which we were able to redirect fairly quickly, thanks to the cooperation of a Democratic president, Harry S. Truman, and a Republican Congress.

All told, it was a good quarter-century run of economic expansion and boom times, ending in the early 1970s. At that time, President Richard M. Nixon took the dollar off the gold standard, leading to the termination of the Bretton Woods system of international financial exchange, and the Arab oil embargo of 1973–74 put a chokehold on the world's energy supplies, contributing to the ensuing stock market crash, a bear market that lasted through 1974. When the Vietnam War ended in 1975, military veterans weren't greeted with hometown parades, though they did receive the same generous taxpayer-funded benefits as their World War II brothers and sisters. While the number of Vietnam vets—just under 9 million—was more easily absorbed into the now larger economy, the war's end did not have the same salutary effect on the U.S. economy; indeed, it severely damaged it. Unwilling to raise taxes to pay for a fruitless war, President Lyndon B. Johnson and Congress unwittingly had unleashed a cycle of inflation that would wreak havoc for decades.

Today's economy looks very different than it did in the days of gas lines and the American evacuation of Saigon. The telecommunications revolution that led to the Internet in the early 1990s brought people, businesses, and countries closer. Mobile communication has become dramatically cheaper and more accessible to nearly all. In 1980, there were five mobile phone subscriptions for every million Americans; today there are more than 90 for every 100 people. Energy prices have dropped in real dollars while energy consumption has tripled; the amount of energy it takes to produce a dollar of goods and services has dropped by about 35 percent since 1990, according to the Energy Department's energy-efficiency index. Since 2000, U.S. productivity has increased by a fourth, and by more than 80 percent since 1980.

Logically, these should be boom times, but they aren't. Real hourly wages were flat for the first 15 years of the new century, mitigated only by modest minimum-wage increases. The housing meltdown in the late

2000s cascaded through credit markets and the banking system, rocking the financial system at the foundation of the world's economy. The country has been clawing its way back ever since.

While some things have gotten better, we're not there yet. The economy is hamstrung by a phenomenon known as deleveraging.

The modern economy experiences two cycles of debt: short-term business cycles that produce the familiar oscillation between expansion and recession—bull and bear markets—and long-term debt cycles, which last roughly 75 years. During these longer cycles, the debt-to-income profile of the economy typically builds up a stock of household, corporate, and government debt that, over time, incomes eventually cannot service. The rebalancing from such indebtedness is called a deleveraging.

The present American deleveraging started in 2007, as rolling mortgage defaults undermined a system of extraordinary household and financial sector leverage, triggering a shift in debt from the financial sector to the debt-burdened federal sector through fiscal and monetary bailouts. Household debt—from consumer loans, credit cards, and mortgages—was not bailed out and remains high. This, in turn, drives household-level austerity, which reinforces a negative cycle of lowered demand, lowered employment, lowered asset values, and lowered tax revenue. As this negative cycle grinds on, middle-class expectations are dramatically reduced.

Other economic trends are also going in the wrong direction. The U.S. poverty rate was 15 percent in 2012, compared to 11 percent in 2000. Children are one of the most poverty-endangered population groups in America: since 2000, the child poverty rate has increased every year, from 16.2 percent in 2000 to 22 percent in 2015. The gap in income between rich and poor is greater in the United States than in any other developed country. America ranks around the 30th percentile globally, meaning 70 percent of countries have a more equal income distribution, according to the *CIA World Factbook*. We're not really looking like the Land of Opportunity anymore.

One result of all this is that aggregate demand for goods and services has dropped off a cliff. For example, the Consumer Price Index dropped from an average level of 3.8 in 2008 to −0.4 in 2009, the first time the CPI had gone into negative territory since 1955. Total home sales dropped two-thirds, from 1.05 million in 2006 to just 375,000 in

2009. The history of recovery is fundamentally a question of how you stimulate or re-create consumer demand so that it is natural and not propped up by government subsidies. That hasn't happened during the recovery. Even $4 trillion of a Federal Reserve monetary policy called "quantitative easing" hasn't been able to stimulate demand to the levels necessary to create a vibrant, self-sustaining economy.

The American dream has given way to an age of uncertainty. As a 2013 Washington Post–Miller Center poll exploring Americans' changing definition of success and their confidence in the country's future put it: "Although most Americans still think hard work and education breed opportunity, their faith in a brighter tomorrow has been eroded by intensifying struggles on the job and at home that have led some to conclude that the United States has emerged from the Great Recession a fundamentally changed nation."

2. OUR VIEW OF NATIONAL SECURITY IS WEDDED TO OUR TWENTIETH-CENTURY PAST, NOT OUR TWENTY-FIRST-CENTURY REALITY.

Up until Christmas Day 1991, when the Soviet Union's hammer-and-sickle flag was lowered for the last time over the Kremlin to be replaced by the Russian tricolor, the global security environment was fairly simple. There had been only three choices: the West, the Soviet Union, and nonaligned nations. For the United States, this meant a bipolar strategic environment. Further simplifying things, national economies were less entwined, and the nation-states exerted relative control over information, which equated to a monopoly of influence over the populations they needed to control. Perceptions could be shaped, media influence of events could be mitigated, and the relatively slower march and consistent familiarity of Cold War events allowed nations to address ongoing and emerging crises in a fairly predictable, even orderly, way.

Today, all that is up for grabs. The strategic environment, and national security in particular, can no longer be viewed strictly in the context of nation-states populating a unipolar, bipolar, or even multipolar world. Rather, the international geopolitical landscape has assumed an "apolar" complexion. We think of it as an interdependent "strategic ecology" with multiple supranational, nation-state, and nonstate actors competing for strategic access, influence, and leverage to address their own interests throughout the global system.

The fact is that "security" in the twenty-first century is not what that word meant in the previous century. National security, as defined in today's terms, can no longer be considered merely an issue of defense that begins at our shores and extends outward. Nor can it be viewed as strictly an issue that falls solely under the purview of our military.

Twenty-first-century security is more about the vibrancy and resilience of the essential systems operating inside and outside our national borders, which are intimately intertwined with the larger global system that constitutes human civilization—food, water, energy, education, industry, mobility, information, the built environment, and public health.

Yet, for some reason, we can't bring ourselves to have an adult conversation about what it means to be "secure" as a nation.

Take climate change. A 2015 Yale–George Mason University poll found that only 52 percent of the 63 percent of Americans who actually believe in climate change—about three in ten—believe that it is the product of human activity. As a result, there is little public discourse, let alone action, to address a problem that more than nine scientists in ten accept as factually grounded. If the French philosopher and mathematician Blaise Pascal were alive today, he would find our wholesale vacillation fascinating. Indeed, he would think we were nuts. Climate change, after all, is our modern-day version of Pascal's Wager, which posits that humans make the safe bet that God exists, even though this cannot be proved or disproved through reason. Clearly, we are not taking the safe bet with the planet's changing climate, even though it is essentially a scientifically proven fact.

Yes, the outcome of the 2015 United Nations climate conference, also known as COP21, appears to be a step in the right direction, but COP21's agreed-upon goals and targets don't get us on track to mitigate the effects of carbon in the atmosphere in this century. Moreover, it remains to be seen whether real action at the necessary scale will be implemented by the 196 signatory nations in a way that can ensure our collective security.

Still, the words *national security* get plenty of attention, particularly in the political season that seems to be constantly upon us. As voters, we collectively demand that politicians stand tough on national security. Yet we limit our definition of this term to those things we can find, track, fix, and finish—that is, whoever the "bad guys" are at any given moment. Accordingly, our political discourse invokes the specters of our worst fears, anxieties, and angst: al-Qaeda, ISIS, China, Iran, North Korea, Russia, or whatever new band of thugs is currently making trouble and headlines. Of course, we do need to vigorously defend ourselves against these threats; that is what defense is all about. But we have blurred the distinction between defense and national security so much that we tend to use the terms interchangeably. Being secure is about much more than vanquishing our enemies, real or imagined.

In a rare case of bipartisanship, this disconnect resounds on both sides of the political aisle. Conservatives want to reestablish American leadership—it's about leading the free world and spreading democracy, the longstanding Cold War mantra. For liberals, it's about strengthening the institutions that were created during the Cold War, with the global order hinging on principle-based decision making.

While those worldviews work reasonably well internally, they don't work outside America's borders. For one thing, they fail to recognize that the twentieth-century status quo really wasn't great for a lot of the world's people. Consider just a handful of statistics on where we are today:

- According to the United Nations Food and Agriculture Organization, almost a billion people suffer from chronic hunger and almost 2 billion are under- or overnourished—that is, malnourished, overweight, or obese. Kids are the most visible victims: Approximately 5 million children die each year because of poor nutrition, the human equivalent of more than 25 fully loaded 747 aircraft crashing every day. Of the world's hungry, 98 percent live in developing countries.
- Around 1.2 billion people, almost one-fifth of humanity, live in areas of water scarcity, and 500 million additional people are approaching this situation, according to the United Nations. Another 1.6 billion people, or almost a quarter of the world's population, face economic water shortage, where countries lack the necessary infrastructure to take water from rivers and aquifers and make it potable. In a warming world, almost half the world's population could be living in areas of high water stress by 2030, including as many as 250 million Africans.

- Around 1.1 billion people worldwide—roughly the population
  of India—lack access to electricity, with most concentrated in
  Africa and Asia, according to the World Bank. Another 2.9
  billion rely on wood or other biomass for cooking and heating,
  resulting in indoor and outdoor air pollution attributable for 4.3
  million deaths each year.
- Around the world, in developing and advanced economies alike,
  cities are struggling to meet the need for decent, affordable
  housing. If current trends in urbanization and income growth
  persist, by 2025 the number of urban households that live in
  substandard housing—or are so financially stretched by housing
  costs that they forgo other essentials, such as health care—could
  grow to 440 million, up from 330 million today, according to
  McKinsey & Co. This could mean that the global affordable
  housing gap would affect one in three urban dwellers, or about
  1.6 billion people.

Bad as they are, all of these situations risk being exacerbated by additional security threats, including cyberterrorism; "plain old" terrorism, including the proliferation of chemical, nuclear, and other weapons of mass destruction, some of which are easily transportable across borders; transnational organized crime, from human trafficking to political corruption; and infectious diseases, from Ebola to MERS.

And, as already mentioned, there's climate change. According to the Pentagon's *Quadrennial Defense Review*, climate change is now recognized by defense planners as a "threat multiplier" or an "accelerant of instability" because of how it influences a range of other, already existing threats. For example, a food shortage exacerbated by rising temperatures and population growth could lead to conflicts over resources, which may drive human migration to a more resource-rich area (as we've seen in Syria, masses of drought-stricken farmers move from rural areas into cities in search of nonexistent jobs, leading to civil unrest, antigovernment protests, and, ultimately, civil war and flight to European countries, overwhelming those nations' support systems). War and mass migration may further stress food and water resources in a given region, a classic vicious cycle.

The American Security Project, a nonpartisan organization created to educate the American public and the world about the changing nature of national security in the twenty-first century, produces the Global

Security Defense Index on Climate Change, an assessment of how much governments around the world consider climate change to be a national security issue, and how their militaries and national security communities have begun to plan for the impacts of climate change. The latest results, published in 2014, were stark: about 70 percent of the world's nations explicitly stated that climate change was a national security concern. Almost all nations with official military planning have stated that their government considers missions like humanitarian assistance and disaster relief to be critical responsibilities of their armed forces. That largely explains how leaders of nearly 200 nations came together in 2015 to agree on a framework for addressing climate change—the largest global agreement in world history.

The United States and most other major economies have little appetite for altering the global order and hence are doubling down on the old system, exacerbating trade imbalances and driving record resource extraction. As commodity prices rise, global powers hedge ever more aggressively, stockpiling resources and increasingly becoming entangled in conflicts in resource-rich areas—conflict minerals in the Congo, rare-earth elements in China, water in the Middle East, timber in Indonesia. As the global economy falters, unrest increases, and the great unresolved conflicts of the twentieth century—the Middle East, South Asia, North Korea, Taiwan, eastern Europe—grow increasingly enmeshed in the power dynamics of this new era.

Absent a new framework, the Washington establishment seeks to force old institutions into a new geopolitical puzzle. It assumes that having regional military commands and bilateral diplomatic missions is still a cohesive and coherent operating system. America's national security establishment can barely see the challenges of today, let alone predict the crises of tomorrow.

The result is that we're effectively undermining our national security in the name of defense by ignoring the unsustainable nature of our national and global system. Simply stated, we're depleting our national resources and bleeding our national strength by seeking to preserve a perceived status quo with an almost obsessive focus on threat and risk. This isn't to say we don't need a strong military. There are bad people in the world who are doing bad things and will continue to do so, and they need to be dealt with in no uncertain terms. But we need to strike the proper balance between national defense and national security.

Today, we try to control the uncontrollable without ever challenging the logic or efficacy of our actions. At the same time, we address only marginally the central root causes of the most problematic, complex, and very real challenges to national security, even though most *are* controllable: an exorbitant national debt and the real possibility of fiscal insolvency; waning global influence and credibility as a result of our perceived national hubris; suburban sprawl incoherently designed to accommodate cars rather than people; a gluttonous national lifestyle that creates systemic, preventable health problems costing us billions of dollars a year; farming techniques that degrade soil and damage natural resources; a food production and distribution system dependent on excessive subsidies; unsustainable energy policies and infrastructures that disregard the limits of Earth's ecosystems; a general disregard for the environment and an overt rejection of the responsibility to bequeath to our children a world worth living in; and a lackluster educational system, which has resulted in a general decline in national capacity to innovate and compete on a global scale. All of these, and more, are part of the security landscape.

We have to face the reality that the manner in which we—as a nation and as citizens—act and live has more to do with our national security than our military's ability to conduct large-scale combat operations abroad. Although we have the finest, most professional, most capable military the world has ever known—and it needs to stay that way—the enduring security of America in the twenty-first century will be found in thinking and designing anew for our current and emerging reality.

And just as America would never fight a twenty-first-century war with Korean War–era weapons, it should not govern with institutions devised for an era long past. The Founding Fathers established a Constitution that allows for the institutions of government to adapt to the knowledge, threats, and opportunities confronting each generation. We need to make use of that foresight.

3. OUR CITIZENRY IS DISENGAGED FROM PARTICIPATING IN THE DEMOCRATIC PROCESS.

An unsteady economy, frustration with the lack of progress in our overseas military operations and diplomatic endeavors, the growing gap between rich and poor, the flight of manufacturing overseas and capital

to the coasts, the seemingly limitless dysfunction of governmental institutions, the vast and growing sums of money being poured into elections—these and other factors have led Americans to largely opt out
of participating in the stewardship of their communities, states, and
nation. In essence, we've lost the visceral connection to what it means
to participate in a democracy—the essence of being an American. Our
relationship to our nation has been dumbed down. At the core, we're no
longer citizens—we're residents. We pay our taxes and that's about it.
(And we even complain about that.) We then consider our civic obligation complete.

We don't even vote, arguably the most fundamental privilege and
duty of a citizen in a democratic society. Americans are rightfully apa-
thetic, angry, and frustrated at the relentlessly negative tone of today's
campaigns, and at the unlimited and opaque contributions political candidates can amass under today's lax campaign-finance laws, leaving electoral power to the richest Americans. The decline in voter participation
over the past quarter century has been well documented, but it's worth
highlighting: general election voter turnout for the 2014 midterm elections was the lowest in any election cycle since 1942, when Americans
were preoccupied with a world war, according to the nonpartisan United
States Election Project. Just 36 percent of eligible voters—slightly more
than one in three—cast ballots in 2014.

Perhaps worse, the Millennials, our youngest citizens and largest
demographic age group, are tuning out. "If you are 24 years old, all you
know is petty partisan politics while big issues aren't getting addressed,
while the economy is still struggling," Trey Grayson, director of the
Institute of Politics at Harvard University, told the *New York Times* in
2013. "So you wonder whether the governing institutions of your country are up to the task." Harvard's survey, of more than 3,000 voters under 30, documented Millennials' antipathy toward government. It found
that faith in most major government institutions—with the notable exception of the military—declined over the past several years. Only 39
percent of young voters trusted the president to do the right thing, as
opposed to 44 percent in 2010. Just 18 percent of voters under age 30
trusted Congress, compared with 25 percent three years earlier.

Nonetheless, 96 percent of congressional representatives were reelected in 2014. This is attributed in part to something called Fenno's
Paradox—the observation that people generally disapprove of Congress

as a whole but support the representative from their own congressional district. It was named for political scientist Richard Fenno, who discussed this in his 1978 book *Home Style: House Members in Their Districts*. (The phenomenon has been applied to areas other than politics. For example, many Americans dislike their public school system but like the public school their children attend.) The reelection rate is also attributed to gerrymandering, in which state legislatures rig congressional districts to be deemed "safe" for whatever political party is in power. Getting a seat in Congress these days doesn't guarantee you a job for life, but in most cases it leads to long-term employment.

That furthers Americans' disengagement. If the incumbents always win, partly because they've rigged both voting and campaign financing in their favor, then why bother to participate? Of course, opting out of voting is itself a means of "voting"—in this case, with one's nonparticipation.

This doesn't bode well for any democracy, an observation noted more than 200 years ago by Jean-Jacques Rousseau, an eighteenth-century Swiss philosopher, writer, and composer. His political philosophy influenced the French Revolution as well as the overall development of modern political, sociological, and educational thought.

Said Rousseau: "As soon as public service ceases to be the main concern of the citizens and they come to prefer to serve the state with their purse rather than their person, the state is already close to ruin."

TAKING ON GLOBAL UNSUSTAINABILITY

So, once again, what is the "cause of America"? What do we stand for?

The cause of America will be found in taking on the immense global challenge of our age, global unsustainability—not by turning our backs on this reality. Our cause is to figure out a sustainable way forward and lead the rest of the world in that direction.

To do so, we need to get on with the hard work of fixing ourselves instead of squandering precious time on ideological debates and ineffectual dithering. This requires that we, with intellectual and emotional honesty, take stock of where we are, where we are going, and from where we've come. We need to look at ourselves not only from the perspective of America as defined by our national borders, but also as an actor in a global system, subject to forces and dynamics of a world in which we represent only about 4 percent of the population.

By demonstrating that we have the courage and vitality to reinvent ourselves, we can revive the quintessential American characteristics of innovation, optimism, and boldness that the world has come to expect from us. And, in the process, perhaps we'll even earn the credibility and influence needed to lead on the global stage in the twenty-first century.

If we can't convince ourselves to get moving, then we should listen to our allies. On behalf of her fellow Australians, Prime Minister Julia Gillard addressed a joint session of Congress in March 2011 with the kind of refreshing, bare-knuckled honesty that comes only from the best of friends:

> In both our countries, real mates talk straight. So as a friend I urge you only this: Be worthy to your own best traditions. Be bold. . . . The eyes of the world are still upon you. Your city on a hill cannot be hidden. Your brave and free people have made you the masters of recovery and reinvention. . . . I firmly believe you are the same people who amazed me when I was a small girl by landing on the moon. On that great day, I believed Americans could do anything. I believe that still. You can do anything today.

Indeed, we are those very same "brave and free people." In the end, we needn't accept that we are condemned to lie down in the collective grave of history's great civilizations. We have a choice to shape our trajectory and our future so that we don't just survive the twenty-first century, we thrive in it. All we need is a new vision, a shared cause worthy of our history and the generations of Americans that have gone before us—a cause that is aligned with the great purpose of America as set forth in the Preamble to the Constitution.

And to make that vision and cause a reality, our country needs a plan. That means we need to dust off the idea of grand strategy.

CHAPTER TWO

FOLLOW THE DEMAND

IN MAY 1940, WILLIAM S. KNUDSEN GATHERED HIS FAMILY IN THEIR Detroit living room and announced he was going to war. Knudsen, president of General Motors, wasn't actually going "over there" to fight—indeed, American troops hadn't yet joined the battles in Europe or the Pacific. Rather, he was going to lead the charge from American shores, helping President Franklin D. Roosevelt transform the American economy to become a driving force behind the war effort.

Signius Wilhelm Knudsen emigrated to the United States from Denmark in 1900 at age 20 and found work in Buffalo, New York, at a metal stamping company that made parts for early automobiles. Ford Motor Company, a leading customer, bought the company in 1911. Knudsen worked for Ford before moving to General Motors, where he became an expert in mass production. In 1924, he ascended to president of Chevrolet, at the time General Motors's worst-performing division, and in less than two years turned it into one of GM's most profitable. It earned him the moniker "the Genius of Production." In 1937, Knudsen was named GM's president.

Three years later, recognizing that government alone couldn't lead the charge to prepare America for what he saw as an inevitable conflict, FDR turned to the private sector to help America's transition to wartime footing. Specifically, he turned to "Big Bill" Knudsen. FDR appointed the 61-year-old executive to the newly formed seven-member National Defense Advisory Commission, created "to coordinate and organize the Nation's resources of men and materials for defense." In addition to Knudsen, Roosevelt assembled a blue-chip roster that included Edward R. Stettinius Jr., former board chair of U.S. Steel; Ralph Budd, president of the Chicago, Burlington and Quincy Railroad; Sidney Hillman, president of the Amalgamated Clothing Workers Union; Chester Davis, a member of the Board of Governors of the Federal Reserve; Leon Henderson, a member of the Securities and Exchange Commission; and Harriet Elliott, Dean of the Woman's College of the University of North Carolina. All were people who could think big and do big.

Given the enormity of their task, they were going to need to think really big and do even bigger. In 1940, the pull of war from beyond America's shores was growing stronger from both Asia and Europe, and America wasn't even close to be being ready. The U.S. economy still hadn't fully recovered from the Great Depression. Unemployment hovered around 14 percent, and exports and the Consumer Price Index were still below 1929 levels (though the gross national product was slightly higher). Beyond the economy, the U.S. military was in dismal condition. The United States could count only around 458,000 uniformed personnel, most equipped with second-rate legacy gear from World War I.

Moreover, given the circumstances—that the National Defense Advisory Commission possessed no formal authority to compel action; that the nation was overwhelmingly against getting involved in yet another European war; that no government official or institution seemed willing to take the political risk of actually leading; and that the private sector was generally not supportive of FDR and his initiatives—Knudsen's task seemed all but impossible. The only viable pathway for the commission members was to use their collective wits and will to redirect the industrial capacity of the nation toward preparing for a war that no one recognized, let alone saw, as necessary. As Arthur Herman noted in his 2012 book, *Freedom's Forge: How American Business Produced Victory in World War II:* "If the country was going to make itself seriously ready for war, neither the politicians nor the generals nor the admirals were willing to take the lead. American business and industry would have to figure it out on their own."

It was Knudsen who took on the burden of figuring it out. His role was to head the Production Division, charged with "obtaining fullest use of all available manufacturing facilities," including adapting existing factories and building new ones "in inland areas away from the usually vulnerable industrial regions," according to one of the commission's founding documents. Standing on, and risking, his personal and professional reputation, Knudsen set out to convince his corporate brethren to take on the burden of orienting the nation toward the national test that awaited it.

What Knudsen needed was the ability to place orders for goods and materiel in a strategic way. He needed to harness the initial Allied demand for war products and use it to prepare the American economy for the inevitable mass production challenge to come. As a businessman, Knudsen knew that American business would not survive if it were asked to pitch in as an act of charity.

The answer was to aggregate the orders for weapons and transport vessels coming from European governments that were placed even before the American entry into the war, and use them to optimize the American economy, turning it essentially into one integrated factory. At the time, Italy, France, the United Kingdom, and some of the Nordic countries had placed orders for a range of weapons, aircraft, and ships. The orders were relatively small and were placed with different companies, each of which had its own designs and parts. At the time, the U.S. Army had six arsenals that manufactured weapons, all with outdated equipment. The supply chain was extremely inefficient.

Understanding that mass production needed scale and standardization, Knudsen set out to convince Washington that the status quo had to change. He needed two principal tools: the cost-plus contract and the Lend-Lease Act. The cost-plus contract allowed civilian businesses to work for the government, convert to war production, and still be profitable. Profitability would be a critical issue because as demand for war production ramped up, the still-fragile levels of post-Depression consumer demand would flatline. The Lend-Lease Act put just enough control in the hands of the commissioners to let them overcome some of the competitive practices that were healthy in peacetime but unnecessary and wasteful in wartime. The act stated that any military orders placed in the United States would be taken over by the government, and the equipment either lent or leased to the foreign powers. That shifted the contractual relationship with American industry from a disparate group of nations to just one government buyer.

Effectively, that buyer was Bill Knudsen. America, Roosevelt announced in 1940, would become the Allies' materiel producer. And Knudsen was CEO.

By the time the Japanese Imperial Fleet surprised the American troops in Pearl Harbor on December 7, 1941, Knudsen knew how to absorb the massive new flow of resources that would be directed to building the American force and arming our allies for victory. As Herman pointed out in *Freedom's Forge:* "By the time of Pearl Harbor, America's war production effort was approaching that of Hitler's Germany. By the end of 1943 it was bigger than that of Germany, Britain, and the Soviet Union combined. By the end of the war, 70 percent of everything the Allies used to win World War II was made in an American factory."

No company exemplified the wartime transformation more than Knudsen's former employer. Seemingly overnight, General Motors plants that had once produced Cadillacs, Pontiacs, and Oldsmobiles were now cranking out tanks, aircraft, and munitions. Fisher Body began assembling the famous M-4 "Sherman" tank. Buick churned out 75,000 ammunition casings a month—12.5 million by the war's end. Cadillac made the M-5 tank. Chevrolet produced shells, gun parts, aircraft engines, and armored cars. Oldsmobile manufactured aircraft machine guns, high-precision aircraft engine parts, and millions of tons of forgings for trucks, tanks, guns, and aircraft. Pontiac made an anti-aircraft gun for the Navy and automatic field guns for the Army.

It wasn't just GM. The entire American truck and automobile industry converted to war production. So did the petroleum and chemical industries, the food and clothing sectors, and others.

In the end, it was Knudsen, a private-sector industrial leader, who spearheaded the notion of America as the "arsenal of democracy," a moniker he coined and that FDR leveraged to awaken a disinterested, if not a willfully unaware, nation to the realities of impending global war. During his Fireside Chat of December 29, 1940, FDR promised the desperate British that America would support their fight against the advancing Nazis, who by then had occupied much of Europe and were heading across the English Channel to threaten America's closest ally. "We must be the great arsenal of democracy," FDR proclaimed, and with that phrase, America set out to become the industrial machine that would sustain the Allied war effort for the duration of the conflict.

Once America was fully immersed in the war, Knudsen was commissioned a lieutenant general in the U.S. Army—the only civilian ever to enter the Army at such a high initial rank—and formally tasked to continue his work of building, expanding, adapting, and sustaining the industrial war machine he had created. In his creation, Knudsen, more than anyone else, set the foundation for a new American strategy—one that was big enough and powerful enough to meet the global challenges of his time.

Whether he knew it or not, Bill Knudsen was doing grand strategy, American-style.

RECLAIMING OUR KNOW-HOW

American grand strategy is about creating the conditions at home and abroad in which we can most effectively preserve and expand the Preamble's six aims. As practiced by Presidents Franklin Roosevelt, Harry Truman, and Dwight Eisenhower, everything was on the table. Grand strategy became *the alignment of America's economic engine, governing institutions, and foreign policy to meet the great challenge of the era.*

But today, in the United States, grand strategy is seen as just too damn hard. It tends to be addressed with excessive academic rhetoric, an aura of sage mysticism, or flat-out cynicism. "The world is too complex" is a common excuse for avoiding the task altogether. The result is that grand strategy isn't considered a pragmatic, actionable discipline by those who most need to practice it. True, Yale teaches a course on it. Numerous big-name, big-scale projects have studied it (such as the Princeton Project, in 2006). The Defense Department's war colleges discuss it. Policy wonks lecture and blog about it. Yet 25 years after the effective end of the last grand strategy, nobody is doing it. America is adrift.

The reason is relatively simple to trace. Washington stopped "doing" grand strategy in 1961. Eisenhower's conception of containing communism was so successful in making America more prosperous and secure that the 1960 presidential candidates, John F. Kennedy and Richard M. Nixon, argued not about differing visions, but which man would implement Ike's plan better.

Ultimately, all presidents from JFK to George H. W. Bush would accept the broad strategy of containment: defeat the Soviets in a contest of economic and political systems while actively containing their moves on the global chessboard. The better we lived the American dream, the greater the contrast with the underperforming Soviet economy, and the more resources we had to stop their international advances, the sooner communism would collapse.

The strategy fit both the external threat and domestic zeitgeist well. So well, in fact, that when he became president, Kennedy, a former Navy lieutenant, dismantled his five-star predecessor's strategy and plans division of the National Security Council, which had paid full-time attention to the strategic horizon and America's grand strategy. Some scholars argue that Kennedy and his whiz kids simply had no experience running a high-level planning staff and did not understand how to use the tool. Whatever the reason, we took our collective eyes off the long-term prize, which, in 1961, had little apparent practical cost.

But there was a cost. The remaining half of the National Security Council staff, the Operations Directorate, focused on emerging and active crises. But focusing only on crises meant we could no longer look to the horizon to identify the slower-moving, higher-mass challenges that shaped the strategic landscape within which America and all nations must operate. The result: Washington has pretty much forgotten how to think strategically. And over time, our inability to see the bigger picture has cost us dearly. We could not see beyond the U.S.-Soviet narrative and missed the deep changes in the global economic environment that led to the lost economic decade of the 1970s, and to the rise of terrorism. Most tellingly, we could not see the end of the Soviet Union.

It's critical to understand that we got through the last century because we knew how to do grand strategy, and do it well. More important, we must recognize that we can and need to do it today. The world is not "too complex." Our past leaders made global decisions without the benefit of computers or the Internet, or really much data at all, compared to the rich insights we can draw on today. To get there, we must keep an eye on our purpose, filter out the noise to focus on the strategic drivers, then make choices that enable, not constrain, innovation at every level.

In other words, we don't have to reinvent the wheel. A quintessentially unique American method of grand strategy already exists. We have leveraged it to great effect in our past and can leverage it now for our future. We just need to update it for the twenty-first century.

AMERICA'S STRATEGIC COMING OF AGE

The two defining examples of American grand strategy are World War II and the Cold War. To meet the global challenges of both, America's leaders had to think on a scale that hadn't previously been contemplated. Everything had to be on the table: foreign policy, governance, economics. And though Hollywood lionizes the military dimensions of these fights, in both cases, we leaned on our economy first. Leveraging the power of industry has always been one of the nation's most effective tools during times of great challenge.

In fact, the key to American strategic success in World War II was to let the economy do the heavy lifting. We had to outproduce the Axis powers before engaging them on the battlefield. At the center was Bill Knudsen's system of production. It was organized by business leaders to deliver an unprecedented volume of armaments while preserving private business. Instead of nationalizing industry, we used the cost-plus contract. But even the government had to pay its bills. In 1942, Washington expanded the income tax, increasing individual and corporate income tax rates, reducing the personal exemption amount, and imposing a 5 percent "Victory Tax" on all individual incomes over $624. With the nation at full employment, it was an effective way of raising revenue and avoiding the kind of debt buildup that could lead America back to a depression.

For that system to succeed, the civilian economy needed some help from Washington. According to Terrence H. Witkowski, professor of marketing at California State University, Long Beach, writing in the academic journal *Advances in Consumer Research*, World War II "required a great mobilization of American society, directed and financed by the federal government and conducted through businesses, the media, and numerous local institutions." The War Production Board allocated scarce materials and limited the production of civilian goods, while the Office of Price Administration imposed price freezes and forced housewives to live with a complex system of rationing. "People were bombarded with messages asking them to be frugal, to recycle, and to produce at home more of what they consumed," wrote Witkowski. "'Produce and

Conserve, Share and Play Square,' exhorted one War Food Administration slogan. Finally, gasoline shortages forced consumers to shop closer to home, helping small grocers, and wartime scarcity necessitated changes in product and packaging materials, forms, and colors."

All of this radically transformed the U.S. economy. Among other things, it definitively ended the Great Depression. By war's end, American manufacturing represented 50 percent of global production, and we were producing 40 percent more food than we could consume. But just as fast as it arrived, it ended. Less than four years after Pearl Harbor, Germany and Japan had surrendered. The great economic engine that had lifted America out of the Depression threatened to sputter to a stop. Whatever the postwar world would look like, America would need a new strategic direction and a massive source of demand to fuel it in order to avoid the reemergence of breadlines and soup kitchens.

We quickly found both the direction and the demand.

A STRATEGIC DIRECTION IS BORN

The Cold War featured a different kind of global adversary: the Soviet Union. Its left-wing ideology approached global expansion differently than the far-right monsters of Nazi Germany and Imperial Japan. Subversion was more appealing than blitzkrieg to the politburo in Moscow. With the advent of nuclear weapons, we recognized that direct military action against the Soviets in their Eurasian stronghold would be foolhardy at best and, once the Russians produced an atomic bomb, potentially devastating to both sides. Instead, we recognized that we had to contain the Soviets and defeat them in a contest of economic and political systems. We had to see which one—communism or capitalism—was more economically and socially sustainable, and could survive the test of time.

Those were the conceptual underpinnings of America's postwar strategy of containment, authored largely by George F. Kennan, an American diplomat and historian.

In early 1946, while serving as America's chargé d'affaires in Moscow, Kennan sent an 8,000-word telegram to the U.S. State Department in response to a request by the United States Treasury to explain why the Soviets were not supporting the newly created World Bank and International Monetary Fund. He began by explaining that his answer "involves questions so intricate, so delicate, so strange to our form of thought, and so important to analysis of our international environment that I cannot compress answers into single brief message without yielding to what I feel would be a dangerous degree of oversimplification." Kennan's five-part response outlined his opinions of the Soviets. His ideas, which became the basis of the Truman administration's foreign policy, first came to public attention in 1947 in the form of an article, which he penned pseudonymously, in the journal *Foreign Affairs.*

"The main element of any United States policy toward the Soviet Union must be that of a long-term, patient but firm and vigilant containment of Russian expansive tendencies," Kennan wrote. To that end, he called for containing "Soviet pressure against the free institutions of the Western world" through the "adroit and vigilant application of counter-force at a series of constantly shifting geographical and political points, corresponding to the shifts and maneuvers of Soviet policy." Such a policy, Kennan predicted, would "promote tendencies which must eventually find their outlet in either the break-up or the gradual mellowing of Soviet power."

For this to happen, Kennan recognized that the U.S.-Soviet contest would be decided by the internal success of America: "It is . . . a question of the degree to which the United States can create among the peoples of the world generally the impression of a country which knows what it wants, which is coping successfully with the problems of its internal life and with the responsibilities of a world power, and which has a spiritual vitality capable of holding its own among the major ideological currents of the time."

It is hard to imagine a public official writing something like this even today, and it was controversial from the get-go, including among those within the Truman administration. The idea of "containment" led to a rift between Kennan and Paul Nitze, Kennan's successor as Director of the Policy Planning Staff at the State Department. Nitze saw the Soviet threat primarily in military terms and interpreted Kennan's call for "the adroit and vigilant application of counter-force" to mean the use of military power. In contrast, Kennan, who considered the Soviet threat to be primarily political, advocated economic assistance—the Marshall Plan was a prime example—and "psychological warfare" through overt propaganda and covert operations to counter the spread of Soviet influence without having to resort to lethal weapons.

The debate over containment wasn't settled until 1953, when Eisenhower called for and directed Project Solarium. Solarium was an exercise in which teams from the Strategy and Plans Directorate of the National Security Council withdrew to Fort McNair, just a couple miles from the U.S. Capitol, to develop the best possible case for three separate strategic options: rollback (then favored by Secretary of State John Foster Dulles), Kennan's version of containment, and Nitze's different, more militaristic version of containment. In August 1953, the three teams presented their arguments to the president in the solarium on the roof of the White House. Two months later, Eisenhower signed NSC 162/2, which outlined the "New Look," or "long haul," strategy that embraced Nitze's more vigorous interpretation. At the same time, the emerging strategy made it clear that the United States would avoid a direct military confrontation with the USSR and that excessive military expenditures could actually hurt U.S. national security by undermining the long-term health and vibrancy of its economy. NSC 162/2 established that we needed to maintain enough deployed and deployable military strength, both conventional and nuclear, to keep the Soviets in a box, but the priority was on maintaining strong alliances around the globe and building our economy to outcompete the Soviets.

STRATEGIC DEMAND: THE ECONOMICS OF CONTAINMENT

By choosing to codify and relentlessly adhere to a grand strategy of containment, Washington essentially chose to embrace interdependent strategic challenges: mobilize the economy and beat the Soviets. Once again, the United States needed an economic engine to do the heavy lifting. Our civilian economy had to outperform and outlast the Soviet civilian economy while supporting a global military presence to contain Soviet influence. Since it was an open-ended contest, America needed to be fiscally prudent: every tax dollar spent on the military was a dollar that could not be spent on civilian services and infrastructure.

To make all this work, the American economy would have to be redefined for a second time in the twentieth century. That's exactly what we did.

The dawn of the Cold War paralleled one of the great boom times in America's economic history, as the postwar economy shifted into a period of unprecedented growth, spurred by pent-up consumer demand, to be quickly followed by the economics of the Baby Boom, the largest generation of Americans up to that point. The auto industry successfully converted back to producing cars, and emerging sectors such as aviation and electronics grew by leaps and bounds. The period just after World War II became known as the "Golden Age of Capitalism."

Our postwar economic boom was not a given. Historically, war debts often lead to periods of deep recession or full-on depression. Far from an accident of history, World War II's postwar boom was in fact manufactured, tailored to meet America's strategic requirements as they stood in the 1940s and '50s.

The end of World War II left America with three major pools of demand within reach, right when they were needed the most. First was housing. War production brought an estimated 5 million people off the farms and into industrial, and increasingly crowded, cities. Second was demand for consumer goods. After 16 years of austerity from depression and war, including four years of saving money to support the war effort, Americans had the financial wherewithal to buy just about anything—and just about everything needed replacing. Third was demand for reconstruction materials for Europe and Japan. Devastated by war and with no ability to produce food or manufactures, Europe and Japan needed American goods to survive.

The good news is that we were ready to take advantage of all this new demand, just in time for the Cold War to kick off. In fact, Washington began looking ahead to the postwar period only months after Pearl Harbor. In order to avoid crushing war debt, Congress enacted the universal income tax in 1942. The GI Bill—passed by Congress in 1944, even before the D-Day landings in Normandy—laid more of the foundation. Written by Topeka lawyer Harry W. Colmery, a former national commander of the American Legion, the bill was designed to make sure that World War II veterans did not have a reason to march on Washington, as their World War I predecessors had in 1932, to secure benefits for their service.

In 1945, the War Production Board became the Office of Temporary Controls, managing the material flows in the economy for another two years after the war's end. In 1951, President Truman pushed American industry into the suburbs to survive a potential nuclear attack, creating the federal incentives that fueled the early days of Silicon Valley and suburban industrial parks. In 1956, Eisenhower signed the

Interstate Highway and Defense Act to facilitate Americans' geographic expansion.

Suddenly, it was boom times. The nation's gross national product more than doubled in real dollars, from $1.27 trillion in 1940 to $3.08 trillion in 1960. The housing boom coincided with a significant jump in postwar births that lasted until the mid-1960s. That "baby boom" increased the number of consumers as more Americans joined the middle class.

Once again, the U.S. economy was leveraged to support America's foreign policy and military efforts around the world. According to the 2014 book *Crisis Without End? The Unraveling of Western Prosperity*, by Andrew Gamble,

> The western sphere of influence was organized as a liberal international market order, and its economy thrived under U.S. leadership, eventually outcompeting and outclassing the economy of the Soviet bloc, contributing to the collapse of the USSR in 1991. The command economy of the Soviet bloc could excel when all its resources were mobilized in pursuit of one goal, such as building a nuclear deterrent or exploring space. But it was poor at developing a diversified economy which could cater for multiple and changing wants, and it became both wasteful and inefficient, and no match for the consumer cornucopia that blossomed in the West.

By the late 1950s, America was a global economic powerhouse. The Big Three U.S. automakers sold more than 11 times as many cars as their three closest foreign competitors. Fully a third of all the machine tools produced in the world were made in America. Meanwhile, foreign direct investment by U.S. corporations skyrocketed, from $7 billion in 1938 to $32.8 billion in 1960, on its way to $82.8 billion by 1970. "The tentacles of U.S. corporate control reached into the interstices of every country outside the Soviet bloc," wrote Dana Frank in *Buy American: The Untold Story of Economic Nationalism*. "Coldly policing the 'free world' against the forces of Soviet darkness, the American corporations bought up the world, and the world bought American."

Back at home, the new consumerism was palpable. High and rising wages, growing families, and affordable cars led many Americans to migrate to the suburbs in search of a single-family home. With interstate highways reducing the cost of travel and technological innovations such as the invention of air-conditioning, the Sun Belt embraced suburban development: Albuquerque, Atlanta, Dallas, Houston, Miami, Phoenix, and other burgeoning metropolises in the South and Southwest all grew rapidly. As new, taxpayer-funded highways created better access to the suburbs, the geography of commerce began to change as well. Shopping centers multiplied, rising from eight at the end of World War II to 3,840 just 15 years later. Many industries soon decamped to the 'burbs in search of less-crowded climes.

The Soviet economy, in contrast, was "always on the defensive," wrote Andrew Gamble, and was forced to adopt severe protectionist measures to succeed, such as building the Berlin Wall to insulate the economy of East Berlin, the Soviets' zone, from that of the western side of the city. The economic success of the West's economy, particularly in Europe but also in East Asia, coupled with the system of military alliances and forceful interventions by the Americans, kept the Soviet Union largely contained and prevented it from expanding much beyond the sphere of influence granted to it by the Yalta Conference, convened in 1945 by the major heads of power to discuss Europe's postwar reorganization.

It took more than 40 years, but the gambit worked. By 1991, the Soviet Union collapsed under its own contradictions while the U.S. economy suffered only a mild recession. Once again, America, driven by its economic might, triumphed on the global stage.

The key to it all was converting a large pool of demand into the economic foundation of a world-changing grand strategy.

AMERICA'S UNDEAD POST–COLD WAR GRAND STRATEGY

Despite the peaceful collapse of the Soviet Union, America didn't demobilize the economy after the Cold War the way we did after World War II. Instead, we doubled down on it.

As Kennan made clear, America alone would not be sufficiently powerful to succeed in thwarting the Soviets. We would need to craft and hold together an alliance of capitalist nations that collectively outperformed the Soviet Bloc. What followed was fairly aggressive economic diplomacy. From the Bretton Woods Conference in 1944 to the General Agreement on Tariffs and Trade in 1947, America's leaders shaped, designed, and managed a new system of trade and exchange among the nations of the West. Representing fully half of the global economy at the end of World War II while at the same time propping up Britain and occupying Germany and Japan, the United States had a lot to say about the shape of that system.

That system had a purpose, of course: to build the capitalist West while ensuring that the American economy continued to enjoy favorable conditions. Sometimes, that meant allowing Japanese and European imports into U.S. markets to help them rebuild. Sometimes it meant opposing our closest allies, like the British during the Suez Crisis of 1956. Sometimes it meant exporting massive quantities of wheat to the Soviets, as we did in 1972. The shape of the international system and the management of it were always decided with one eye on the East-West conflict. But since the end of the Cold War, those policies have largely continued, sometimes boomeranging on America in a perverse way.

If we were going to make a post–Cold War economic transition, the textbook time to do it would have been just after the end of the Cold War, in the 1990s. Instead, after the wise moves of trying to smooth the transition of the Soviet Union and balancing the budget, we were distracted by Saddam Hussein's adventurism and the irrational exuberance of the dot-com bubble while Washington tried to turn the Chinese into capitalists and democrats through the same kind of trade and economic engagement that worked with Japan. Instead of a grand strategic reset, we got incremental changes in both the domestic and foreign policy.

That incremental approach turned out to be spectacularly misguided on both fronts. On September 11, 2001, 19 hijackers killed 3,000 people, shocking America into a series of ill-considered military interventions backed by rhetoric that conflated al-Qaeda and the global war on terror with the past challenges of World War II and the Cold War. Absent an economic strategy to underwrite multiple theaters of armed conflict, debts mounted. When oil prices doubled in 2007 in response to rising Asian demand, at the same time that interest rates were being reset on subprime adjustable loans, the Cold War economy finally collapsed.

For 25 years, since the fall of the Berlin Wall, the components of America's Cold War economic engine have been allowed to continue. Today, that economy is on monetary life support, incapable of serving the objectives of the Preamble we are honor-bound to advance. Misaligned with America's twenty-first-century landscape of risk and opportunity, that economy is, on balance, extracting wealth instead of creating it. Overseas, great economic imbalances are building to such an extent that no amount of military force can keep them from weakening America. The net effect has been that our economic, social, environmental, and political indicators are headed in the wrong direction. This is the world Admiral Mullen observed in that summer of 2009, when he summoned Colonel Mykleby and Captain Porter to reenvision America's grand strategy.

THINK ANEW, ACT ANEW

World War II and the Cold War presented both threat and opportunity, and applying grand strategy allowed America to align the two: you could defend the country while doing well. Consumer spending and consumption—and, by extension, industrial production—became so much a part of the American psyche that it rose to the level of patriotism. In effect, our national "operating system" leveraged the inextricable linkage and interdependence of the enduring national interests of prosperity and security. One feeds the other, and when they become imbalanced, it is time to update the operating system.

This is where grand strategy comes into play. Grand strategy is effective only to the extent it reflects the dominant conditions of the time. It needs to be refreshed from time to time, lest it become an outdated legacy of an era that has passed, dragging us down instead of lifting us up. "The dogmas of the quiet past are inadequate to the stormy present," wrote Abraham Lincoln in his annual message to Congress in December 1862. "The occasion is piled high with difficulty, and we must rise with the occasion. As our case is new, so we must think anew and act anew. We must disenthrall ourselves, and then we shall save our country." Lincoln was referring to the freeing of the slaves—this was just a month before the Emancipation Proclamation—but the words are just as relevant today when it comes to assessing America's place in a changing world.

Today, our operating system is out of balance. The enduring interests of prosperity and security are not working in concert, mostly because we are looking behind us, not forward. We have allowed threat and risk to become the drivers of our existence—so much so that we are expending our prosperity in the (mostly futile) pursuit of security that is mostly defined by our twentieth-century past, not our twenty-first-century reality.

Suffice to say, today's world has changed. There are no longer two sides defined by clear, conflicting interests. Rather, today's world is marked by a complex blend of conflicting, diverging, and, most important, converging interests that are being acted upon by nation-states, nonstate organizations, and even individuals. It's a global economy built of regional components, where centrally controlled commodities can roil world markets—witness Russia's use of natural gas as a pawn in its chess game with eastern and western Europe, the geopolitical leverage China enjoys through its majority control over rare-earth elements, or Saudi Arabia's insistence on doubling down on oil production even amid a global oil glut. Yesterday's grand strategy of "containing" competing superpowers is as outmoded as vacuum-tube TVs.

So, can we "think anew and act anew" about America's purpose? Arguably, we must if we are to regain our economic strength at home and our political leadership in the world.

To do that—to think and act at the scale needed to redirect America's economy, and to build the strength at home that gives us credibility and influence abroad—requires new visions and tools.

It's time to reboot America's operating system. And the good news is, we can start right now.

CHAPTER THREE

UNLOCKING THE NEXT BOOM

THE SINGLE QUESTION FACING AMERICANS TODAY IS NOT HOW TO strengthen the middle class or preserve American freedoms, though both are essential outcomes of any grand strategy. The core question is, What is America's role in the world? What strategy should replace the remnants of containment and ensure prosperity and security in the twenty-first century?

In our judgment, the answer is clear: America must lead the global transition to sustainability.

Why? The four strategic antagonists—the rapid economic inclusion of 3 billion people, climate change and the depletion of our natural capital, the contained economic depression, and the resilience deficit—are stressing our global systems and tearing at the fabric of our nation. The status quo cannot be maintained and is, arguably, already unraveling. Further, these four problems are fundamentally linked, forming the great global challenge of the era. Solving one requires solving them all. And, as we have seen throughout America's history, only when we address the cause of all mankind can our values and our interests converge.

What do we mean by sustainability? It's not just "green," though environmental issues are one part of it. Rather, sustainability describes a broad range of economic, security, social, and environmental concerns expressed throughout society. For example, American economists see the lack of aggregate demand and high levels of debt and are worried about the sustainability of the American economy. American political observers see the low voter turnout and low educational levels and are worried about the sustainability of our form of self-governance. Our military leaders see the high operations tempo and extended tours of duty and are worried about the sustainability of the all-volunteer force. Engineers see America's fragile infrastructure and the lack of funds to fix it and worry about the sustainability of basic public services. Our farmers see the loss of up to 75 percent of America's topsoil and worry about the sustainability of our food supply. And that's just here at home.

Our use of sustainability as the basis for a new operating system for America stems from the clear-eyed pragmatism seen in Colonel Mykleby and Captain Porter's original 2009 *National Strategic Narrative*. For the purposes of America's new operating system, we use their definition of "sustainability," which is rooted in science: an organism's ability to remain diverse and productive over time. This is true for any organism, from a simple plant or animal to a complex system with interdependent parts—from a gnat to a nation. So, America's new operating system must ensure that the United States remains diverse and productive over time.

Let's unpack that.

Diversity means we need depth, redundancy, elasticity, and resilience. In Mykleby's Marine mind that means, "We need to have the capacity to take a gut punch and come back swinging," whether that "punch" comes from a physical attack, extreme weather, a financial unraveling, an uncontrollable disease vector, political turmoil, or social unrest. But it's not just about the sudden jolts to the system. We also need to recognize and adjust for slower-moving punches that can be destabilizing, from the steadily incremental weather shifts of climate change to our crumbling infrastructure to the growing inequity between rich and poor. All of this is a part of what constitutes security in the twenty-first century.

We also need to be productive, but we can no longer afford to define productivity in strictly quantitative terms of GDP—a metric established in the caldron of the Great Depression that is primarily focused on money, goods, and services. We also need to think of productivity in qualitative terms, such as the long-term vibrancy, health, and prosperity of the nation and its people. The issue of quantity versus quality isn't a philosophical argument; it's an issue of math and science. We don't have unlimited resources, no matter how much money we have. Growth isn't always an option—or an improvement. It's really that simple.

Finally, we must do this "over time." We take that to mean indefinitely, without end, in the same way as President Eisenhower insisted on budgetary discipline in the face of that era's "long twilight struggle." Any new grand strategy must be prudent, stay within our means, and leave future generations in better shape as a result. After all, living the good life and improving the lot of our children is a key part of a sustainable American dream.

The challenges we face in the twenty-first century can be resolved only if America is able to count on the economy as a wind at our backs, a force that inspires a broad alliance of nations and peoples because it serves not only their core interests but also their greatest dreams. This is central to the American way of strategy. When we are at our best, we harness the American experiment in the pursuit of the long-term, enduring interests of prosperity and security for our citizens and, in so doing, for the rest of the world. An unsustainable international order represents the primary threat to our prosperity and security. Therefore, the United States has the right and obligation to lead the transition to a new order that creates the conditions conducive to long-term prosperity and security for all.

LEADING AGAIN

In the face of the present challenges and in the best tradition of the Republic, America's response must be to lead. The nation must put its own house in order and, with willing global partners, author a prosperous, secure, and sustainable future. And to lead the global transition to sustainability, we must walk the talk.

America can and must start at home. For a limited time, we will be able to transition our domestic economy to generate sustainable prosperity from deep pools of demand and underutilized capital. But this time, business must initiate the economic transition. Washington is too fractured and myopic, too unfamiliar with strategy, too cumbersome, and too cynical to take on this important task. The inertia of political ideologies from the left and right, still anchored in the logic of the last grand strategy, is too much to overcome through traditional advocacy. Business, however, is already experiencing the disruption, navigating the uncertainty, and eyeing the extraordinary opportunities to be had in a new economic engine. As we will describe in the following chapters, the way is clear for business to initiate the transition without any changes in current policy. And as business leads, Washington will inevitably follow. That's representative democracy at work.

Once America commits, with its credibility on the mend and its economy as a driving force, we must then lead a new global partnership of major economies to adapt the international order. The slow, incremental commitments included in the Paris climate accord, for example, can be supplanted by harnessing the greater force of economic self-interest. With our markets aligned, the United States will have to work with its partners to forge, implement, and verify a durable transition framework among the world's major economies.

Suffice to say, this won't be easy. The task at hand is to develop a pragmatic, actionable framework that not only addresses our enduring interests of prosperity and security, but also aligns our immediate self-interests of personal well-being and short-term gratification with the long-term interests of follow-on generations.

AMERICA'S PROSPERITY FORMULA

At the most basic level, the question our grand strategy asks is, How can our economy do the strategic heavy lifting? We're not talking about the economy doing the work on a trivial or partisan project. And it is not about redistributing wealth or causing money to "trickle down." We're talking about how the economy can help solve the great challenges of our time while delivering widespread prosperity.

We submit that there is a straightforward economic formula that has allowed American leaders of the past to address real opportunity and long-term risk through effective action. This formula can be written as

Demand + Capital − Stranded Assets = New Growth Scenario

Demand is the call on goods and services we produce here at home. *Capital* is how we finance the equity and infrastructure to allow demand to be met. *Stranded Assets* are those that are difficult, politically or structurally, to devalue. Align all three and you get a powerful scenario for growth.

The formula emerged out of World War II. As we described earlier, before Pearl Harbor, industrial wizards like Bill Knudsen were able to organize demand for arms, munitions, ships, planes, and trucks to prepare American business for a wholesale conversion of our industrial ecosystem from civilian to military production, while financiers like Bernard Baruch created the mechanism to aggregate capital, the Lend-Lease Act, providing the financing necessary to be ready for the declaration of war in December 1941. After Pearl Harbor, capital for industrial conversion was combined with massive government purchase orders, via the cost-plus contract. The implementation of the universal income tax in 1942 paid for those contracts. Coming out of the Great Depression, the primary stranded assets to be absorbed were labor (unemployment) and factory equipment and capacity.

The Cold War was fundamentally a different era, yet the growth scenario followed the same pattern. We tapped into the biggest pools of demand in the system—housing, consumer goods, and reconstruction materials for Europe and Japan—and deployed them to address the new challenges of Soviet and Chinese communism. Washington aligned capital through the use of subsidies and infrastructure investments. We financed highways, expanded access to suburban mortgages, and enticed workers to relocate outside city centers by pushing government-funded activity into the suburbs.

The stranded-asset challenge at the time was America's excess wartime production capacity and returning veterans. The growth scenario— suburban expansion—addressed that by unleashing demand for housing and automobiles. America's expanded industrial capacity was well utilized. Returning veterans found work in civilian manufacturing factories at the same time their soon-to-be spouses left some of those same war-production factories and settled in at home to raise families.

Suffice to say, we don't think like this today. Instead, we frequently confuse the designs of Cold War–era economic engineering with the mystical and mythical actions of a free market.

To understand that, it helps to understand some basic macroeconomic principles. Federal economic policy is thought of as having only two modes: monetary and fiscal. Monetary policy focuses on interest rates and is managed by the Federal Reserve, a semi-independent arm of the government whose goals are to manage inflation and ensure full employment. In the absence of any new growth scenario or fiscal stimulus, the Federal Reserve has been leading macroeconomic management over the past few years, spending more than $4 trillion since 2009 to prop up the American economy.

Fiscal policy is set by Congress. It centers on how money is collected in taxes, fees, royalties, and other mechanisms, and how that money is spent by the government. Fiscal policy can redirect American interests in any number of ways. During the Great Depression, FDR's public works programs put unemployed Americans back to work while building new infrastructure. Ronald Reagan's fiscal policy during the 1980s came in three forms: defense spending, corporate tax reduction, and the home mortgage tax deduction. President Obama's American Recovery and Reinvestment Act focused on health care, education, infrastructure repairs, and clean energy.

At the end of the day, monetary and fiscal policy are tools that focus on the management of the economy and its business cycle. While both are vitally important, there is little these tools can do if the underlying growth scenario is broken, besides slowing and softening the inevitable unwinding. At that point, it's time for a new growth scenario.

That is precisely where America sits today. Our old growth scenario is exhausted. The post–World War II economy ran out of fuel back in the early 1970s. Despite the lack of demand, President Reagan, in his 1984 campaign commercial, declared, "It's morning again in America," but hooked the economic engine to consumer debt and federal deficits, stimulating demand artificially, allowing industry to leave rather than innovate, and in the process hollowing out America's middle class. Ever since, we've been inflating one speculative bubble after the other, draining wealth from the middle class and reversing the hard-earned postwar gains.

A NEW AMERICAN GROWTH SCENARIO

Our economic scenario reverses that trend. Thanks to large-scale demographic shifts over the past 20 years, the United States is sitting astride three vast pools of pent-up demand that can fuel an economic engine for a new U.S. grand strategy: for walkable communities, regenerative agriculture, and resource productivity. The cumulative impact of these three pools of demand, if harnessed by the private sector, is potentially transformational.

WALKABLE COMMUNITIES

The first pool of demand is homegrown. American tastes have changed, from the splendid isolation of the suburbs to what we'll call the "half-mile lifestyle"—work, school, transit, doctors, restaurants, playgrounds, and entertainment all within a short walk of the front door. Between now and 2030, Baby Boomers and their children, the Millennials, will converge in the housing marketplace, seeking smaller homes in "new urban" communities. In its 2013 consumer preference survey, the National Association of Realtors found that 60 percent of homebuyers want their next home purchase to have the attributes of what is commonly referred to as "smart growth." That is, they want right-sized homes in a broader range of housing types (single-family, townhouse, live-work, condo, apartment) and they want them in walkable, service-rich, transit-oriented, mixed-use, opportunity-dense neighborhoods. That represents roughly three times the demand for housing after World War II—a demand signal that was a primary driver of our economy until the 1970s. Today's demand for smart growth is of truly historic proportions.

The demand exists across the country. Boomers are downsizing and working longer, and they fear their car keys will be taken away as old age creeps in, leaving them stranded in the car-dependent suburbs, eventually to be housed away in a nursing home or retirement community. Millennials were raised in the isolated suburbs of the 1980s and 1990s, and 77 percent say they don't want to go back there. Prices have already flipped, with exurban property values dropping and those in walkable neighborhoods rising. Yet legacy federal policies—from transportation funding to housing subsidies—remain geared toward the Cold War imperative of population dispersion and exploitation of the housing shortage, and they are stifling that demand. Only a fraction of housing starts have the attributes of smart growth, and new homes represent only 1 percent of the residential real estate market.

REGENERATIVE AGRICULTURE

The United States cannot become sustainable, nor can it support global sustainability, without addressing agriculture. To meet rising population and income levels, according to the Organization for Economic Cooperation and Development, the world needs to increase global food production by 60 percent by 2050, and 100 percent of that will need to use farming techniques that restore soils and cleanse waterways. For American farmers, the increase in demand for food is already translating to record prices, but the heartland is held back from capturing additional gains from regenerative methods, which provide up to three times the profits per acre and 30 percent higher yields during drought, because of federal policies set during the Nixon administration.

It is time to restore America's heartland and breadbasket. Instead of depleting soils and polluting rivers, American farming must adopt modern methods that bring more land into cultivation, keep families on the land, provide employment to a new generation of American farmers, and build regional food systems that keep more money circulating locally, all while helping to feed the world.

RESOURCE PRODUCTIVITY

To bring 3 billion new middle-class aspirants into the global economy requires a revolution in resource allocation. Energy and material intensity per person will need to drop dramatically while simultaneously delivering the higher income and lifestyle expectations that come with global connectivity.

That revolution will provide the logic to power innovation in material sciences, engineering, advanced manufacturing, and energy production, distribution, and consumption. In the United States, the high-wage, high-skill jobs emerging from this revolution will restore and strengthen America's middle class and national competitiveness for decades to come. In the end, America will learn how to "make things" again.

We'll discuss each of these pools of demand in depth in Part II.

THE $1.3 TRILLION BUSINESS OPPORTUNITY

Redesigning an economy to run on new sources of homegrown demand does far more than adjustments in fiscal and monetary policy ever could.

The scale and duration of these three pools of demand will ease investor uncertainty, unlock capital, tighten the job market, and raise wages—all via market forces. This, in turn, will address consumer debt: as Americans' paychecks revive, they will pay off or pay down their household debts and will be able to reengage in and reinvigorate the American dream. And this time, with their consumption once again aligned with the nation's strategic imperatives, Americans can blaze a new path forward for the rest of the world to follow.

There is a limited window of opportunity, however. For example, the demographic convergence of Boomers and Millennials in the housing market runs until 2030. During this time, both generational cohorts, each about one-quarter of the U.S. population, will be in the housing market seeking to make a change. Concurrently, the world's 3 billion new middle-class consumers in emerging economies will gain access to the formal sector of their economies, where studies by the International Monetary Fund forecast their incomes will spike 300 percent, with a concomitant spike in demand for goods and services. China's urbanization challenge alone, bringing 292 million people out of the countryside and into cities over the next 20 years, is a daunting resource- and energy-intensive prospect, and one that will happen at the same time America is building residential housing for half our 2030 population.

The financial outcomes are accordingly impressive, according to our calculations:

- Meeting demand for walkable communities would increase annual residential construction by 80 percent over 2014 figures, a gain of approximately $225 billion a year in residential sales alone. Reduced sprawl will save local governments another $23 billion annually in avoided public-service expenditures—roads, water, sanitation, schools, et cetera.
- Meeting global food demand and sustaining an extraordinary level of production while protecting our soils and waterways will require a transition to regenerative agricultural methods that could triple farm profits. Growing regional food systems and urban agriculture would increase overall U.S. exports to meet the 60 percent increase in food supply required by 2050. This would translate to approximately $190 billion annually in additional revenue to farm operators.

- Embracing and hosting the resource productivity revolution
  would deliver a boost of more than $850 billion annually, or
  5 percent of U.S. GDP. America would be both capturing the
  savings from reducing and eliminating waste and producing a
  new era of innovative materials, goods, and services for domestic
  and global markets.

As the new foundation for the economy, this roughly $1.3 trillion annual opportunity would have significant and cascading positive effects, as increased employment, new household formation, new business creation, and new infrastructure development would follow, restoring consumer demand at home while restoring global demand growth. The new American dream would align with middle-class purchasing power while staying within planetary boundaries.

One example of a positive effect is unlocking investment in renewable energy capital equipment—the hardware for massive deployment of wind, solar, and other clean-energy sources. Using WWF research that mapped a 95 percent global renewable energy scenario by 2050, we estimate that total U.S. renewable energy expenditures could run between $187 billion and $657 billion annually. As a comparison, U.S. capital expenses for the oil and gas sector in 2013 were approximately $200 billion.

PRIVATE, NOT PUBLIC, INVESTMENT

In contrast with most other plans for reviving America's economy, we believe the best way to finance this new growth scenario is through private investment, not public funding. There are trillions of dollars of liquidity sitting on the sidelines of the productive economy: $3.5 trillion in corporate cash, plus another $10 trillion in private equity and hedge fund cash. And $30 trillion of Baby Boomer wealth is in the process of being transferred to Millennials (that's on top of the $17 trillion changing hands between the World War II generation and their Boomer offspring). All of these players need a new investment hypothesis for America, and this opportunity could be compelling.

In the absence of policy, how would investors be able to channel their funds into the right investments in a coordinated way to enable the new economic engine to take hold? We will explore this concept later in this book, but the simple answer is a new kind of investment bank for the American dream, chartered deliberately to keep its eyes on the long term and return a solid 3 percent interest on the trillions of assets it will need to manage.

Our rationale for private-led investment is pragmatic, not ideological. Public spending at the scale necessary is just not likely to happen. The undeniable truth is that Congress has rolled back spending on infrastructure, and the electoral math does not appear to lend itself to any meaningful change in the time frame we have to capture this opportunity and avoid the worst of the environmental and geopolitical impacts.

UNSTRANDING ASSETS

We also have to deal with today's stranded assets. There are two looming types: unburnable hydrocarbons and unprepared human capital.

To stay within the limits of planetary warming that the overwhelming scientific consensus views as tolerable, the International Energy Agency estimates we can burn only about one-fifth of the untapped oil and gas currently on the books of publicly traded companies and state-owned enterprises. The remaining 80 percent needs to remain "stranded" in the ground, unable to be burned for combustion. Depending on the price of oil and gas, this could amount to $25 trillion worth of wealth being written off. You simply can't do that without crashing the markets or causing a global recession, or worse.

There is a way forward. We believe it is time to solve the stranded hydrocarbon issue by executing a feedstock shift, moving oil and gas out of combustion and into materials. We'll talk more about this later. For now, suffice to say that this offers far better carbon-abatement opportunities than simple carbon taxes or cap-and-trade schemes.

It's not just hydrocarbons that are being stranded. Many American workers are already stranded, due to a mismatch between the millions of available jobs and the skills of the existing workforce. The economic meltdown of 2007–2009 led to the unemployment of 8.7 million Americans. The jobs that came back were generally lower-skill and lower-wage with fewer benefits. At the time of writing, while the official unemployment indicator stood at around 5 percent, involuntary underemployment still affected more than 10 percent of the total workforce, according to the Department of Labor, not including those who have stopped looking for work altogether. Household income, flat since 1979, is barely breaking even with expenses. For the American dream to come back, employment and household income will need to improve dramatically, but American workers are ill-trained to do the higher-skill jobs we will need to restore economic mobility. This reserve labor pool is going to be needed as our economy kicks back into gear. Again, more on that later.

NOT WAITING ON WASHINGTON

Put it all together and America is poised for a new economic boom. Simultaneously, new pools of demand, vast stores of pent-up capital, and a workable set of stranded-asset challenges are aligning with the four strategic antagonists of the coming decades.

The next question is how to implement. Over the past 25 years, policy-led pathways have been tried and have, for the most part, failed, especially at the national level. Indeed, we see America facing a situation not unlike what the nation experienced at the onset of World War II: We are in need of an economic engine that must be implemented so rapidly that it must be crafted by business itself. We just cannot repeat the kind of gratuitous uncertainty witnessed around Obamacare or the Simpson-Bowles commission to identify medium- and long-term strategies to cut the national debt. We don't have time for the set-piece lobbying battles in Congress, testing in the Supreme Court, or the threat of legislative reversal every two years. Those are dead-end paths.

Our new growth scenario, rooted in a powerful demand-plus-capital business case rather than a threat-plus-regulation policy framework, has the advantage of being able to be implemented under current policy by private businesses investing and producing at the speed of commerce to harness the best of the private sector's efficiency. By preserving and enhancing the value of assets that would be stranded by policy-led efforts, we may be able to proceed even more rapidly into a sustainable, prosperous, and more secure America than ever imagined.

That isn't to say that government policy is not important. It is, and the large package of Cold War policies that have ossified around the old economic engine will eventually need to be redirected to support the transition to sustainability. What we are saying, however, is that for now we have to expect Washington to act as a representative democracy, but only begrudgingly, "leading" only after American citizens and businesses have established a solid new direction. We fully expect that as this plan kicks into gear, Washington's elected officials will see the proverbial parade and will rush to be at the front of it.

The key is demand. Reset America around deep pools of demand, and suddenly we're looking at a new American century.

PART II

THREE POOLS OF DEMAND

CHAPTER FOUR

WALKABLE COMMUNITIES

THE FUTURE OF AMERICA'S COMMUNITIES IS TAKING SHAPE IN Detroit's New Center neighborhood, a few hundred feet from the historic Fisher Building and the former General Motors headquarters. That's where an organization called Detroit Future City has set up shop, the nerve center of an effort to bring together disparate voices in one of America's most downtrodden cities and create a vision of what's possible.

"A lot of big changes are happening in Detroit," says Dan Kinkead, the group's director of projects. The changes are coming as much from necessity as will. The storied epicenter of the automotive world— America's richest city just a half century ago—has traveled a bumpy road for decades. Just since the turn of the millennium it has suffered the financial defaults of General Motors and Chrysler, the exodus of tens of thousands of residents and businesses, inept or corrupt city officials, exploding debt, a declining tax base, and, in 2013, the nation's largest municipal bankruptcy.

Today, the city of 700,000—down from 1.8 million in 1950—has 90,000 vacant lots and 70,000 abandoned buildings as well as a 36 percent poverty rate and 23 percent unemployment rate, both the highest in the nation. Motown is, arguably, a city that has run into a ditch.

So, why is Dan Kinkead hopeful—and why are we? There are hundreds of initiatives, from tiny start-ups to massive public-private partnerships, aimed at jump-starting the beleaguered city and putting Detroit squarely on the road to recovery. The idea isn't necessarily to re-create the "old" Detroit. Rather, it's to reinvent it as a dense, diverse, walkable, transit-friendly city. As such, Detroit may be on the leading edge of where American cities and suburbs need to be heading.

The reason is simple but fundamental: demand for the Ozzie-and-Harriet suburban American lifestyle is declining. American tastes have changed from the "splendid isolation" of the suburbs (a term popularized in a song by the musician Warren Zevon, who borrowed it from nineteenth-century British foreign policy) to the "half-mile lifestyle," where work, school, friends, doctors, dining, playgrounds, entertainment, parks, and more are within a brief walk, bike trip, or transit ride of one's front door. The large-lot, new single-family house, which so epitomized domestic consumption in the latter half of the twentieth century, no longer rules.

Boomers and Millennials—more than half the population—now want an "urban" lifestyle, even if it's in the suburbs. Indeed, in some areas, suburbs are finding new life, especially when they offer more urban-like amenities—shopping, entertainment, community activities, and the like, all in close, walkable proximity to where people live. The 'burbs may lack the excitement of downtown Manhattan or Chicago, but for those for whom "excitement" is overrated, there are new urban design principles that can help achieve the right balance. It turns out that the suburbs can be transit-friendly and experience-rich, just like a big city. Moreover, the opportunity is huge. We have approximately 2.8 million acres of what urban and suburban design expert Ellen Dunham-Jones calls "underperforming asphalt" available for redevelopment across the American suburban landscape. If we redeveloped even a quarter of that, we could meet half of America's future housing needs.

The paradox is inescapable. Federal subsidies, state laws, and local ordinances still incentivize ever-more-isolated, car-dependent communities. Yet since the 2008 economic crash, developers, faced with growing demand and minimal government support, have poured more than 50 percent of real estate investment into the 1 percent of metropolitan land that was already walkable. There remains a paucity of such housing, making vibrant, walkable communities available primarily to those who can afford to pay the premium, even though a majority of Americans would prefer to live in these places. According to a 2016 analysis by the online real estate database and brokerage firm Redfin, just 14 percent of America's neighborhoods are at once affordable, walkable, and near decent schools—and most of those were in Austin, Seattle, San Diego, and Washington, D.C.

This need not be the case. We are facing an unprecedented opportunity to revitalize our communities—both urban and suburban—in a way that doesn't merely address a variety of social and environmental challenges, but also represents one of the biggest economic opportunities in history: about $225 billion annually in residential sales, plus billions more in avoided public expenditures—roads, water, schools, sanitation, and other infrastructure and institutions that might otherwise have gone into supporting sprawl. By bringing the concept of walkability to communities across America, we can grow vibrant, diverse communities in a way that isn't just economically feasible for the public sector, but highly profitable for the private sector. And better for all who live there.

Which is why the first of our three massive pools of economic demand is homegrown—literally. By focusing local planning, construction, and market development on making communities walkable, we can simultaneously address several big issues:

Decarbonization: create communities that require less driving, dramatically reducing energy use and its associated greenhouse gases and other pollutants.

Economic development: spur domestic activity in construction and other professions, with millions of low- and medium-skilled jobs.

Financial returns: absorb billions in excess liquidity and deliver healthy returns over the medium and long term.

Upward mobility: redefine the American dream and make it widely accessible to working- and middle-class Americans.

Social fabric: strengthen American communities, civic participation, and social resilience.

Health and wellness: improve Americans' physical and psychological well-being.

Walkable communities are part of a growing lexicon of terms that, individually and collectively, reflect a desire to rethink how we design and build the cities and towns in which Americans live, work, play, and shop. There are sustainable cities, green cities, smart cities, eco-cities, carbon-neutral cities, resilient cities, "new urbanist" communities, and something called neotraditional development. The U.S. Green Building Council, which developed the LEED Green Building Rating System that has become the dominant benchmark for environmentally responsible buildings, has created LEED for Neighborhood Development, or LEED-ND, a standard to help guide the development of sustainable and walkable communities. Each of these is a slightly different take on a singular idea: with planning, partnerships, and persistence, both existing and new communities can stimulate economic growth, grow wealth, increase security, reduce poverty, improve health, cut pollution, increase resilience, and generally be nicer, more convenient places to spend our time.

CONVERGING GENERATIONS

The movement of companies and residential housing to urban cores, along with the slower development of suburbs, to re-create the walkable urban experience, represents a 180-degree turn from the development strategy in place for the past 70 years. Today's housing and economic strategies were fused by the Cold War. As part of America's strategy to contain the Soviets so that we could ultimately defeat them in a contest of economic and political systems, subsidized suburban growth competed with the politburo's central planning.

And it worked. During the 1950s and '60s, Americans, feeling secure in their near-term prospects, got married, bought homes, and started having children. In the late 1970s and early 1980s, those children, the Baby Boom generation, started having kids of their own, peaking during the last two decades of the twentieth century, and producing the Millennial generation.

Today, Boomers and Millennials are roughly equal in size, around 78 million people each, together composing nearly half of the overall U.S. population. The housing preferences of these two groups are now converging, pivoting decisively away from the monochrome subdivisions that have long pervaded the American landscape. Boomers are downsizing and working longer, and, as we mentioned earlier, they don't want to get stranded in car-dependent communities. For them, reaching the symbolic age of 65 means shunning multibedroom, large-lot homes in the suburbs, which don't support the active lifestyles many in this generation want or need. Large homes require too much maintenance and time; car-dependent suburbs become untenable when driving becomes challenging or unsafe. The data suggests that Boomers who are downsizing are relatively well off. Harvard University's Joint Center for Housing Studies found that those aged 55 and older accounted for 42 percent of the growth in renters over the past decade. Besides, it's more fun to be near stores, restaurants, museums, galleries, cinemas, concert halls, stadiums, and other stimulating venues, particularly when one finally has the time to enjoy them. The retirement dreams of their predecessors—whether isolated sunbaked communities in Florida or Arizona or golf courses in California or the Carolinas—are either less affordable or less desirable than they once were.

Millennials, for their part, have had enough of the suburbs—at least how we currently think of them. The Millennials "are fueling an urban revolution looking for the vibrant, creative energy cities offering a mix of housing, shopping, and offices," says a 2014 report by Nielsen, the market research company. "They're walkers and less interested in the car culture that defined Baby Boomers." A 2015 survey of adults in the 50 biggest U.S. cities by the National Association of Realtors and the Transportation Research and Education Center at Portland State University found that Millennials utilize public transit more than any other age group, are more likely to walk or bike for transportation purposes, and prefer attached housing like apartments and condos to standalone houses—so long as the loss in interior space comes with increased walkability. Millennials currently live in urban areas at a higher rate than any other generation: 62 percent say they prefer to live in the type of mixed-use communities found in urban centers. And with diminished economic prospects, owning a car, let alone a house, is off the table for the foreseeable future, so it pays to live where you already want to be. Besides, the action—and the jobs—are increasingly found in urban centers.

These two generations will overlap and compete in the home-buying market until about 2030. Millennials, beginning to settle down and raise families, will be looking for starter homes. Boomers will be looking to downsize from single-family houses to something more manageable and convenient. Increasingly, both will be showing up at the same open houses and bidding against one another for the same apartments and townhouses. It is already a heated competition in many markets. "Millennials aspire to stay in the cities rather than moving to the suburbs or rural areas, presenting a potential problem for Boomers who will eventually want to downsize and sell their large suburban McMansions," says Nielsen.

Nielsen makes it clear that this isn't just about cities. The concept of urban 'burbs has taken on currency in redevelopment circles as suburban communities transform to more urban environments, with walkable downtown areas and everyday necessities within reach, according to Leigh Gallagher, author of *The End of the Suburbs: Where the American Dream Is Moving.* (The *New York Times* coined this phenomenon "Hipsturbia.") There's also Peter Calthrope's vision of New Urbanism, articulated in his book *The Next American Metropolis: Ecology, Community, and the American Dream,* which takes proven urban design principles and applies them to suburban development, including an emphasis on diversity in both community design and population, being pedestrian- and transit-friendly and environmentally conscious, with mixed housing types (single family, townhouses, and apartments) available to a mixed spectrum of household income, along with plenty of public green space.

The transformation of America's housing stock couldn't come too soon. As Christopher Leinberger points out, the "drivable suburbanism" development pattern that followed World War II is unsustainable. It "actually narrowed consumer options, consumed land at six to eight times population growth and produced 'could be anywhere' places," says Leinberger, who is president of LOCUS, a national coalition of real estate developers and investors who advocate for walkable urban development; he also is the Charles Bendit Distinguished Scholar and Research Professor at the George Washington University School of Business. Moreover, he says, the suburban formula has been reinforced by real estate finance, "which has turned what for thousands of years was a 40-year asset class into a product with a 7–10 year life."

The result, he says, hasn't been healthy for Americans or their economy. Among the unintended social, economic, health, and environmental consequences: dependency on a car/truck-only transportation system that is putting financial pressure on household budgets, social segregation, and the secession of financial elites; the dependency of about a third of the U.S. population that do not drive; subsidized drivable suburban public and private infrastructure that is too expensive to continue building and maintaining; and an indirect impact on American foreign policy, which is skewed toward securing oil from countries that are hostile to the United States.

The increased focus on making cities and suburbs more housing-dense isn't just a nice idea. It's an economic and environmental necessity. According to the U.S. Census Bureau's estimate, America will add another 130 million people to its population by 2050, which translates to roughly 50 million new households. It's unlikely that the bulk of these will be created on virgin greenfields in suburbs and exurbs. That's not even what people want. The National Association of Realtors' 2013 Community Preference Survey found that 60 percent of American homebuyers want their next home purchase to have the attributes of what is commonly referred to as "smart growth." Currently, there's simply not enough available housing of this type to go around.

AN INDEX FOR WALKABILITY

So, what, exactly, is a walkable community? While the term itself may seem intuitively obvious—it's a place where you can walk easily and safely to wherever you want to go—there have been a variety of efforts to add some metrics to that rather squishy definition. An obvious one is "walkability," which quantifies how amenable an area is to walking, based on such things as the presence and quality of sidewalks, paths, trails, and other pedestrian routes; the presence of trees, landscaping, and other greenery that provide both beauty and shade; the proximity of residences to schools, shopping, community centers, and places of worship; the ease of traffic and road conditions for drivers and nondrivers alike; street signs and other way-finding measures optimized for walkers and bicyclists, not just drivers; the presence of benches and other resting places for walkers; and the overall safety conditions for walkers and bicyclists, from adequate crosswalks and signals to reasonable protection from crime. In other words, a walkable community is designed to meet the needs of people, not cars.

There are now scores and indices that tally these and other factors down to the neighborhood and street level, with lists of "most walkable communities" published on a regular basis. Among the best known is Walk Score, a Seattle-based company that provides data to real estate firms and websites. It assigns a score of between zero and 100 to millions of addresses in the United States, as well as to neighborhoods and entire cities, based on an algorithm that awards points based on the distance to things like businesses, parks, theaters, schools, "and other common destinations." (It also publishes separate Bike Scores and Transit Scores.) The company claims to serve up about 4 million scores a day to more than 10,000 websites and smartphone apps, making it accessible to just about anyone anywhere.

Aside from informing renters and homebuyers about a key quality of a prospective residence, Walk Score's data has helped demonstrate the financial value of walkable communities. Houses with above-average levels of walkability command a premium of between $4,000 and $34,000 over houses with average levels of walkability in the typical metropolitan areas studied, according to a 2009 study by CEOs for Cities, a nonprofit alliance of U.S. mayors, corporate executives, university presidents, and nonprofit leaders. And not just for residential properties: Walk Score found that a ten-point increase in walkability increases commercial property values by 5 to 8 percent.

Companies like Walk Score are democratizing data that allow walkable communities to put their best foot forward. And while New York, San Francisco, Boston, and Philadelphia are among the larger cities cited as "most walkable," many smaller communities are stepping up. Cities such as Kingsport, Tennessee; Dunedin, Florida; Vancouver, Washington; and Pontiac, Michigan, tout their walkability, often serving up studies showing the myriad benefits to those who live and work there.

Those benefits are plentiful. A succession of surveys, research projects, and economic analyses has concluded that walkable communities not only are convenient and aesthetically pleasing to Americans, but they also provide attractive personal, economic, and societal benefits.

For starters, a substantial body of evidence has shown that automobile-centered communities—with segregated commercial and residential land uses, low density, disconnected street networks, and insufficient pedestrian and bicyclist infrastructure—are associated with reduced physical activity in outdoor spaces, leading to negative health outcomes. Indeed, the built environment "has become a leading cause of disability and death in the twenty-first century," according to *New York Times* health writer Jane Brody. "Physical activity has been disappearing from the lives of young and old, and many communities are virtual 'food deserts,' serviced only by convenience stores that stock nutrient-poor prepared foods and drinks." The impacts on our children are most pronounced. Dr. Richard Jackson, author of *Designing Healthy Communities* and former chief public health officer of California, illustrates the severity: "We are seeing severely overweight 17-year-olds who have diseases of 77-year-olds: difficult to manage diabetes and other disorders like asthma, fatty liver disease, hypertension, and heart failure." Just to put a statistic around it, a child born today stands a one in three chance of developing diabetes in his or her lifetime.

In contrast, walkable communities have been linked to increased physical activity in daily routines, contributing to positive health outcomes. Consider some of the evidence:

- Residents in walkable neighborhoods were "at less risk of being obese or overweight," according to a 2008 study from the University of Utah, published in the *American Journal of Preventive Medicine*. It linked the body mass index of nearly a half-million Salt Lake County residents to 2000 Census data and found that a man of average height and weight weighed ten pounds less if he lived in a walkable neighborhood versus a less-walkable one. His female counterpart weighed six pounds less.

- Residents of neighborhoods with walkable access to shops and services have "higher levels of social capital such as trust among neighbors and participation in community events," according to a 2010 study of 20 neighborhoods in two New Hampshire communities by the Natural Resources and Earth System Science program at the University of New Hampshire, which was published in the journal *Applied Research in Quality of Life*.

- Older people who perceive their neighborhoods as safer and more walkable are less likely to develop severe depressive symptoms, and the effects may be long term, according to a 2014 study published in the *Journal of Aging and Health*. Researchers examined links between the onset of depressive symptoms in 570 Latino adults age 60 to 90 and various characteristics of the Los Angeles neighborhoods they lived in, including crime, the availability and quality of sidewalks, traffic safety, and aesthetics.

- There's a correlation between the frequency of street intersections, a measure of urban compactness, and human health, according to a 2014 study published in the *Journal of Transport & Health*. It analyzed the street network configuration of 24 California cities with populations between 30,000 and just over 100,000, and used health-survey data to see how the intersection designs affected rates of obesity, diabetes, high blood pressure, heart disease, and asthma. The more intersections, the lower the obesity rates at the neighborhood level, and the lower obesity, diabetes, high blood pressure, and heart disease rates were at the city level, the study found.

There's more, but you get the idea. Walkable communities engender health and well-being among their residents. But the business and economic benefits are nothing to sneeze at, either.

Chris Leinberger has been assessing real estate values in walkable communities—or, more specifically, what he has dubbed "walkable urban places," or WalkUPs. For rental apartment and for-sale residential, the price premiums associated with WalkUPs are even greater, says Leinberger in a 2013 report, *The WalkUP Wake-Up Call*. He found that multifamily rental apartments in WalkUPs achieve rents per square foot approximately 28 percent higher than in drivable suburban areas. For-sale residential prices are 57 percent higher in WalkUPs than in drivable subdivision locations. Moreover, he says, a growing proportion of income property development—including office, retail, hotel, rental apartments, and for-sale residential—is concentrating in WalkUPs. "Although WalkUPs and walkable neighborhoods make up only 3 percent of the metropolitan Washington, D.C. region's land, they have accounted for 25 percent of income property development in the latest cycle, up from only 6 percent from 1992 to 2000."

Leinberger adds, "Walkable urban regions in the U.S. have a 41 percent higher GDP over non-walkable regions." That's equivalent to the difference between countries like Germany and Romania, he says.

In fact, one of the biggest winners of walkable communities is commercial real estate. That's why hundreds of companies across the United States are moving to and investing in walkable downtown locations. According to a 2015 report, "Why American Companies Are Moving Downtown," from Smart Growth America, "As job migration shifts towards cities and as commercial real estate values climb in these places, a vanguard of American companies are building and expanding

in walkable downtown neighborhoods." Leinberger was a key partici-
pant in the study.

The study examined the motivations of companies that relocated,
opened new offices, or expanded in walkable downtowns between 2010
and 2015. It was a diverse group of companies covering 170 specific
industries, including 15 software developers and 29 information technology companies, 45 manufacturers, 11 universities and colleges, seven
food production companies, six advertising agencies, and six oil and gas
companies. Fifty-two were part of the Fortune 500, and 12 were among
Fortune's "100 Best Companies to Work For" for 2015.

There were six common themes explaining why companies chose
to locate downtown: to attract and retain the talented workforce being drawn to the restaurants, cafes, cultural institutions, and nightlife
downtown; to build brand identity and company culture by literally being at the center of things; to support creative collaboration by locating
in dynamic, creative, engaging neighborhoods; to be closer to customers and business partners, facilitating in-person meetings; to centralize
operations, particularly when operations were spread out over a single
region; and to support sustainability, including an opportunity to demonstrate corporate citizenship and a way to use their sizable investing
power for good.

WHY SUSTAINABILITY NEEDS CITIES

As such, cities and business long have had a symbiotic relationship. One
provides purpose and place, the other brings people. Not sure which is
which in the preceding sentence? That's the point.

From a business perspective, the question related to cities and sustainability is clear and compelling: Can you have a healthy company
in an unhealthy city? Arguably, no. And vice versa. Companies need
healthy cities to provide reliable infrastructure, an educated and vital
workforce, a vibrant economy, and a safe and secure environment to survive and thrive. Cities, of course, need business as an economic driver.
As such, the sustainability of cities and business are interdependent and
inextricably linked.

A pair of "Citystates" reports produced in 2012 and 2015 by the
think tank and consultancy SustainAbility put forth a compelling hypothesis: sustainability needs cities as much as cities need sustainability.

The contrast between the overwhelming and dispiriting state of the broader world and the more concentrated, dynamic energy of cities led the reports' coauthors, Chris Guenther and Mohammed Al-Shawaf, to explore the current and potential nexus between cities and sustainability, including what risks and opportunities sustainability might hold for both global and local companies as they face ever-rising pressure to deliver social as well as financial value around the world.

"In the twenty-first century, cities will increasingly be the frame through which we understand and shape our shared economic, political, and cultural circumstances," they write. "They will also be ground zero for the collision of economic, environmental, and social imperatives that define sustainability. Together, these facts suggest that in proactively addressing the challenge of urban sustainability, business and others may have an opportunity to harness the power and positive characteristics of cities to drive sustainability more widely."

The symbiotic relationship between companies and cities can have a highly salutary effect. Businesses, as engines of innovation and ingenuity, can play critical roles in engendering sustainability at the local level. Given the right system conditions, a thriving business community can offer a wealth of solutions to provide clean air and water, a robust transportation network, food and energy security, adequate and ample housing, and the environmental, social, and economic success that is at the heart of sustainability.

From an innovation standpoint alone, the city-company combo can't be beat. In his book *Where Good Ideas Come From: The Natural History of Innovation,* Steven Johnson points out that when viewed from every aspect of innovation—patents, R&D budgets, inventions, inventors, jobs, et cetera—innovation in cities follows what Johnson calls "superlinear scaling": as cities get bigger, they get more innovative, not on a linear basis, but on a positive quarter-power law basis. If a city was 10 times bigger than another city, it wasn't 10 times more innovative, it was 17 times more innovative.

SustainAbility's 2015 report acknowledged that "more companies are engaging and innovating for sustainability within and across cities, as are cities with companies. But the potential of such engagement has only begun to be understood, much less realized." The report offered a "Corporate Urban Sustainability Progress (CUSP) Maturity Model," a five-step framework with actionable steps companies can take to better understand the opportunities and how to seize them. The goal is to recognize the connections between urban and business goals; analyze which urban trends will specifically impact a company's industry or business; work with or without partners to develop experimental products, services, and initiatives; evaluate the pilots' impact; and develop a growth strategy to take what's working to scale.

"We see sectors like energy, infrastructure, real estate, transportation, all quite engaged with cities," says Guenther. "But we're really interested in how other industries like food, retail, consumer products—you name it—can find ways to accelerate their own sustainability ambition and agendas in cities and with cities." In their research, Guenther and Al-Shawaf found that companies tend to be narrow and short-term in their interest in cities. So, they wondered, "How do we make it a more expansive conversation that involves longer time horizons and bigger initiatives? How do we find a vocabulary and a framework that allows us to understand, 'Hey, you're working in the city; we're working in the city. How do we coordinate our efforts?' It's really getting at the idea of systems change and systemic impact."

CATCHING UP TO THE TIMES

The convergence of sustainability and cities represents a massive business opportunity. For example, today's market for walkable communities represents a demand three times larger than that created by returning vets and their new spouses after World War II. That's the same demand that fueled our economy in the form of suburban sprawl until the late 1970s and early 1980s. It was huge. It is also over. The upshot is that we can capture all this new demand if we just activate it by catching policies and investments up with the times.

Right now, government policies and funding are doing little to support that demand. Quite the opposite: federal subsidies—which paid for the interstate highways and kept gas prices reasonable—are now a key source of the bottleneck. Seventy-seven percent of Fannie Mae's $2.9 trillion book of mortgages were added between 2009 and 2013—mortgage products that require many buyers to drive increasingly farther from city centers to qualify for a home loan. The group Smart Growth America calculates that the federal government spends $450 billion a year on real estate programs, from tax expenditures to loan guarantees to low-interest loans and grants—largely aimed at buttressing the suburban lifestyle. The $305 billion, five-year federal transportation bill known as the Fixing America's Surface Transportation (FAST) Act, signed into law in 2015, fell far short of the $478 billion bill the White House asked for. The law provides $230 billion for highways but only $60 billion for public transportation, one of the keys to walkable communities. Taken together, the federal intervention in the housing and transportation markets, once a strategic necessity, is now contributing to the pent-up private demand for walkable communities.

Things aren't that much different with local governments. Counties on the suburban fringe often see suburban development as the path to increased tax revenue, unaware that after the wave of buyers passes through they will be left with a heavy infrastructure burden and a thin tax base. Incredibly and ironically, after subprime mortgages and high gas prices triggered the Great Recession, publicly traded home builders were able to go back to Wall Street investors with an argument that, even though home prices had declined, agricultural land prices had dropped even further, thereby maintaining or even increasing builders' profit margins.

Meanwhile, Wall Street is resting on an equally large reservoir of liquidity that is looking for "certainty" before investing. For investors, uncertainty comes in many forms: licensing and regulatory requirements, interest rates, the price of carbon and energy, tax policy, and demand ambiguity, to offer a partial list. A decisive policy that sets a clear framework for investment can tap this pool of capital through a new era of right-sized mortgages, municipal bonds, and equity investment in the businesses building the next American dream.

It's not just that developers and investors are missing out on an untapped real estate boom. There's also a price tag on getting it wrong. Suburban sprawl costs the American economy more than $1 trillion annually, according to a 2015 study by the Global Commission on the Economy and Climate, established to examine how countries can achieve economic growth while dealing with the risks posed by climate change. The study found that Americans living in sprawled communities directly bear $625 billion in extra costs, plus an additional $400 billion to the greater society, regardless of where one lives and works. Included in those figures are a range of direct and indirect costs: the displacement of agriculturally and ecologically productive lands, increased infrastructure costs, and increased transportation costs, including increases in per capita facility costs, consumer expenditures, travel time, congestion delays, traffic accidents, and pollution emissions, plus reduced accessibility for nondrivers and reduced public fitness and health. The report concludes:

> To the degree that sprawl degrades access by affordable modes (walking, cycling, and public transit), these impacts tend to be regressive (they impose particularly large burdens on physically, economically, and socially disadvantaged people). To the degree that sprawl concentrates poverty in urban neighborhoods, it tends to exacerbate social problems such as crime and dysfunctional families. To the degree that it reduces agglomeration efficiencies, increases infrastructure costs, and increases expenditures on imported goods (particularly vehicles and fuel), it tends to reduce economic productivity. Sprawl also provides benefits, but these are mostly direct internal benefits to sprawled community residents; there is little reason to expect sprawl to provide significant external benefits to non-residents.

Much of the preference for sprawl reflects economic and social factors, such as the perceived safety, affordability, public school quality, prestige, and financial security of suburban neighborhoods. But that turns out to be an illusion. For example, the commission found that sprawled suburban areas typically have two to five times the traffic fatality rates as in smart-growth communities.

Some of this is driven by building codes, which provide incentives for car ownership and driving. One example is parking. Regulations in some jurisdictions mandate that every housing unit have two surface parking spaces, which increases the amount of land committed to asphalt and reduces the number of residences that can be built on a given site, meaning lower density. Wider roads similarly reduce the amount of land available for housing and green space. It's not that we need policies to force people to abandon single-family homes for cramped and crowded apartments or otherwise give up the good life—far from it. Well-designed neighborhoods can include detached houses and townhouses with yards, apartments with shared play areas and rooftop gardens, public parks and gardens, plus studios, workshops, and garages included in residential buildings or available for rent nearby. In fact, research shows that this is exactly what people want.

ALL TOGETHER NOW

There is a better way to create vibrant and healthy communities. Getting from here to "walkable" requires planning and partnerships. By bringing together a region's city and suburban planners and stakeholders to focus on an integrated strategy, it is possible to bring the benefits of walkable communities and smart growth to both urban and suburban neighborhoods, addressing the housing demands of the next quarter century and beyond. And, in the process, improve everyone's quality of life, along with the area's economic vitality.

We already know this can work. In the 1980s, for example, as part of its strategy to constrain sprawl and retain the vitality of its urban core, Portland, Oregon, built a $100-million light-rail network called MAX (for Metropolitan Area Express). Since the streetcar route was identified, more than $8 billion of new development has occurred in light-rail-station areas, according to Trimet, the agency that operates MAX. Another study found that property values in Portland increased by $75 for every 100 feet closer a home is to a light-rail station. Such data underscores why the past decade or so has seen a boom in light rail, particularly in the Sun Belt, including Dallas, Houston, Los Angeles, and Phoenix, cities that have traditionally defined "sprawl" and have lacked adequate transit systems.

At the other end of the political spectrum from liberal Portland is another example: Salt Lake City. Expecting Utah's population to double by midcentury, and the bulk of that to affect the Salt Lake region, the state and various municipal governments came together with the Salt Lake Chamber and stakeholders from across the political spectrum to figure out how the region could double its population without diminishing the quality of life. In 1997, a public-private coalition called Envision Utah was formed, setting in motion a process that profoundly changed urban growth in the region. The first two years involved several hundred workshops and some 18,000 citizens.

Envision Utah developed four scenarios and settled on some of the more aggressive aspects of two of them to create the Quality Growth Strategy, which included 47 development goals and a 280-page "toolkit" manual on how to implement them. The goals included investing in a massive multimodal transportation network, transforming zoning codes, and modernizing energy and water distribution systems. The result minimized vehicle miles traveled, preserved farm- and wildlands, and will save $5 billion in local government expenditures over 20 years. Among the outcomes: Utah has decreased driving and increased the amount of passenger rail, providing new options for commuting along with improved air quality.

And then there's the aforementioned Detroit Future City, funded by the city's indigenous foundation community and working closely with city officials. It is one of the largest civic engagement projects in the United States. Since its founding in 2010—funded to "create a comprehensive framework to strategically coordinate, guide, and maximize the impact of the powerful work we are all doing every day"—the organization has held hundreds of community meetings and boasts 163,000 "interactions" with Detroiters—survey responses, conversations, town hall meetings, and the like—as part of a multiyear planning process.

In 2013, informed by all that input, the group published a strategic framework—"an integrated approach to transforming the city and its neighborhoods." It aims to balance land use, the city's existing infra-structure, its network of neighborhoods, its existing building stock, and the capacity of its civic organizations and government—all while spur-ring jobs and economic growth. "The idea was that we weren't there to make decisions for people or tell people what to do in the typical way you see a master plan, but rather to provide the frame through which people can make decisions," says Dan Kinkead.

It's a hat trick, to be sure. And less-hobbled cities have stumbled trying to address all these things amid a diverse and unruly group of stakeholders. But Detroit has several things working in its favor.

One is Mike Duggan, who became the city's mayor in 2014. The affable mayor—a former prosecutor and health-care business execu-tive, and the first white mayor of the majority-black city since the early 1970s—has been juggling the basics of keeping the lights on with the more aspirational goals of growing Detroit's economy. "I'm trying to get the buses to run on time, the street lights to come on, and the ambu-lances to come, and I think we're making progress," he told an audience of out-of-towners in 2015. Beyond that, Duggan seems to be using every tool at his disposal to lure business back, leveraging a network of busi-ness and foundation connections he's built over his career. Among his goals: "To encourage more people, especially young people, to live in town." He's been known to cajole total strangers to set up businesses in Detroit, and some of them do.

SUSTAINABILITY + SECURITY: REINVENTING GREENSBURG

As cities as diverse as Portland, Salt Lake City, and Detroit make clear, there's a lot that can happen when local residents, business owners, elected officials, neighborhood activists, and others come together to hash things out and envision a better future. No one knows this better than the residents of Greensburg, Kansas, a hamlet in the south-central part of the state, about 110 miles due west of Wichita on U.S. Highway 54.

On the evening of May 4, 2007, an F5 tornado—the highest category on the Fujita Scale used to rate tornado intensity—swept through town. Measuring 1.7 miles wide, wider than the town itself, and with winds peaking at 205 miles per hour, it killed 11 people and, essentially, Greensburg itself. During 65 minutes, the twister knocked down 95 percent of the town's businesses and residences. The remaining 5 percent were seriously damaged.

In the storm's immediate aftermath, Kathleen Sebelius, the state's governor at the time, called Bob Berkebile, a principal in the Kansas City architectural firm of Berkebile Nelson Immenschuh McDowell, better known as BNIM. Berkebile and BNIM had developed an international reputation for sustainably designed buildings and communities, especially those hard hit by natural disasters. In 1993, for example, after the great Mississippi and Missouri rivers flooded, causing some $15 billion in damages across some 30,000 square miles of the American Midwest, Berkebile convened a panel of national experts to reconsider the federal government's policy about rebuilding after a flood. BNIM was later hired to relocate a couple of communities out of harm's way. Tropical Storm Allison in 2001, Hurricane Katrina in 2005, the Haiti earthquake in 2010—the hard-hit communities from those and other calamities turned to Berkebile and BNIM for help in rebuilding.

When Sebelius called Berkebile about rebuilding Greensburg, he and his colleagues were initially reluctant to visit the devastated town, fearing they would be saying, in effect, "We're from the governor's office and we're here to help." Berkebile and a small team agreed to go to

Greensburg "as volunteers and to listen, and just become a part of the community for a while," as he explained. When they arrived in Greensburg, or what was left of it, the BNIM team initiated the process they had developed 14 years earlier in Valmeyer, Illinois, and Pattonsburg, Missouri, two towns nearly wiped out by the 1993 floods. The process involved gathering the entire town together to have a community dialogue about the future.

That was no easy task in Greensburg. There were no community halls or school gymnasiums remaining in the town. So, Berkebile asked the Federal Emergency Management Agency—FEMA—to erect a giant circus tent just outside of town and cater lunch for the thousand or so displaced citizens of Greensburg. It was the first time everyone had been together since the storm. That gathering—the first of what would become weekly tent meetings held throughout the summer of 2007—included an exercise called "Community Treasures," where the BNIM team asked residents three questions:

What do you love about your community?
What are the barriers of your community?
What would you create, if you could, in your community?

"These open-ended questions came with a lot of very rich dialogue about that community, its quality, and how to create something for their children in the future that would be more powerful than what they currently were experiencing," recalls Berkebile. "They were throwing out lots of ideas, and we were trying to listen and define those for them and then help them forecast what the outcomes might be."

What ultimately emerged from the conversations was, in many respects, a blueprint for a sustainability-infused town: a new Greensburg, powered by renewable energy, filled with energy-efficient buildings designed to provide healthy spaces to live and work. Affordable, resilient buildings, able to withstand the next tornado or flood, or whatever nature threw at them. They called for a "progressive, inclusive" town that respected the local environment and provided opportunities for young people to live, learn, and work.

Consciously or not, the citizens of Greensburg, who are, by and large, politically and socially conservative, were describing a vision for their rebuilt community using the language of sustainability. And the town they eventually rebuilt was an icon of environmental attributes, boasting the largest number of buildings per capita in the world to achieve LEED Platinum certification, the highest level offered by the U.S. Green Building Council. They included City Hall, a K–12 school, and the county hospital, the town's biggest employer. Greensburg's LEED Platinum John Deere dealership was designed to capture and recycle water, use geothermal heating, and draw power from its own wind turbine.

Indeed, the whole town became renewably powered. The city partnered with John Deere Renewable Energy and the Kansas Power Pool, a consortium of cities and towns that pool their electricity-buying power, to construct a wind farm five miles outside of town that could deliver power to the regional power pool, providing Greensburg with enough renewable energy credits to enable it to claim that it gets 100 percent of its power from the wind—the same force that knocked the town down in the first place.

In May 2008, a year after the tornado, Greensburg's city council adopted the 20-year Sustainable Comprehensive Plan, produced by BNIM, "a framework to ensure that Greensburg enjoys a socially vibrant, economically viable, and environmentally rich future." The master plan "memorializes the hopes and dreams of the community." They were collective dreams, born of a rich dialogue about the future. Among other things, the plan noted that "the desire to create a walkable community was clear from Greensburg's residents. It helps create the small town feel that was cherished for generations in Greensburg."

Berkebile began to wonder how to replicate such conversations in other cities, including those not necessarily facing devastation. "How do you raise the question about the future in every community in America?" he asks. "How do you participate in a dialogue at the community scale that embraces the level of change and opportunity that is appropriate?"

It remains an open question. Berkebile admits that he hasn't been able to pull off a community-scale dialogue effectively without a natural disaster, though he views climate change as a slow-moving natural disaster that could force the question in many towns. Meanwhile, he remains hopeful that if you can start a conversation, creating the conditions conducive for community members to invest their personal time to create scenarios about the future based on their values and passions, there are ample opportunities to build communities that are resilient to whatever blows their way.

That's what Greensburg did. And the proof is in what the town looks like nearly a decade after the tornado. The population is smaller, but it's also younger, a rarity among small midwestern towns. Now, there are reasons for young people to stick around Greensburg, or to come back after college to start a family and a career. "Before the tornado, if you asked most of the high school kids about their plans for the future, they'd say the same thing: 'I'm going to go away to college and never come back,'" says Greensburg school superintendent Darin Headrick. "Now, they say, 'I'm going to go to college and then come back.' They see things here that they can impact."

But there is an even deeper lesson for America to learn from Greensburg. Its shift to a sustainability-based design was essentially forced. The entire community was devastated by an unpredictable act of nature and, when faced with the reality of rebuilding, chose to design for their present and future reality and use the opportunity to revitalize and reinvigorate the community they love. Right now, our nation is in a position of free choice: the ability to shape ourselves to our emerging reality given what we know about climate change, water scarcity, soil erosion, waning public health, burgeoning socioeconomic stress, and the other forces shaping us. Eventually we will have to deal with these dynamics, but we shouldn't wait until we're forced to, as Greensburg was. Today, we not only can shape our future, but also make a buck doing it. In the aftermath of a tornado—whether a literal or figurative one—decisions will be more costly, and a lot more painful.

As Greensburg demonstrates, how we rethink the sustainability of our communities, from walkability to livability to security, will play a key role in how we think about sustainability overall, not just in the United States but globally. And there's a case to be made that, for all of the social, environmental, and economic challenges of today's cities, they are vital living laboratories for a sustainable future.

THE BUSINESS OF RESILIENCE

There's big money in all this systemic change. According to BCC Research, the global market for smart-city technologies is forecast to grow to $668 billion in 2019, more than triple what it was in 2013, for modern power grids, upgraded and efficient water treatment systems, transportation management systems, and energy-efficient buildings. "The major cities in the world have transformed into massive cosmopolitan regions with considerable cultural diversity," reports BCC. It defines a "smart city" as

> an innovative city that uses information and communications technologies (ICTs) and other means to improve the quality of life, the efficiency of urban operations and services, and competitiveness, and ensure that it meets the needs of present and future generations with respect to economic, social and environmental aspects. . . . ICTs can act as a platform to help overcome these challenges and take advantage of emerging opportunities as cities advance toward becoming smarter and more sustainable places to live.

"The growing awareness of our fragile ecology and the evolving environmental compliances and regulations have made it difficult to govern these large cities," wrote BCC's analysts. Smart cities, they note, make extensive use of communication technologies to improve the quality of life of their citizens, as well as building so-called green infrastructure, such as restored or constructed wetlands, or planting trees to soften the punch of storms. Green infrastructure incorporates both the natural environment and engineered systems to provide clean water, conserve ecosystem values and functions, and provide a wide array of benefits to people and nature. It can address not only storm-water management, but also flood mitigation, air-quality management, and other factors—usually at a fraction of the cost of digging and laying pipes. Such techniques are already being used extensively in Chicago, Dallas, Houston, Los Angeles, New York, Philadelphia, San Jose, and other cities.

Another burgeoning market is for community microgrids, small energy systems specifically designed to meet some or all of the energy needs of a campus, neighborhood, or small community. Microgrids can either be connected to the larger electricity grid or operate independently from it. They contain embedded intelligence that allows them to be managed in real time, providing electricity where and when it's needed, including tapping into the main grid if necessary. According to a 2015 report from Navigant Research, worldwide annual revenue from community microgrid implementation is expected to total nearly $7 billion from 2015 to 2024.

Add to this the growing market for renewable energy purchases by cities to power their buildings, infrastructure, and even to resell to businesses and residences. The 2015 list of the largest green-power purchasers among U.S. cities, published annually by the U.S. Environmental Protection Agency, includes cities not typically associated with green issues: Houston, the District of Columbia, and Dallas. Cities typically associated with progressive environmental agendas—Portland, San Francisco, Seattle—didn't even make the cut. Even Buffalo, New York, is becoming a green-energy hub, with the combination of wind turbines and Niagara Falls's clean, cheap hydroelectric power being credited with generating an economic turnaround and lowering the region's unemployment rate. Meanwhile, Hawaii governor David Ige signed a bill in 2015 calling for the state's electricity sector to transition entirely to renewable energy in 30 years, the first U.S. state to commit to 100 percent renewable energy. Some experts believe it can happen much faster.

The push for green infrastructure, green power, and microgrids addresses a range of community needs, including job creation and economic development, as well as the carbon-reduction goals being implemented by cities around the world. In 2015, for example, New York City mayor Bill de Blasio set a goal of powering 100 percent of the city's government operations from renewable energy, part of a commitment to reduce the Big Apple's greenhouse gas emissions by 80 percent by 2050. Doing so also will take a big bite out of the city's annual electricity bill, currently more than $600 million a year.

But for all these benefits—job creation, economic development, pollution reduction, and cost savings—there are additional compelling reasons for companies to embark on these projects. In a word, resilience: the ability of cities to more effectively handle the kind of extreme weather events—hurricanes, tornadoes, blizzards, and all the rest—that are occurring with greater frequency. That is, to avoid becoming the next Greensburg, Kansas.

Undoubtedly, mayors, city councils, and public works departments are reading reports like the 2014 *National Climate Assessment,* produced by a team of more than 300 experts, guided by a 60-member advisory committee, and reviewed by the public and experts, including federal agencies and a panel of the National Academy of Sciences. It summarized the impacts of climate change on the United States. Among its findings:

> Heavy downpours are increasing nationally, especially over the last three to five decades. The heaviest rainfall events have become heavier and more frequent, and the amount of rain falling on the heaviest rain days has also increased. Since 1991, the amount of rain falling in very heavy precipitation events has been significantly above average. This increase has been greatest in the Northeast, Midwest, and upper Great Plains— more than 30 percent above the 1901–1960 average. There has also been an increase in flooding events in the Midwest and Northeast, where the largest increases in heavy rain amounts have occurred.

Resilience isn't just about flooding, of course. As we said earlier, it's about "the capacity to take a gut punch and come back swinging." Somewhat more formally, city resilience "is the capacity of individuals, communities, institutions, businesses, and systems within a city to survive, adapt, and grow no matter what kinds of chronic stresses and acute shocks they experience," according to 100 Resilient Cities, a non-profit organization. It is also, says the group, about "the stresses that weaken the fabric of a city on a day-to-day or cyclical basis." The goal of 100 Resilient Cities, pioneered by the Rockefeller Foundation, is to fund 100 cities around the world to hire a "chief resilience officer." It's a new job title that typically exists in or around the mayor's office, and its holder acts as the city's point person for building resilience, helping to coordinate all of the city's efforts to prepare for, and respond to, extreme weather or other shocks, including economic and social turmoil. The CRO, as this position is being called, is intended to work across departments to help improve internal communications and bring together a wide array of stakeholders.

To the extent CROs can improve communications and collaborations among various city departments—not to mention with the citizenry and other stakeholders—they will be performing a near-Herculean task. Like most bureaucracies, cities are notoriously siloed—they barely collaborate among themselves, let alone with the private sector or local universities to identify partnership opportunities, business models, and creative financing that can upgrade or strengthen city infrastructure;

procure renewable energy; install "smart" lighting, parking, traffic, and other systems; finance and operate transportation systems; or any of a number of other things that can enhance cities and towns.

When it happens successfully, public-private partnerships can be a potent driver of projects that promote sustainable communities. In Detroit, for example, former race car driver and billionaire Roger S. Penske—owner of auto racing's Team Penske, the Penske Corporation, and other auto-related businesses—led a consortium of businesspeople that raised $1 billion to build the M-1, a three-mile streetcar system down Willard Avenue that connects the riverfront, downtown, and the New Center–Midtown neighborhoods. It's the first urban rail transit line in the United States to be built and operated by a private, nonprofit organization, with most of the funding coming from individual investors and foundations. (In addition to Penske are Quicken Loans founder and chair Dan Gilbert and Compuware founder Peter Karmanos.) The project quickly became a development magnet: nearly all the buildings along the M-1 corridor are being renovated, and there's a six- to eight-month waiting list for some of the condos being built.

Similarly, in Denver, the Eagle P3 Project brought together the Regional Transportation District with companies like Fluor and Aberdeen Global Infrastructure Partners in a $2 billion project to build a 36-mile electrified commuter rail system with 15 stations. The public agency owns the system while entering into a long-term lease with a consortium of companies, giving them the right to use the property and make improvements to operate the rail system. The public agency owns all revenues, advertising, and naming rights. Meanwhile, the private group is responsible for costs of operation and maintenance, including repairs, replacements, and updates. All are part of what's being called "smart" transportation systems—or "mobility" systems, a newer term, which integrates walking, biking, public transit, car sharing, and driving. The goal is to create a seamless (or, in Silicon Valley lingo, "frictionless") experience for community residents and visitors, enabling them to access multiple and coordinated modes of transportation to get from here to there. According to Navigant Research, the global smart urban mobility infrastructure and services market is expected to grow fivefold over the next decade, from $5.1 billion in 2015 to $25.1 billion in 2024.

The partnerships needed to build these things—whether a fast and efficient transportation system, a clean and reliable energy system, a safe and plentiful water system, or other keystone infrastructure—underscore the fact that urban needs are far too great for traditional public funding. Public-private partnerships, once considered a wonky novelty, are now becoming a necessity, both for governments and for private companies.

INVESTOR-READY CITIES

Such projects don't happen without a lot of TLC. To get private-sector investment, cities will need to take inventory of their policies and political institutions and aim to realign them with the needs of investors. That is, to be "investor-ready," in the words of a 2015 report from Siemens, PwC, and the law firm Berwin Leighton Paisner: "Cities are now more reliant than ever before on private-sector support to scope, finance, and deliver projects. It is becoming much more common to see private-sector finance help to cover the cost of delivery with long-term management contracts for maintenance and operation to secure the investment and provide confidence to the public sector in sustained delivery."

Nearly all cities have limited access to funds and ways of financing their plans. Some lack even the most basic legal and institutional frameworks to facilitate access to financing from the capital markets. Federal grants can get cities only part of the way to the finish line. On the other hand, investors want and need such things as streamlined regulatory and licensing processes, stakeholder buy-in, reliable governance structures, and a clear vision among city leaders about the goals of a project.

There are a growing number of innovative funding solutions that tap the vast pool of capital available through pension funds and other sources. For example, there's West Coast Infrastructure Exchange, or WCX, founded in 2012 and operating in California, Oregon, Washington, and British Columbia. It targets union and public-employee pension funds, which represent "patient capital"—that is, they typically have longer-term investment horizons and less interest in turning a quick profit. As such they can afford to let investment in an infrastructure project take years, even decades, to pay dividends. It doesn't hurt that the creation of new jobs and economic growth from the investment often align with the fund managers' interests and mandates. So far, WCX has raised $18 billion, a sizable sum, but that is only a small slice of the $1 trillion or so these three American states and one Canadian province will need in infrastructure upgrades in the coming decades, not to mention America's overall $3.6 trillion price tag for infrastructure improvements.

Even when there's funding, public-private partnerships are not always easy. Often, the two sectors speak different languages and operate at different speeds. At the annual VERGE City Summit produced by GreenBiz Group, cities and companies come together to discuss how to overcome the mismatch in public-private partnerships aimed at energy, transportation, water, and other infrastructure. Among the barriers frequently cited are that governments tend to have longer time horizons for projects, while private companies want to move quickly. Likewise, cities often get bogged down in dealing with day-to-day problems at the expense of addressing the bigger picture, which can be frustrating to private-sector minds that just want to "get it done."

Such challenges notwithstanding, such partnerships will increasingly become table stakes for communities as they address their smart-city, carbon-reduction, and resilience goals, many of which will require new, more efficient technologies and practices, often secured with innovative financing models that address many cities' bleak budget realities. Already, dozens of U.S. cities are making bold commitments: Boston, Boulder, New York, Portland, San Francisco, Seattle, and Washington, D.C., are among the Carbon Neutral Cities, an alliance of municipalities committed to an 80 percent reduction in their cities' greenhouse gas emissions by midcentury. That will require these cities to dramatically scale up renewable energy purchases, retrofit city fleets with electric and other alternative-fuel models, equip buildings with energy-efficient technologies, replace streetlights and traffic signals with highly efficient bulbs, and upgrade wastewater treatment plants and other infrastructure—in most cases requiring significant investments. And it's not just big cities. The towns of Dewitt, New York; Carrboro, North Carolina; Saline, Michigan; Salisbury, Maryland; Columbus, Wisconsin; South Daytona, Florida; Hurricane, Utah; and Lancaster, California, are among hundreds of smaller American cities and towns that have committed to reducing their energy use and carbon footprint, along with other initiatives intended to align their operations with the goals of a more livable, safe, and operationally efficient community.

And then there's the tiny town of Bloomfield, in southeast Iowa, with a population of 2,640, last we checked. Just over half the town—51 percent—is considered low to moderate income, and like many small

American towns, Bloomfield has experienced its share of brain drain as local kids go off to college and pursue careers, never to return. The town suffered a dearth of well-paying jobs and opportunities.

Still, when it comes to energy, Bloomfield is a shining light among American cities, both big and small. It began when town leaders decided to tackle a minor symptom of decline: the decaying streets and sidewalks in Bloomfield's downtown. A consultant recommended installing a ground-source heat pump solution to serve buildings on the town square while they were digging things up. That engendered a conversation that eventually led to Bloomfield declaring a goal of energy independence, rooted in the community's values of jobs, durability, and up-by-the-bootstraps self-sufficiency. Working with the Rocky Mountain Institute, city leaders devised a plan to achieve that ambitious goal. For example, they realized that local hog farms generated a great deal of methane, a global-warming gas that also had the potential to generate power. The school system explored alternative fuels for its buses. All in all, city officials discovered that efficiency measures alone could reduce Bloomfield's energy consumption by nearly a fourth, and create jobs along the way.

Doug Dixon, the president of Bloomfield Main Street, a business group committed to the town's revitalization, put it this way: "By utilizing our resources responsibly and keeping and creating energy dollars in our community, we intend to attract new energy initiatives that will create jobs and position us as a community for the twenty-first century."

This is no utopian vision. Bloomfield—like Greensburg, Detroit, and thousands of other American communities—will always have its challenges. Rather, theirs is a pragmatic and purposeful approach applicable to cities and towns of all sizes and geographies, grounded in the understanding that America is strongest, safest, and most prosperous when our communities are healthy and sustainable, in every sense.

CHAPTER FIVE

REGENERATIVE AGRICULTURE

WHEN YOU LOOK CLOSELY AT THE STATE OF AMERICAN AGRICULTURE and the policies behind it, *strategic* and *adaptive* are not words that come to mind. In fact, American agriculture looks downright oblivious to the changing environment, the global markets, and the times. Farming in the United States is, for all intents and purposes, centrally planned and heavily subsidized by the federal government, currently to the tune of around $20 billion a year—"farm income stabilization," in D.C.-speak. But that's just the tip of the subsidy iceberg.

There's also $8 billion in crop insurance subsidies, with private-sector providers pocketing more than $1 billion annually in "administrative expenses," despite the fact that the crop program is largely paid for by the government and is extremely lucrative for insurers. The beneficiaries of this largess are a handful of companies, including Starr Indemnity & Liability, run by former AIG CEO Maurice Greenberg; Wells Fargo, the nation's fourth-largest bank; Zurich-based ACE Group; and units of American Financial Group, Deere & Company, and Archer Daniels Midland.

There's Price Loss Coverage, a program through which farmers receive payments when prices for corn, soybeans, and 12 other crops drop below a certain level; countercyclical payments, similarly triggered when market prices fall below thresholds; Average Crop Revenue Election, or ACRE, a revenue assurance program that provides for overall profitability for a given crop if a farmer meets strict guidelines; marketing loans that offer favorable terms through instruments known as loan deficiency payments and commodity certificates; and disaster assistance programs to help farmers recoup large losses resulting from nature's wrath.

There's more—millions more annually in conservation subsidies (helping farmers reduce soil erosion and enhance groundwater recharge), for the Agricultural Research Service (the U.S. Department of Agriculture's R&D lab), and in Farm Service Agency loans (for farmers who cannot otherwise get funding from a commercial lender). There's nearly $2 billion in annual irrigation subsidies provided by the Department of the Interior's Bureau of Reclamation. There's something called shallow loss programs, a series of three programs—Agriculture Risk Coverage, the Supplemental Coverage Option, and the Stacked Income Protection Plan—designed to kick in when revenue drops as little as 10 percent from a predetermined level. Did we mention subsidies for tobacco farmers—the ones whose products are frowned upon by the very same federal government?

That adds up to a lot of money. Indeed, up to half of every dollar farmers receive is a direct or indirect federal subsidy. Half. It's important to ask just what we're getting for that investment and massive market intervention. On the one hand, the industrial food system has produced increasing quantities of affordable food for both domestic and foreign markets, grown by farmers who are continually upping their productivity, if not their profits. And food prices, at least in the United States, are certainly less volatile than they were just a few decades ago.

On the other hand, modern agriculture's negative effects are bad and worsening: nutrition is dropping, toxicity is rising, soils are being depleted, pollinators are dying off, carbon is being dumped into the atmosphere, water use is draining aquifers, runoff is polluting waterways, monocropping is decreasing resilience, and food distribution leaves major underserved groups hungry at the same time that 40 percent of food is going to waste.

It is hard not to conclude that current federal intervention in the food system is harming America and Americans. Worse, this is happening at a time when we need to be firing on all cylinders to meet rising global demand. As 3 billion people come into the global middle class over the next two decades, and as the world population goes from 7 billion to 9 billion, the Organization for Economic Cooperation and Development and the United Nations Food and Agriculture Organization estimate that the world will have to increase its food supply by 60 percent by 2050—and that 100 percent of that will have to be regenerative. America's agricultural heartland should be preparing for a new era of agricultural innovation, productivity, and profit, but under business as usual, we're headed instead for depletion and disruption. One need only look at the years-long drought in California's Central Valley for evidence that we are unable to handle even a modest disruption in weather and climate.

China's changing diet gives a sense of the scale we're dealing with. The country has 20 percent of the world's population but only 8 percent of its arable land. According to a 2014 report by the Earth Policy Institute, Chinese meat consumption went from being one-third of America's in 1978 to more than double our intake today. And there's plenty of room for growth, given that China has four times America's population. Indeed, some Chinese may be eating too well: the Middle Kingdom now accounts for a third of all the new diabetes cases worldwide, according to a 2013 *Journal of the American Medical Association* report. With its seemingly insatiable appetite, China is now dependent on global markets for its food supply. America delivers one quarter of China's agricultural imports, worth approximately $24 billion annually, according to 2013 USDA figures, making China our largest agricultural export destination. Like it or not, our agricultural futures are fundamentally linked.

In the next two decades, the world will triple the number of people who will leave behind subsistence farming to draw on global food markets. China alone will bring 292 million more people into its cities in the next 20 years, nearly the current population of the United States, and we must find a way to meet that demand while turning agriculture from an environmental liability into a force for the regeneration of natural capital and ecosystem services. It's an enormous strategic challenge that does not allow for error in the design of our agriculture system. We have a long way to go.

SETTING THE TABLE

It did not get this bad overnight. In fact, it's been building for a long time. So what happened?

The first modern agricultural subsidies cropped up in the 1930s, with the New Deal and the Agricultural Adjustment Act of 1933. It paid farmers not to plant on part of their land and to kill off excess livestock in order to reduce crop surplus and effectively raise the value of crops. The bizarre mix of payments to variously grow and not grow certain crops made little sense.

The coming of global war changed things. By the end of World War II, American agriculture was an unqualified success story, producing around 40 percent more food than could be consumed domestically. American farmers worked miracles to get food to our troops and allies, increasing production, processing it for shipment to distant theaters of war, and doing it amid a massive reduction of farmworkers, many of whom had been shipped off to the front lines.

There were two great drivers of this success: innovations in irrigation and improvements in farm machinery. World War II coincided with the advent of the motorized aquifer pump, allowing farmers across the Great Plains to tap into the great underground sea of freshwater known as the Ogallala Aquifer, which undergirds eight states across America's middle, from South Dakota to Texas. With plentiful water, American farm yields reached skyward, leaving the hardship of the Dust Bowl behind. Second, American companies such as John Deere and International Harvester mass-produced gasoline-powered tractors and a host of plows, threshers, and combines that allowed a reduced number of farmworkers to outproduce their predecessors. With consistent irrigation and the substitution of fossil-fuel energy for horse- and people-power, America fed the Allied effort and the homeland.

Producing a 40 percent surplus of food helped win the war, but it became a liability in peacetime, when the law of supply and demand dictates that prices will fall, and rapidly, as the result of large surpluses. With farmers taking loans to purchase their new equipment and the fuel to run it, Washington needed to find a way to buy a lot of food, and needed a place to send it.

Farmers did not have to wait long. Even before the war's end, it was clear that Europe's entire population was at risk of mass starvation, since the continent's own agricultural production had halted because of the fighting on the eastern, western, and Mediterranean fronts. War-affected regions had to contend with poisoned water supplies from human and animal casualties, cratered fields, and unexploded ordnance, from bombs and land mines to mortar shells and hand grenades. Those farmers who could produce crops found that road and railroad transportation was largely disrupted, with most trucks destroyed or pressed into service to move the displaced and refugees. Food-processing plants had been decimated by aerial raids or retreating ground forces. Markets in cities and towns were often inaccessible or had been pounded to rubble. The food systems would not be able to meet the population's needs for years. The same went for Japan, the Philippines, and much of urban, coastal China.

America's farmers had plenty of foreign mouths to feed, but until Europe and Asia began to rebuild and start producing goods and services, they would have no way to pay. Surplus war rations, repackaged as CARE Packages, would be the first American aid to arrive in postwar European ports. But it was the Marshall Plan and a series of reconstruction assistance programs by the Truman administration that would keep America's excess production from going to waste. It was critical and strategic assistance. With millions displaced and hungry, with insufficient heat, electricity, and water in Europe's devastated cities, the continent was extremely vulnerable to communist insurgencies. By demonstrating America's commitment to basic needs and reconstruction, even of Germany's industrial capacity, America secured essential allies at Western Europe's moment of greatest need.

By 1970, the global agricultural system had changed dramatically. After European and Japanese reconstruction, populations across the developed world began to increase their consumption of meat, poultry, and bread, with a concomitant increased demand for corn, soy, and wheat. By the early 1970s, fully 60 percent of the world's grains were going into livestock feed, and consumer prices were rising.

In 1972, the Soviet Union revealed to the world that its grain harvest was in trouble. To remedy this, the Soviets made secret deals with the five biggest American grain companies to purchase more than 24 million tons, worth almost $1.5 billion in 1972 dollars (equivalent to about $8.5 billion today). This happened just as a widespread drought hit the Midwest. It is unclear whether Earl Butz, Secretary of Agriculture at the time, was aware that the Soviets were buying up fully a fourth of America's entire wheat crop, but he did nothing to stop the sale.

Since the sale essentially involved the equivalent of the entire U.S. grain reserve, grain prices jumped and farmers scrambled to plant as much as they could to take advantage. Butz—a conservative Republican politician who had been appointed by Nixon—fanned their frenzy, advocating increased production. He envisioned a hyperefficient, centralized food system, one that could profitably and cheaply feed the world by producing endless mountains of corn and soy from America's Grain Belt. In 1973, Butz went on a speaking tour, prodding farmers to "plant fence row to fence row" to meet the global demand. He brooked no dissent in the belief that bigger farms were more productive and therefore in the national interest.

The high grain prices resulting from the exports and drought contributed to a period of spiraling inflation: American workers demanded higher wages to pay for food and other necessities, so companies passed the increases on to consumers, who then demanded higher wages to keep up. By 1973, the inflation rate for groceries reached 20 percent in just one year. The impact roiled food buying, and shoppers organized protests at supermarkets. Public school systems, even in farm states like Iowa, substituted peanut butter and beans for more expensive meat dishes. A headline in *U.S. News & World Report* asked, "Why a Food Scare in a Land of Plenty?"

Of course, what was bad for consumers was good for the farm industry. U.S. farm income skyrocketed, from $2.3 billion in 1972 to $19.6 billion just a year later, and farm income stayed high for most of the decade.

But it didn't last forever. Livestock producers found themselves caught in a price squeeze as feed prices jumped. Millions of hogs, cattle, and chickens were sold for slaughter as producers reduced their inventories. Butz's admonition to "get big or get out" led farmers to tear out various land conservation tools and processes such as shelterbelts (windbreaks designed to protect crops, soils, and livestock from wind and blowing snow). Millions of midwestern farmers spent the 1970s taking on debt to buy more land, bigger and more complicated machines, new seed varieties, more fertilizers and pesticides, and generally producing as much as they possibly could. For a few years, those actions seemed like good bets.

By the 1980s, farms were cranking out much more than the market could bear, depressing prices at a time when interest rates had spiked, turning all of those loans farmers had taken out during the 1970s into a paralyzing burden. The bubble burst. Farm incomes plunged and tens of thousands of farms went under. Butz's great policy change had given rise to the deepest rural crisis since the Great Depression. It had also created a deeply rooted, monolithic agricultural system that is alive and not so well today.

SHIFTING GROUND

Today's agricultural industry is clearly a remnant of Butz's era, but if it is so bad, why hasn't it changed? One big reason is that the staying power of such huge government intervention in the farming sector is partly a product of the disproportionate clout given to farming states in America's political system by the Electoral College and the Senate: western and midwestern states like Iowa, Kansas, Nebraska, and Wyoming punch way above their weight in national elections.

It's easy to understand their motivation. When you put it all together, we're talking about big money. A 2010 analysis by Grey, Clark, Shih and Associates, a Canadian consultancy, estimated the total value of USDA programs alone at $180.8 billion—not small potatoes. And once subsidies are in place, they become addictive; they take root politically and become a sacred cow for politicians, farmers, and consumers. The sad thing is, at the end of the day, all that money doesn't buy much except acres of dysfunction.

We're essentially keeping a dying system on life support. In the words of Adam Moody, founder and CEO of Moody's Butcher Shop and a fifth-generation farmer from Montgomery County, Indiana, who has been practicing sustainable farming since 1987, "Subsidies are nothing more than antibodies for an anemic system."

What has changed? For starters, Earl Butz's policies and farming technology have driven massive consolidation. Since 1979, more than 300,000 small farms have disappeared in the United States, and since 1946 the number of Americans employed in agriculture has dropped by 70 percent, from about 10 million to less than 3 million today, while the U.S. population more than doubled, from 141 million to 320 million. Some of that is because of gains in productivity, but all that "progress" isn't paying off for most who make their living off the land.

Today's farm households earn most of their income from off-farm sources: 91 percent have at least one family member working at a job outside the farm fence, according to the U.S. Department of Agriculture's Economic Research Service. That's essential, given that the majority of farms operate at a loss; median farm "income" was negative

$1,558 in 2015, though average total income among farm households was $113,251, meaning average nonfarm income was nearly $115,000. Farmers are getting older, more so than workers in almost any other occupation. According to the Labor Department, the median age for farmers and ranchers was 58.3 years in 2012 (stats are published every five years), second-oldest among tracked occupations and up from 50.5 years over the past three decades.

Despite all this, the productivity of American farms continues to climb. Agricultural production in the United States has increased by an average of 5 percent annually since 1990. For example, according to Agriculture Department data, between 1950 and 2000, the average amount of milk produced per cow more than tripled, from 5,314 pounds to 18,201 pounds per year, while the average yield of corn nearly quadrupled, from 39 bushels to 153 bushels per acre. Each farmer in 2000 produced on average 12 times as much farm output per hour worked as a farmer did in 1950. But there are limits, and since the turn of the millennium, agricultural productivity has been essentially flat.

The greater use of agricultural inputs, such as fertilizer and machinery per acre, was partly responsible for this bounty, along with the development of new technology, which made inputs more effective or allowed inputs to be combined in new and better ways. But the main drivers of U.S. agricultural productivity are in large part the basic strategies of industrialization: specialization, standardization, and consolidation. Creating a new system that meets our strategic imperatives will require us to understand how these industrial strategies have translated into three attributes of the current agriculture system—industry consolidation, soil depletion, and proprietary seeds—then design a business-led pathway that meets our strategic needs while strengthening farming families and communities as they produce affordable and nutritious food.

INDUSTRY CONSOLIDATION

To be a farmer in America today is to tend a vast acreage of specialized monocrops—a single species that's grown year after year. Fully two-thirds (67.6 percent) of the 300 million acres of farmed land in the United States are devoted to just two crops, corn and soy, according to 2015 data from the USDA's Farm Service Agency. It's a simple matter of following the money. According to the department's Economic

Research Service (ERS), "Broadly speaking, payments tend to follow production: Farms with greater production of a program commodity—either because they have more acreage of the commodity or higher yields on their acreage—receive greater total payments."

Consolidation means fewer farms are producing more and more. Today, large-scale and nonfamily farm operations account for just 8 percent of farms but 60 percent of the value of production, according to a 2014 USDA *Economic Information Bulletin*. Three big companies—Deere & Company, AGCO, and the Italy-based CNH Industrial—control 77 percent of the world's $65 billion farm machinery market. Things are even more concentrated in the food production part of the industry, according to a 2012 report from Food & Water Watch, an advocacy group based in Washington, D.C.:

> The agriculture and food sector is unusually concentrated, with just a few companies dominating the market in each link of the food chain. In most sectors of the U.S. economy, the four largest firms control between 40 and 45 percent of the market, and many economists maintain that higher levels of concentration can start to erode competitiveness. Yet according to data compiled by the University of Missouri–Columbia in 2012, in the agriculture and food sector, the four largest companies controlled 82 percent of the beef packing industry, 85 percent of soybean processing, 63 percent of pork packing, and 53 percent of broiler chicken processing.

One of the most striking consolidations has been in the agricultural seed business, where three companies—Monsanto, DuPont, and Syngenta—control slightly more than half of the global market, more than double the 22 percent that the top three firms controlled in 1996. Enforcement of federal antitrust laws has slackened in recent years, with few meaningful investigations into mergers and acquisitions of large agricultural producers, suppliers, and processors. According to Phil Howard, an associate professor in the Community, Agriculture, Recreation and Resource Studies program at Michigan State University, since 2008 "there have been more than 70 seed company acquisitions by the top eight firms, as well as a number of biotech company acquisitions and joint ventures." Moreover, he says, the six biggest chemical and seed companies have increased their cross-licensing agreements to share genetically engineered traits, "strengthening the barriers to entry for smaller firms that don't have access to these expensive technologies." It is likely that further consolidation will eventually turn those six big seed companies into just two or three, says Howard. Indeed, at the end of 2015, Dow and DuPont agreed to merge, one of the largest corporate hook-ups in the history of business.

Such concentration harms both producers and consumers. Farmers pay more for supplies when only a few firms sell seeds, fertilizer, and tractors. They also sell into a highly consolidated market, and the few firms bidding for crops and livestock can drive down the prices that farmers receive. While consumers have a cornucopia of brand choices (which is mostly a variation in advertising and labeling), they actually have fewer choices at the supermarket when it comes to origin, quality, processing, and packaging. Moreover, food processors and retailers are quick to raise prices when farm prices rise, such as during oil price hikes or a drought, but are slow to pass savings on to consumers when such conditions ease.

Once again, subsidies play a role. One unintended consequence of subsidizing farms is inflated land prices and the consolidation of farmland in the hands of a few profitable landowners. The USDA's ERS reports that when agricultural subsidy payments increase income from farm production, "the expectation of future payments may be capitalized into the value of farmland." The agency also found that "cropland consolidated more rapidly in those zip codes with higher levels of government payments." All told, farmland values grew 15 to 25 percent due to farm subsidy payments, benefiting all farm households regardless of whether they are direct recipients of farm subsidies. Crop insurance subsidies and loan deficiency payments further enhanced cropland values.

The outcome is clear: when Uncle Sam designs the menu, farmers plant what the government wants instead of what consumers want, let alone need.

Consolidation is having an impact beyond fertilizer, seeds, and tools. Modern genetics allows businesses to reproduce animals with a preferred package of desired traits, and without variation. Long used in the poultry sector, the practice is coinciding with increased frequency of pandemics. One harsh example came home to roost in 2015, when an avian flu epidemic, called H5N2, swept 15 midwestern states and two Canadian provinces, the worst bird flu epidemic in American history. It caused ranchers to destroy some 40 million chickens—more than 10 percent of the national chicken inventory—25 million in Iowa alone, representing 40 percent of that state's egg-laying capacity. The outbreak of a particularly infectious version of the bird flu was believed to have come from wild ducks and geese that migrated across the Pacific Ocean before infecting domestic fowl. U.S. egg production fell in 2015 for the first time since 2008, and the month of June 2015 saw a 17.8 percent increase in egg prices over the previous month, the largest one-month increase in 42 years. The high prices persisted for several months after the epidemic was contained.

This wasn't the first major chicken-and-egg epidemic. A similar, albeit less virulent, strain of influenza caused a multistate outbreak in 1983–84, when 17 million birds died or were killed, including nearly all the chickens in Pennsylvania. It took more than two years to eradicate the flu strain.

Both epidemics pointed out the importance of diversity and resilience in our food system. The poultry raised on industrial poultry farms in the United States are largely monotypic, all exact replicas of one another. A single pedigreed cockerel, a male chicken, has the reproductive capacity to sire 2 million chickens in its life as a breeder on a poultry farm. The entire chicken genome was published in 2004, which informed us that commercial chickens have lost 90 percent of their genetic variations compared to native and noncommercial hybrids.

The same is true for most other livestock, as well as crops raised on American farms. According to the American Association of Swine Veterinarians, "As genetic improvement falls into the hands of fewer companies and the trend towards intense multiplication of a limited range of genotypes develops, there is mounting concern that large populations may have increasingly uniform vulnerability to particular pathogens."

Talk about putting all your eggs in one basket!

SOIL DEPLETION

For all the benefits derived from growing food locally or organically, or even replacing monocrops with a cornucopia of fruits and vegetables, these practices are still not necessarily regenerative. As we said, one key to ensuring a bountiful supply of meat, milk, fruits, vegetables, and other foods is to restore our soils.

"Soil is a living and life-giving natural resource," says the USDA's Natural Resources Conservation Service. "As world population and food production demands rise, keeping our soil healthy and productive is of paramount importance. So much so that we believe improving the health of our nation's soil is one of the most important conservation endeavors of our time."

To the extent that America's agricultural soil is a national treasure (and a buried treasure at that), industrial agriculture has been squandering it for decades. Today, the quality and quantity of soil in the United States represents, by some measures, a looming national catastrophe. According to the University of Michigan's Global Change Program, 96 percent of North America's soil erosion comes from food production (66 percent from agricultural activities; 30 percent from overgrazing). The majority occurs in the central portion of the United States, right where we produce the bulk of our food. Significant portions of this region have been designated as "Areas of Serious Concern," where up to 75 percent of the topsoil has been lost, mostly due to modern farming techniques.

Healthy soil provides a number of essential biological functions. It regulates water, helping control where rain, snowmelt, and irrigation water goes. It filters, buffers, degrades, and detoxifies pollutants, including industrial and municipal runoff. It stores, transforms, and cycles carbon, nitrogen, phosphorous, and other nutrients. It anchors the roots of plants and trees. And it ensures the diversity and productivity of plants and critters that live in soil. All told, soil provides 11 distinct services, according to the United Nations Food and Agriculture Organization.

The microbial content of soil is no small matter. It is where much of the planet's biodiversity resides. According to the Earth Institute at Columbia University, an acre of soil may contain 900 pounds of earthworms, 2,400 pounds of fungi, 1,500 pounds of bacteria, 133 pounds of protozoa, 890 pounds of arthropods and algae, and even sometimes small mammals. (Kudos to the grad students who counted all this stuff.) A single gram of soil may hold a billion bacteria, of which only 5 percent have been identified. Bacteria are able to perform an extremely wide range of chemical transformations, including breaking down organic matter and manufacturing nutrients inside roots. These processes are crucial to growing a healthy food supply.

So, if our topsoil is eroding, we'll just make some more, right? Not quite. It can take 500 to 1,000 years to create just a single inch of topsoil through the interaction of bedrock, climate, topography, and living organisms. Soil erosion has always occurred naturally, but sometime during the nineteenth century, the rate of topsoil loss from erosion due to agriculture surpassed the rate of soil formation, according to Lester Brown, founder of the Worldwatch Institute and the Earth Policy Institute. We've been losing ground ever since.

Federal policy and subsidies that promote monocropping, combined with intensifying storms from a shifting climate, are washing away the rich dark soils in the Midwest that made the nation an agricultural powerhouse. Since soil formation is an extraordinarily slow process, erosion poses a serious problem; over time, it can cause fertile farmland to become unsuitable for agriculture. In extreme cases, erosion can lead to desertification, a process that causes soil to become barren and incapable of sustaining plant growth for many years.

However, even low rates of soil erosion can severely damage agricultural land and decrease its productivity by reducing soil's water-holding capacity and stripping away nutrients and organic matter. In fact, soil removed by erosion contains about three times more nutrients and up to five times more organic matter than the soil that remains behind.

The National Sustainable Agriculture Information Service notes that erosion is the single greatest threat to soil productivity, and it levies a significant economic toll. According to a 2006 study published in the *Journal of the Environment, Development and Sustainability*, the loss of soil and water from U.S. cropland decreases productivity by about $37 billion per year, and $400 billion worldwide. The study found that the United States is losing soil ten times faster than the natural replenishment rate. It could be worse: China and India are losing soil 30 to 40 times faster.

PROPRIETARY SEEDS

Soil degradation is one way we are squandering America's agricultural treasure. Seeds are another. As we noted earlier, the seed industry has undergone consolidation to the point that just three companies control more than half of the market, with further consolidation likely. That's a problem in and of itself, but it's not the whole story. It turns out that seed companies and their allies have been trying to stymie efforts by farmers seeking a workaround in the form of seed libraries.

Seed libraries are a type of agricultural commons where users can borrow and share seed varieties. They are part of a tradition dating back centuries, where farmers saved seeds from one year's crop to plant the next year or traded them with other farmers. (Arguably, farmers invented what we now call the sharing economy.) Today's seed libraries—by making a wide range of both common and "heirloom" fruit, vegetable, and flower varieties available to gardeners and farmers—help preserve and enrich species biodiversity. A growing number of libraries have taken root in recent years in the United States, from only a handful in 2010 to more than 300 today.

In some towns, public libraries that once exclusively housed books and other published materials are being repurposed to include seeds. For example, Arizona's Pima County, home to Tucson, launched seed libraries in 2012 in eight public libraries. Anyone with a library card can check out up to six seed packages a month, much as they would books, DVDs, or other materials. The barcoded packets typically contain enough seeds to grow five to ten plants. Since borrowers don't return the same seeds, there are no due dates or overdue fines, though there's an expectation that borrowers will contribute seeds from their harvest the following year. Similar public library programs exist across the United States, from Richmond, California, to South Sioux City, Iowa, to New Port Richey, Florida.

It sounds simple enough, not to mention downright civic: citizens in both urban and rural communities sharing seeds, enhancing biodiversity, saving money, and growing nutritious varieties of fruits and vegetables for their families and community.

Not so, it seems. In Pennsylvania, such activity was viewed as downright criminal. In 2014, the Cumberland County Library System, in the south-central part of the state, received a letter from the state's Department of Agriculture stating that Mechanicsburg's Joseph T. Simpson Public Library, which loaned heirloom and organic seeds, was in violation of the Pennsylvania Seed Act of 2004. Citing concerns that seeds may be purposefully or accidentally mislabeled, that they might contribute to the growth of invasive plant species, or cross-pollinate with other plants or contain poisonous species, the department told the library it could not operate the seed library unless its staff tested each seed packet for germination and other things. This was not something the library's staff was willing or able to handle.

Pennsylvania's Seed Act, which applies to entities "offering for sale, selling, *bartering or otherwise supplying seed*" (emphasis added), was aimed at big seed companies, which are subject, under section 111.1 of the law, to "sampling and testing of seeds." Seemingly, this regulatory and oversight kerfuffle was an issue of security. One state agriculture commissioner noted that seed libraries on a large scale could pose a danger, stating that "agri-terrorism is a very, very real scenario."

Agri-terrorism? Not the most pressing scenario. But even if it were, one thing we have learned since 9/11 is that addressing the threat of diffuse and loosely coupled terrorist organizations through increased centralization and bureaucratic controls simply doesn't work. It's far more effective to set standards, decentralize control, and provide support capacity to facilitate localized prevention and response.

In the end, however, the seed library, not wanting to flout the law, shut down, opting instead to occasionally host seed-swap days where local folks could get together and exchange seeds among one another, unaffiliated with any institution.

Warning: This may sound like a quirky local story involving overzealous bureaucrats, the kind of laughable government overreach we all like to point to from time to time but prefer not to believe is the rule.

Not so fast.

It turns out that the Pennsylvania effort is part of a larger, multistate effort by the American Legislative Exchange Council, a "nonpartisan, voluntary membership organization of state legislators," according to its official description. And, we might add, a controversial one. The group produces "model bills," many of which end up verbatim in state legislation and laws. In this case, ALEC drafted model legislation reserving "exclusive regulatory power over agricultural seed, flower seed, and vegetable seed" to the state, forbidding local government to "enact or enforce . . . an ordinance, regulation, control area, or quarantine to inhibit or prevent the production or use of agricultural seed, flower seed, or vegetable seed or products." This section includes such specifics as "regulating the display, distribution, growing, harvesting, registration, storage, transportation, or use of agricultural seed, flower seed, or vegetable seed" and so on. There's enough key words there to scare off any local librarian.

Why ban seed-sharing libraries? It might be that seed libraries threaten some of ALEC's members—who include Dow, DuPont, Deere & Company, and Monsanto—which profit from systems in which farmers must license proprietary seeds and are contractually for-bidden from saving, let alone sharing, them. Sharing seeds not provided by these companies threatens their product lines and profits. Why else would a corporate-funded trade group want to prohibit an age-old farm-ing practice?

Threatening seed libraries is a perfect example of vested interests working against the public interest under the guise of protecting pub-lic health and well-being. There are others—oil and coal companies "protecting" the public against climate change regulations; automobile companies "protecting" us from clean-air or fuel-efficiency mandates; manufacturers "protecting" citizens from rules that mandate disclosure of ingredients in consumer products. It's a fairly long list.

A HOUSE OF CARDS

The industrialization of agriculture, along with the consolidation of the food-processing industry, is unhealthy over the long term, says John E. Ikerd, professor emeritus of agricultural economics at the University of Missouri. The fundamental purpose of industrialization is to enhance productivity and economic efficiency by making it possible to produce a greater value of output from a given amount of input, he says. But that assumes the industry in question is accounting for all of the associ-ated costs. That's simply not the case with America's food system. He explains:

> While industrialization has brought tremendous economic benefits by reducing cost and increasing the availability of food, it has done so by imposing significant costs on nature and society through environmen-tal degradation and growing social inequity. Public concerns about the American food system have mounted as the ecological and social costs have increased and have become increasingly visible. The emerging public consensus is that an industrial agriculture is simply not sustainable over the long run. Consequently, as the industrialization of food approaches its pinnacle, it is also approaching its end.

The end? Really?

Well, it's possible. For starters, it seems we have too much food. American households currently throw away approximately 40 percent of their food each year. At the same time, two-thirds of Americans are overweight (over a third are clinically obese), according to the Centers for Disease Control and Prevention, which reports that, in 2009, over 70 percent of the approximately $2.5 trillion we spent on health care went to preventable diseases, many of which are linked to obesity. As a nation, we've let ourselves go so much that the average American stands about a one in five chance of dying from an obesity-related cause, according to research released in 2013 by Columbia University's Mailman School of Public Health. Compare that to a 1 in 20 million chance of dying in a terrorist-related event, according to data from a United Nations al Qaeda–Taliban monitoring team. (Good thing we're all on the lookout for terrorists while we sit in a McDonald's drive-thru). Beyond what we consume as food, we put over 40 percent of our yearly corn harvests into our gas tanks in the form of ethanol, and in the process, we've tied the price of food to the price of oil.

Clearly we have plenty of food. But how long can our gluttony continue?

Most likely, not for long. Consider the collapse of the 500-year-old Atlantic cod industry, following record yields in the late '70s and early '80s. It is a stark reminder of how Mother Nature reacts to our mindless mismanagement of resources. Given the soil depletion, the industry consolidation, the reduction in diversity, and the misallocation of resources, how much time do we have until we hit the ecological wall? No one really knows, but considering the data, and the fact that the electorate doesn't particularly like being hungry, we may want to jump on this problem with a bit of urgency.

TALKING ABOUT REGENERATION

We do have productive and profitable alternatives that not only can set a new course for how America gets its food, but can lead a food revolution to meet the growing global demand in a manner that keeps us square with Mother Nature and gives us the depth and resilience we need to handle the perturbations that a changing climate promises to deliver. Almost since the beginning of industrial agriculture, we've seen a steady parade of alternative ideas and approaches aimed at improving the sustainability of agriculture and food production—that is, minimizing their ecological, social, and economic costs.

There's organic, of course, championed by J. I. Rodale, one of the first advocates of a return to organic farming in the United States. In 1948, in *The Organiculturist's Creed,* he wrote, "The organic farmer and gardener must realize that fertilization is not the only measure for success. He must treat the soil as a living, breathing entity. He must rotate crops. He must fallow the land at regulated intervals. The organiculturist must not practice one-crop monoculture but must engage in a balanced agriculture with cattle as part of the general program. He must be smart in the ways of soil and crops, observing the reaction of the land to the actions of man."

Starting in the 1960s, organic agriculture gained popularity as a counterculture activity, becoming mainstream in the 1990s, though it still represents only a small fraction of American farmland: Just over 2 percent of America's roughly 234 million acres of farmed land is certified organic under the federal government's definition. Organic food sales represent double that—about 4 percent of total food sales in the United States in 2014, according to the Organic Trade Association, an industry trade group.

However small that may seem, the case remains compelling. In 2011, the Rodale Institute released the findings of its 30-year study, "The Farming Systems Trial," launched in 1981, to study the impact on farms that transition from chemical to organic agriculture. The trial surprised a food community that still scoffed at organic practices. After an initial decline in crop yields during the first few years of transition, the organic system rebounded to match or surpass the chemical-based system. In fact, organic techniques beat chemical-based farming methods in every category, most importantly in productivity and profit per acre. Even controlling for premium pricing, organic production brought in three times as much revenue per acre per year. Organic farming also rebuilds soils and retains 15 to 20 percent more water, which improves farms' drought resistance. Moreover, it consumes 45 percent less energy and emits 29 percent fewer global-warming emissions than traditional large-scale farming methods, according to Rodale.

These days, some see "organic" as a low bar, especially given that the USDA's organic standard is the product of compromise and contention. Whole Foods co-CEO and cofounder John Mackey is among those who find the "organic" label wanting. For example, it doesn't take into consideration factors like energy conservation, waste reduction, and farmworker welfare, all of which should be considered by conscientious eaters, he believes. In 2014, Whole Foods introduced a rating system called Responsibly Grown, in which food no longer has to be organic to be "good." It's been controversial, to say the least: both organic and conventional growers have protested.

Responsibly Grown joins a fertile crop of other farming terms, trends, and technologies, including, in alphabetical order, agroecology, aquaponics, biodynamic farming, biological farming, conservation tillage, controlled environment agriculture, good agricultural practices (or GAP), holistic management, integrated pest management (and its offshoot, biointensive IPM), low-input agriculture, natural (or nature) farming, permaculture, sustainable agriculture, and whole-farm planning. Each offers an approach that counters industrial ag's relative blunt-force use of inputs—fertilizers, pesticides, and water—in favor of limited inputs used with precision in harmony with natural cycles and conditions. And while some large-scale "conventional" farmers may claim to do these things—employing technologies that enable yet another technique, "precision agriculture"—it is differentiated from most other alternatives as a matter of degree: precision ag may use fewer inputs than most of today's farmers, but it still uses more than most other alternatives, and it allows for chemical-based fertilizers and pesticides.

We've chosen the term *regenerative* agriculture, which represents the second leg of our grand strategy. The term was coined by Robert Rodale, J. I. Rodale's son, in the 1980s. "Regenerative" made sense to Robert Rodale because "enhanced regeneration of renewable resources is essential to the achievement of a sustainable form of agriculture" and because "the concept of regeneration would be relevant to many economic sectors and social concerns." It makes sense to us as well because we'll need to restore our soils and clean our waterways en route to feeding Americans, never mind the rest of the world, to ensure the vitality and resilience of our agricultural systems. Increasing our food production via today's input-intensive and environment-degrading industrial agricultural techniques just isn't sustainable.

(As an aside, it's worth noting that the idea of what "conventional" agriculture even means is debatable, at least at the global scale. Most people refer to the status quo as conventional, and other options—organic, biodynamic, et cetera—as "alternative." But food activist and former *New York Times* columnist Mark Bittman, speaking at a 2014 food conference hosted by the newspaper, explained it this way: "In terms of feeding people, land use, and commonality, peasant farming is far more conventional. Peasant farming produces more than two-thirds of the world's food. In its reliance on high-tech, fossil fuels, overuse of resources, monocropping, and chemicals, industrial ag is, in fact, completely unconventional. It's downright anomalous." Food for thought.)

Agriculture, more than anything else, embodies the convergence of economic, environmental, and social needs, and regenerative ag embodies the thinking that allows us to address those needs thoughtfully, responsibly, and profitably. In fact, by rethinking how and where we source food, we stand to simultaneously address five key issues facing America:

Decarbonization: harnessing innovative farming techniques that sequester carbon while restoring topsoil health and improving crop yields.

Detoxification: reducing nitrogen, phosphorous, and other chemical runoff into rivers, lakes, and streams.

Population health: improving the quality, affordability, and access to healthy foods, including in urban "food deserts."

Job creation: attracting and equipping the next generation of American farmers, in both urban and rural settings.

Food security: increasing resilience within the American and global food systems.

To address these five issues, we need to think about the logic of America's food system.

The system we have is a single continental market. This was, to a great extent, part of the intent behind President Eisenhower's advocacy of the Interstate Highway System. Before interstates, America's food systems were regional, rotational, and seasonal. Each region had its specialty products, and while certain crops like wheat had been shipped long distances, most regions produced their own produce, dairy, and meat.

High-speed, refrigerated highway transportation created the possibility for agriculture to scale to the continental level and, for the first time, a single national market. As this design became a reality, the farmers of California's Central Valley exploited their comparative advantage in vegetables, stone fruit, and tree nuts, just like other producers around the country would exploit their own advantages, whether Florida (citrus), Wisconsin (cheese), Texas (cattle and cotton), or the Midwest (corn, wheat, and soy).

By focusing on a region's comparative strengths, and "going big," we segregated the production of livestock from crops, and as fertilizers advanced, we stopped rotating crops. And that's where we started mining our soils instead of managing them. And it's here that we need to look for solutions.

We believe America needs to rebalance its current system to create regenerative agriculture at three scales:

- **Community.** From window boxes to urban farms, America can put much more land into production, design new kinds of communities around gardens and farms, and grow fresher, tastier, and healthier food.
- **Regional.** More regional production will keep money circulating locally, provide more jobs, more resilience, and the demand needed for the products of crop rotation. This is critical in many parts of the country. For example, Indiana imports approximately 95 percent of the food it consumes, even though it is largely agrarian.
- **National.** National systems create economies of scale, though we need to move away from brittle and vulnerable centralized systems. Instead, the focus should be on incenting more healthy foods, not just from a nutritional perspective but also ecologically, and on promoting exports of food and technology that help meet global needs. In essence, the national system should integrate community and regional systems and plug into the global system.

Such proposals may sound ambitious, perhaps even risky: Should we even tinker with America's food supply? It's a valid question. After all, it took about 40 years to build the food system we have now, and from the average consumer's perspective, it seems to be working just fine. But the bigger risk may be to do nothing, as our industrial means of producing food becomes more reliant on chemical inputs, more susceptible to disease and other disruption, and less able to feed millions of hungry bellies with affordable and nutritious foods, either at home or abroad.

The need to make food systems sustainable—again, using the definition of sustainability as "diverse and productive over time," but adding the social dimension of widespread accessibility to affordable and nutritious food—becomes especially acute in the face of a changing climate. "The global balance between grain supply and demand is fragile and depends largely on climate," says Lester Brown. "With 80 million more mouths to feed each year and with increasing demand for grain-intensive livestock products, the rise in temperature only adds to the stress." It is only a matter of time, he says, before the types of major downturns in grain stocks seen in Russia become commonplace in the United States and around the world. Brown, not one prone to rosy scenarios, points out that food scarcity and the resulting higher food prices are pushing poor countries into chaos and that such "failed states" can export disease, terrorism, illicit drugs, weapons, and refugees.

The good news is that we are gaining both the technology and the know-how to produce food more sustainably and to harness nature's genius to sequester carbon, leveraging agriculture to draw down the heat-trapping concentrations already in the atmosphere—that is, to be regenerative. And we are gaining the ability do all this in a more distributed, less centralized fashion, producing healthy food closer to where it is consumed, even inside poor urban neighborhoods, affordably and at scale.

THE REGIONAL FOOD REVOLUTION

To see how we can make the transition to a more regenerative agricultural system, we should look toward America's regional food movement. That movement has been evolving over the past quarter century or so, as consumers have taken increasing interest in understanding the provenance of their food, and marketers have been all too eager to indulge that interest with stories, labeling, and marketing that emphasizes where and how food is sourced. Today, we may know the name of the farm from which something came, perhaps even see a picture of the farmer's family and pets, along with stories from the farm.

According to a 2012 survey by A. T. Kearney, grocery shoppers value local foods even more than organic foods, in part because they associate local with being fresher and of higher quality. Sixty-eight percent said local food contributes positively to sustainability, compared to only 50 percent for organic foods. (It should be noted that there is no definition of "local" food, unlike "organic," which is legally defined under federal law.) Shoppers also said they were willing to pay a premium for local food, including 63 percent of lower-income grocery shoppers, and almost 30 percent said they would consider shopping elsewhere if their preferred stores don't carry local foods.

America's largest grocery chains—Walmart, Target, Kroger, Publix, Safeway, and others—have tried, to various degrees, to capture a piece of the "locavore" market, and some specialty chains, notably Whole Foods, have more or less bet the farm on consumers' interest in locally sourced foods. Walmart, America's largest grocer, encourages its managers to buy produce grown within 450 miles of its distribution centers, even if local peaches, for example, cost more than those produced across the country. One reason: reducing the "food miles" that produce travels cuts fuel costs (it currently takes about 10 calories of petroleum energy to get one calorie of food energy to an American stomach) and reduces spoilage. It also doesn't hurt community relations.

Walmart is simply listening to its customers. Interest in local foods has ramped up in recent years, the result of a convergence of issues and concerns: the environment, especially climate change; health and wellness; access to fresh, healthy, and affordable food, especially in marginalized urban and rural communities; and the higher number of malnourished children and adults, in the form of both hunger and obesity, even in the presence of plentiful food. There is also increased concern about food safety: the chemicals used to produce it, the sanitation of the facility where it was processed, how well it was kept cold and free of contaminants en route to market, and, now in the post-9/11 world, how secure it is from potential tampering along its extended production and delivery chain. Almost two out of five Americans report that they have given food and beverage safety a lot of thought, according to the 2015 Food and Health Survey produced by the International Food Information Council Foundation. This is surely far more than would have said so in 1955.

You can also find the changing demand beyond the grocery store. According to a report from USDA's ERS, U.S. farmers sold just over $6 billion in locally marketed foods in 2012, the most recent year for which data is available. More and more local food is coming from sales to retailers, institutions, and restaurants rather than through farmers' markets and community supported agriculture programs, known as CSAs. That is despite the fact that between 2006 to 2014, the number of farmers' markets in the United States jumped 180 percent to 8,260, according to USDA data. The rapid growth is due in part to the USDA's increased commitment to local and regional food systems under President Obama, but also to the growing interest in local foods. Today, these markets give farmers opportunities to diversify their revenue sources while meeting the evolving demands of customers and consumers.

And consumer restaurant trends reflect growing food consciousness, notably the decline of fast-food sales and the rise of so-called fast casual restaurants—higher-end chains like Baja Fresh, Panera Bread, and Shake Shack—that offer higher-quality ingredients, often attached to a sustainability story. (For example, Panera swears off chicken that's been fed a diet of antibiotics to fatten them up before slaughter, and its ham, roasted turkey, and breakfast sausages come from animals raised in "reduced-stress" environments.) Despite its higher price, the market for fast casual food grew by 550 percent between 1999 and 2014, more than 10 times the growth of the fast-food market over the same period, according to market research firm Euromonitor.

Indeed, signs of the local food boom abound, with programs sprouting up around the country that offer some combination of access to local foods, business creation, job training, and address nutrition security in impoverished communities. In 2015, Boston became the first city in the United States to feature an all-local, year-round major public market; almost everything sold at the new Boston Public Market is produced or originates in New England. Also in 2015, Vermont's legislature enacted Farm to Plate, a statewide food system plan to improve the profitability of farms and food enterprises, maintain environmental resilience, and increase local food access for the state's residents. In Dallas, the historically black Paul Quinn College, struggling financially, cut its losing football team and replaced the playing field with a thriving vegetable operation. The school's organic farm now produces 30,000 pounds of food, has donated up to 20 percent of its produce to local food charities, and has put the college on the map as an area food producer. Cuyahoga County, Ohio, has Cleveland Crops, an agriculture and food-processing training and employment program designed to create innovative work opportunities and new career choices for adults with developmental disabilities. In Louisville, Kentucky, a 24-acre site formerly occupied by the

National Tobacco Company, is home to a local food hub aimed at supporting small farmers and building a local food economy. In the South Bronx, a teacher named Stephen Ritz created Bronx Green Machine, an organization that teaches some of America's most impoverished and malnourished school kids how to grow and cook food, all while improving their academic performance. There are hundreds of nonprofits across America dedicated to building backyard organic gardens, teaching young people how to grow food or cook nutritious meals, or boosting the availability of fresh produce in local stores.

The benefits for local economies are just beginning to be understood. The growth of "local" is unearthing some of the infrastructure bottlenecks that, perversely, can make it more economical for farmers to ship their products out of state, or even out of country, than to sell it locally. And there are good, sound economic development reasons for nurturing local food systems. For example, the business of creating and maintaining all the links in the local supply chain—aggregating, processing, packaging, storing, and transporting products—translates into jobs that cannot easily be outsourced. From a national perspective, we can tap into an enormous economic opportunity by opening up the agricultural sector and markets to a wider swath of American workers, investors, and retailers if we recognize that ag is second only to manufacturing in terms of ancillary sector output value: we can get $1.20 of ancillary economic productivity for every dollar the ag sector puts out. And given the fact that the average age of the American farmer is 59 (and rising), it seems to make sense to open the agricultural space to a whole new generation of young, ambitious, and innovative farmer-entrepreneurs.

Numbers-wise, what could these benefits look like? Consider Illinois, 80 percent of whose landmass is agricultural (and 90 percent of that land is "prime" agricultural, the highest classification of soil fertility and health). Few places on Earth possess such an optimal combination of soil types and fertility, climate, and rainfall. The state's agricultural economy generates commodities valued at more than $9 billion a year, according to a 2009 report to the Illinois General Assembly prepared by the Illinois Local and Organic Food and Farm Task Force. Billions of additional dollars flow into the state's economy from ag-related industries, such as farm machinery manufacturing, agricultural real estate, and the production and sale of value-added products. Food processing is the state's largest manufacturing activity, with more than 950 companies adding another $13.4 billion annually to the value of Illinois's raw agricultural commodities. Illinois ranks second nationally in the export of farm commodities, with nearly $4 billion worth of goods shipped to other countries each year.

According to the report:

> Studies show that money spent at local businesses creates a multiplier effect, internally circulating the same dollars up to eight times within the local economy. Using the conservative economic multiplier of two to three cycles, a 20 percent increase in local production, processing, and purchasing will generate $20 to $30 billion of new economic activity annually within the state's borders. Thousands of new jobs will be created for farmers and farm-related businesses. Pre-agricultural production includes seeds, soil amendments, tools, equipment, and maintenance. Post-agricultural production includes aggregation, storage, processing, packaging, and distribution.

The Illinois report doesn't address it, but there's additional economic value, not to mention human value, from leveraging local agricultural assets to enhance food security. As many as 90 percent of Americans could eat food grown within 100 miles of their home, according to a 2015 study by professors Andrew Zumkehr and J. Elliott Campbell, who teach engineering at the University of California, Merced. More than 80 percent of mouths could be fed with food grown within 50 miles.

As markets for local foods continue to grow, farming communities may find themselves moving away from large acreage of monocrops in order to supply the diversity of produce consumers demand. A study by Iowa State research scientist Dave Swenson found that expanding fruit and vegetable production in the upper Midwest could bring significantly more economic benefits than conventional corn and soybean production on the same acreage. Swenson looked at the potential for produce production in Illinois, Indiana, Iowa, Michigan, Minnesota, and Wisconsin and identified 28 kinds of fruits and vegetables farmers could grow in the region. The report concluded that increased fruit and vegetable production in those six states could mean $882 million in sales at the farm level and more than 9,300 jobs. Corn and soybean production on that same acreage would support only 2,578 jobs. Moreover, only 270,025 acres—roughly equivalent to the average amount of cropland in one of Iowa's counties—would be needed to grow enough fruits and vegetables for the six-state region.

THE RISE OF URBAN AG

It may seem paradoxical or counterintuitive to think that cities may play a key role when it comes to increasing the sustainability and resilience of America's food system, let alone of some of America's poorest neighborhoods. But the rise of urban agriculture is not to be brushed off as a passing fad. The growing interest in local food, combined with some clever technologies, is enabling city residents across the economic spectrum to grow food at scale. And in the process, hundreds, maybe thousands of local organizations and programs, both for-profit and not, stand to increase food and nutrition security, increase urban resilience, and reduce environmental impacts—all while producing healthy, affordable, accessible food.

For most people, "urban ag" conjures up images of community gardens, where groups of people come together to grow food, flowers, and herbs, primarily for their personal consumption. They come from a long line of such projects dating back more than a century: vacant lot cultivation associations in the late 1800s, school gardens in the early 1900s, War Gardens during World War I, relief and subsistence gardens during the Depression, Victory Gardens during World War II (which the Department of Agriculture fought until Eleanor Roosevelt planted one at the White House; by 1944, Victory Gardens produced 40 percent of the nation's vegetables), and, starting in the 1970s, community gardens. Today, "community gardens" refers to a variety of arrangements, from small, temporary plots on vacant land waiting to be developed to larger parcels leased or owned by local groups or land trusts. The National Community Garden Association tracks about 2,100 such gardens in 49 states and two Canadian provinces, but that's probably only a fraction of what's out there.

Whatever the size or exact number, Americans seem to be plowing new ground when it comes to growing their own food. According to a 2014 report by the National Gardening Association, some 42 million U.S. households participate in food gardening, up from 36 million in 2008. The NGA statistics include urban, suburban, and rural food gardening.

A big boost came in 2009, when participation in food gardening increased by 4 million households, or about 11 percent, in just one year. Perhaps not coincidentally, 2009 was the same year that the White House Kitchen Garden and the "Let's Move" initiative were launched by First Lady Michelle Obama, along with other USDA initiatives encouraging Americans to grow and eat healthy foods. Some of those budding city farmers had dropped out by 2010, according to NGA's national surveys, but steady growth followed, driven in part by Millennials digging into their first food gardens. In 2013, 18- to 34-year-olds were the second-largest group of food gardeners, 13 million households strong; those 55 and older were the largest group, at 15 million households. "We were also encouraged by the 38 percent increase in food gardening households with less than $35,000 annual income," said NGA.

For years, urban ag happened more or less organically—that is, there were few coordinated or formal movements to propagate gardens and food growing in and around cities. But that's changing, as urban agriculture is incorporated into cities' sustainable development goals and even city planning documents, according to a survey conducted by the Urban Sustainability Directors Network, comprising sustainability officials from more than 130 North American cities. USDN members are finding themselves addressing a growing number of issues related to urban agriculture: understanding land use and city ordinances, including cumbersome laws that thwart garden development; access to capital to build and support gardens, such as for water and irrigation systems; promoting institutional procurement of local foods by government agencies, universities, and others; and a range of liability issues related to community gardens and edible landscaping, such as who is responsible if someone is injured while gardening or gets sick while eating city-farmed foods.

When cities find their way through this thicket and get behind urban garden initiatives, the results can positively impact neighborhoods and entire regions. As Will Allen, CEO of Milwaukee-based Growing Power, says, "If people can grow safe, healthy, affordable food, if they have access to land and clean water, this is transformative on every level in a community. I believe we cannot have healthy communities without a healthy food system."

Allen's vision already is taking shape around the country. For example, in Oakland, California, the historically African American West Oakland neighborhood of about 25,000 has faced decades of unemployment, poverty, and high crime rates, as well as high obesity rates and lower life expectancy than surrounding neighborhoods. Urban gardens began cropping up there in the 1960s, promoted by the Black Panther Party, which operated social programs aimed at improving the access to healthy food for city residents by providing breakfast in local schools, churches, and community centers. Some of the food came from small local gardens planted by party members. According to Nathan Crane McClintock, a professor of urban studies at Portland State University who runs a website called urbanfood.org, "The Panthers used gardening as a coping mechanism and a means of supplementing their diets, as well as a means to strengthen community members engaged in the struggle against oppression."

According to McClintock, the creation of the People of Color Greening Network in the 1990s was a pivotal moment for urban agriculture in West Oakland. It served as a vehicle for fusing social justice with urban ag as citizens planted gardens in vacant lots to promote green space. About that time, a school garden movement began in area schools, teaching basic gardening skills and food education; credit for the school garden movement is attributed to Alice Waters, owner of the restaurant Chez Panisse, a food mecca in nearby Berkeley. By the late 1990s, Oakland's Office of Sustainability had proposed a Sustainable Community Development Initiative that spurred further growth of community gardens. In the early 2000s, the city's pledge to become a sustainable city led the city council to create the Food Policy Council, a 21-seat volunteer body that works with local organizations to "create a healthy and resilient local and regional food system."

One of those organizations is City Slicker Farms, which since 2001 has worked with the West Oakland community to grow and distribute roughly 9,000 pounds of fresh produce a year. After years of farming on nearly a dozen different small plots of land, in 2015 the group leveraged a $4 million state grant to purchase an empty West Oakland lot that at various points housed a junkyard and a paint factory. The new farm plan includes a greenhouse, a fruit tree orchard, and a community garden where local residents who don't have their own garden can maintain a small plot. The group also has helped to create more than 300 back-yard gardens, at no charge to local residents. City Slicker has helped spur a network of West Oakland food justice organizations, including Mandela Food Cooperative, a worker-owned and worker-operated full-service grocery store and education center that sources food from small producers in the region; and People's Grocery, which runs several other food-related projects, including Mobile Market, a truck that traverses the neighborhood selling fresh foods as well as offering nutrition, health, and job-training programs.

What's taking place at City Slicker Farms and elsewhere around West Oakland is part of a vast network of food-justice groups taking root across America. In Baltimore, Boone Street Farm operates on two vacant plots in the center of East Baltimore's Midway neighborhood, producing thousands of pounds of affordable produce, for which residents on food assistance pay only $5 or $10 a bag. The community plots are used for gardening workshops and offer classes in nutrition to students at the nearby public school. In Camden, New Jersey, a city of 80,000 with only one full-service supermarket, community gardeners at 44 sites harvested almost 31,000 pounds of vegetables during an unusually wet and cold summer—enough food during the growing season to feed about 500 people three servings a day. Miami's Liberty City, a predominantly black neighborhood northwest of Miami's central business district, provides environmental projects and food security programming to underserved urban communities throughout South Florida by growing vegetation in neglected and vacant lots and tending to an urban forest—all while giving jobs to the neighborhood's residents. The Last Organic Outpost is building a local food economy in Houston's underserved neighborhoods through urban farming and using sustainable agriculture to teach residents to produce safe and healthy food. Roosevelt Growhouse is a quarter-acre property in downtown Phoenix on a formerly vacant, blighted property that now houses a sustainable community garden supported by hundreds of members and volunteers.

While urban ag isn't limited to the nation's poorest communities, that is where it has the biggest impact. Inner-city gardens and greenhouses help address the plague of food deserts, a term that refers to low-income urban and rural areas where it is difficult to find affordable or high-quality fresh food, where fast-food restaurants and convenience stores, not grocery stores, dominate the landscape.

According to the advocacy group Food Empowerment Project, "People's choices about what to eat are severely limited by the options available to them and what they can afford—and many food deserts contain an overabundance of fast food chains selling cheap 'meat' and dairy-based foods that are high in fat, sugar and salt. Processed foods (such as snack cakes, chips, and soda) typically sold by corner delis, convenience stores and liquor stores are usually just as unhealthy."

The issue of food deserts is part of the larger issue of food security—the availability of healthy food to all who need it. Nationally, 14.3 percent of Americans were food insecure in 2013, meaning "they lacked access to enough food for an active, healthy life for all household members," according to the USDA. These Americans experience a range of diet-sensitive chronic ills, including hypertension, hyperlipidemia, and diabetes. People in poor health tend to take more days off work, making it all the harder to climb out of poverty.

There's a cost to this in both human and economic terms. A 2015 study of 67,000 adults in the Canadian province of Ontario and published in the *Canadian Medical Association Journal* found that health-care costs were significantly higher for food-insecure people, even after adjusting for other socioeconomic and demographic variables. Households with low food security—those that faced uncertain or limited access to a nutritious diet—incurred health-care expenses 49 percent higher than those who were food secure. And health-care costs were 121 percent higher for those with very low food security—households that missed meals or ate smaller meals because they couldn't afford food.

Children are hit hardest. Kids who are food insecure are more likely to require hospitalization and may be at higher risk for chronic health conditions, such as anemia and asthma. Food insecurity among young children is associated with poor physical quality of life, which may prevent them from fully engaging in daily activities such as school and social interaction with peers.

It doesn't take vast swaths of land to overcome these challenges. There's a lot that can be done even in small spaces. According to the Community Food Security Coalition, during a 130-day temperate growing season, a 100-square-meter plot (just over 1,000 square feet, or about one-fortieth of an acre) can provide most of a four-person household's total yearly vegetable needs, including much of the household's nutritional requirements for vitamins A, C, B complex, and iron.

GOING VERTICAL

Community gardens are just one piece of the urban ag puzzle. There is a growing amount of for-profit commercial farming underway within city limits, taking advantage of new agriculture technologies—"agtech" for short—that allow for intensive growing in small spaces, including vacant buildings, unoccupied rooftops, and shipping containers plopped down in small lots.

A great deal of the technology that enables indoor produce growing was developed and honed over the past two decades by cannabis growers, who have learned how to grow plants at scale in confined (and usually hidden) spaces. Many of these growers use hydroponics and other forms of controlled-environment agriculture. Hydroponics—the growing of plants without soil—is a science as ancient as the fabled Hanging Gardens of Babylon, thought to be the first example of soilless growing. During World War II, American troops overseas grew vegetables hydroponically to ease the burden of transporting perishable food to barren islands in the Pacific theater and the arid regions of the Middle East, according to a history of hydroponics published—where else?—in *High Times* magazine. Thanks to hydroponics, the island of Iwo Jima, rocky and barely inhabitable, was transformed from a blood-drenched battleground to a nourishing garden of life. Soldiers protecting vital oil fields on the Arabian Peninsula ate vegetables produced locally in the harshest of desert environments. Today, hydroponics is used on the International Space Station to study plant growth outside the Earth's atmosphere and how best to supply food and oxygen for future colonization missions to Mars and beyond.

Even on Spaceship Earth, hydroponics makes sense. Growing leafy greens, specialty herbs, tomatoes, and other produce indoors using hydroponics uses up to 90 percent less water than growing them outdoors and uses fewer pesticides—and sometimes none at all. Hydroponics has long been central to the Dutch and Japanese food systems, but the relatively cheap cost of land and water in the United States, combined with the costly energy intensity of lighting, made hydroponics too expensive for growing anything but a high-value cash crop like cannabis.

Today, there is the new breed of tricked-out shipping containers designed for growing—again, some born of necessity by pot growers but now migrated to commercial food farming. They come from companies with names like GrowPod, VertiFresh, FusionPharm, Freight Farms, CropBox, and Growtainer. FusionPharm, for example, consists of stackable steel shipping containers that use a combination of LED and fluorescent bulbs and a simple continuous-flow watering system. Environmental controls ensure that temperature, airflow, carbon dioxide, and humidity levels remain optimized. And there's vertical farming, another take on indoor ag, where racks of produce grow from floor to ceiling. In the Chicago area, Whole Foods Markets provided funding to FarmedHere, a vertical farm start-up that also raises tilapia, with the nutrient-rich by-products of fish farming filtered off to grow produce.

Then there's "aeroponics," in which racks of crops are grown indoors, but in neither soil nor water. Instead, plant roots dangle in the air and are sprayed with nutrients, while LED lights play the role of the sun. In the East Ward neighborhood of Ironbound in Newark, New Jersey, a company called AeroFarms built the world's largest vertical farm using aeroponics, a term coined by former Cornell University professor and aeroponics pioneer Ed Harwood, who serves as AeroFarms's chief technology officer. Most of the seed money for the operation came from Goldman Sachs's Urban Investment Group.

AeroFarm's 69,000-square-foot facility, in a former steel factory on Rome Street, has the ability to grow 2 million pounds of leafy greens annually—all without using a speck of dirt or a ray of sunlight. The company says it can take the exact same seed that would take 30 to 45 days to grow in the field and instead grow it in 12 to 16 days, enabling up to 30 crop turns a year. Overall, vertical farming offers up to 75 times greater productivity per square foot than traditional farming, and it uses no pesticides and 95 percent less water.

Operations like AeroFarms offer benefits beyond the food and reduced environmental footprint. Of course, there's also the roughly 78 jobs it has created in the middle of a high-unemployment neighborhood. Beyond the neighborhood, AeroFarms is helping build the region's food resilience.

In fact, it is a perfect example of a distributed network that is providing security and resilience in the face of unpleasant surprises. Most of the food that finds its way into New York City—cabbage from New York, oranges from California, blueberries from Chile, bell peppers from the Netherlands, beef from Australia, and fish from Nova Scotia—passes through a single facility: the Hunts Point Food Distribution

Center in the South Bronx. It is the largest food market in the United States and second largest internationally, feeding more than 23 million people throughout the region, while generating $3 billion in revenues and employing more than 3,000 workers. The city describes the million-square-foot facility as "not just critically important, but also vulnerable." The reason: it sits on a peninsula with the East River on two sides and the Bronx River on the third and is subject to storm surge during high tides. In fact, the city notes, if Hurricane Sandy had hit 12 hours earlier, during high tide, "Hunts Point would have been flooded, the facility would've lost power, and food supply chains to the entire New York City region might have been disrupted." AeroFarms offers an alternative, another route to bring food into New York—food produced locally, year round.

Note that none of these urban ag operations relied on federal dollars or subsidies to grow their businesses. Indeed, when it comes to creating the new menu for how America grows and consumes food, Uncle Sam isn't even at the table. These are classic American innovators and entrepreneurs chasing market opportunities, helped along by nonprofit and for-profit incubators, food aggregation and distribution centers catering to smaller operators, and local tax breaks for landowners who lend or lease their property to urban farmers—and, of course, a demand for locally grown food that will continue to increase.

CARBON COWBOYS

Despite all of these innovations for growing food in nontraditional environments, like empty city lots or shipping containers, we're not going to give up on America's farmers. They continue to stand tall in their fields, producing food at a scale and quality envied by much of the world. Indeed, today's farmers may even become our environmental saviors.

Given all the damage that agriculture does to the environment, it may be hard to believe that it could someday repair the Earth, but a handful of farmers are learning how to do exactly that. The early results of their efforts offer great hope for the regenerative potential of agriculture. The more we can incorporate these methods into the large-scale production of our national and export crops, the more rapidly we can bring our own economy back within planetary boundaries, including healing the soil.

Consider Albert Straus, a second-generation dairy farmer in Marshall, California, a small coastal town in Marin County, just north of San Francisco. The farm was started by his father, Bill, a Dutch Jewish immigrant whose family escaped Amsterdam before the Nazi invasion of 1940. Bill Straus studied agriculture at the University of California, Berkeley (following in the footsteps of his own father, also named Albert, who was one of the first Jews in Germany to receive a PhD in agriculture), then purchased the ranch in 1941 and began with 32 cows, all of them named after friends and relatives.

In 1994, Bill's oldest son, Albert, converted the farm to become the first organic dairy operation west of the Mississippi River. Over two decades, Straus Family Farm became a leading light in Northern California's organic and locavore food movement. Today, the milk from 275 or so cows on Albert's 500-acre farm is combined with that from eight other nearby organic farms and sent to Straus Family Creamery, where it is turned into milk, yogurt, ice cream, and butter, distributed in California and other western states.

In 2013, Straus Family Farm became one of three farms and ranches selected to participate in the Marin Carbon Project, a bold and slightly audacious effort to tweak farming methods to sequester global-warming gases while improving the soil and the quality of milk.

In essence, carbon farming works like this: Farmers spread cow manure on their fields, which increases the amount of nutrients in the soil, enabling the growth of lush foliage, which captures carbon dioxide in plants as well as the soil. They also divvy up their land into smaller parcels called paddocks, perhaps an acre each, which are cordoned off by temporary fences. Cows or other livestock are herded into each paddock, where they eat the foliage, then are moved on to the next paddock. That gives plants time to recover, enabling them to produce 30 percent to 70 percent more forage. (Think of a blade of grass as a tiny solar panel: the more surface area, the better it can process sunlight, in this case to create more plant matter via photosynthesis.) The increased forage draws more carbon out of the atmosphere and sends it down into the roots and soil, where it is sequestered. Fewer days on the same paddock per year also produce less soil compaction. Soil compaction decreases soil fertility, water absorption, and the ability of forage plant roots to penetrate the soil. The process has been dubbed carbon farming.

The process drives carbon deep into the ground, where it can sit for years, even a decade or more, locking down carbon while helping to heal degraded soil by infusing it with vital nutrients such as nitrogen, the mineral element most demanded by plants. The process also eliminates the need for disposing of animal manure through other means, turning what had been a waste product and potential liability into an asset. In addition, there are water-retention benefits: carbon-rich soils soak up heavy rainfalls; carbon-depleted soils don't. The result is that the soil improves, yields increase, water is saved, and carbon is captured from the atmosphere and kept underground for long periods of time.

All this may sound too good to be true, but the evidence is showing that it works. Farmers like Albert Straus are serving as guinea pigs to test how to optimize carbon farming techniques, and to help quantify the results in order to make the process reliable and predictable and, just as important, scalable—that is, if you spread X amount of manure on the ground, you should expect to sequester Y amount of carbon and increase your yield by Z percent. Farmers operating in states that have carbon trading markets—where a business that reduces carbon emissions can sell credits to companies that need to reduce their emissions in order to meet a regulatory cap—can further milk the carbon credits by turning them into cash. The Marin Carbon Project's protocol has been approved by the American Carbon Registry for use on the voluntary carbon trading market, and by the California Air Pollution Control Officers Association, which means California counties can offer greenhouse gas emitters the ability to purchase credits from ranchers like Straus. The state of California is likely to create subsidies and financing arrangements for carbon farmers.

Techniques like carbon farming have trade-offs. For example, they are more labor-intensive than industrial-strength monocropping. There are upfront costs. For example, Straus Family Farm installed hedgerows that help keep wind from drying out the soil, thereby retaining more moisture. But the benefits that inure to the land and the cows give Straus assurance that the farm can remain profitable for as long as he wants to farm it. "It might reverse a trend where after World War II, 40 percent of the population were farmers; now it's just 1 percent," he says, sitting in the small office on his property. "Maybe we need a lot more farmers that are doing small-scale farming that is viable and offers them a good quality of life."

If a few relatively simple, cost-effective farming techniques can improve soil, enhance yields, and sequester vast amounts of carbon, we have a rich opportunity in front of us. Soil carbon expert Rattan Lal, who directs the Carbon Management and Sequestration Center at Ohio State University, estimates the potential for soil carbon sequestration across the world is huge, "equivalent to a drawdown of about 50 parts per million of atmospheric CO_2 by 2100." That is, widespread carbon farming could help bring CO_2 levels down from, say, 550 ppm to "just" 500 ppm—still potentially havoc-wreaking, but less so. Whatever the number, the reality is that sequestering carbon in soils is one of the few practical means currently available to reduce global greenhouse gas concentrations in the atmosphere, potentially reversing climate change. In 2014, rancher John Wick, cofounder of the Marin Carbon Project, testified before Congress that, if replicated across just 5 percent of California's rangelands, "this practice would offset all of the state's annual agricultural and forestry [carbon dioxide] emissions." Beyond that, says Wick, there are 3.5 billion hectares of grasslands globally. "The most conservative estimate shows that if we do this with 2.7 billion hectares, it would get atmospheric carbon down to 350" parts per million, a level that just might prevent global warming from reaching dangerous levels.

For farmers, it's also good business. Spreading manure on fields makes the ground more fertile, creating a cornucopia of grasses and grains that enable cows to graze outdoors more of the year, as opposed to being sent inside and fed grasses and grains purchased from other farmers. Straus once purchased all of his feed from others. Now, half of his cows' feed comes from his flourishing farm. Eventually, he might need to purchase as little as a fourth from others. Carbon farming also can boost crop yields. Research by Lal found that an increase of soil carbon by one ton could increase crop yield by 20 to 40 kilograms per hectare for wheat and 10 to 20 kilograms per hectare for corn. For farmers, both large and small, such financial gains can help tip the scale between profitability and not.

In that light, the carbon farming of Straus and his pioneering brethren farmers in the Marin Carbon Project are part of a critical, life-giving experiment. But such efforts aren't limited to Marin County. The filmmaker Peter Byck, whose 2010 documentary *Carbon Nation* demonstrated how climate change solutions were being embraced by Americans of every political stripe because they made good business sense, has been focusing his efforts on "soil carbon cowboys" in places like Mississippi and North Dakota.

One cattle rancher Byck encountered is Gabe Brown, who purchased a 5,000-acre ranch just east of Bismarck, North Dakota, from his wife's parents in 1991; he began using soil-friendly techniques, like no-till farming, in 1993, as part of a larger move to what he calls holistic management. His farm's tagline is "Regenerating Landscapes for a Sustainable Future." Brown is now sold on carbon farming. "Why would I want to go out and spend thousands upon thousands of dollars every year for synthetic fertilizer, when I can grow the plants, and they, along with soil biology, will make the nutrients available for me, and my livestock will come around, eat these plants, and convert it to dollars?" he asked Byck in *Soil Carbon Cowboys*, a documentary short Byck produced in 2014. "I'm getting all my fertilizer basically for a profit, because I'm making money off these crops." Brown has now eliminated the use of synthetic fertilizers, fungicides, pesticides, growth hormones, and antibiotics on his farm.

Can all this entrepreneurial activity and agtech wizardry disrupt traditional, industrial agriculture? The status quo is unsustainable, and the opportunity to adopt lower-cost methods makes for a compelling business case. There is unlimited potential for America to demonstrate to the world how to produce foods at the necessary scale in resource-efficient and environmentally responsible ways, closer to where it is consumed, and to make sure it is available and affordable to all who need it.

There can still be great efficiency in producing amber waves of grain and green valleys of produce in vast tracts of open fields, and it is possible for large-scale farms to adopt techniques like carbon farming that could redeem them environmentally. What's clear is that there's a revolution taking place, and the world's largest food companies are taking note, watching closely the new generation of food production methods and technologies, and the companies that deploy them at home and abroad.

And, in the process, America can lead by example, as farmers once again become stewards of the soil and the environment, all while feeding people the wholesome food they deserve.

CHAPTER SIX

RESOURCE PRODUCTIVITY

IF YOU WANT TO GET A GLIMPSE OF THE FUTURE OF MANUFACTURING in America, poke your head into the lobby at 236 West Boardman Street in Youngstown, Ohio, just a block off the main drag, West Federal Street. Just inside the nondescript two-story brick building is a lobby filled with metal and plastic objects: machine parts, meshed gears, an exhaust manifold, an intricate block of woven plastic lace, a few decorative doodads. All were made by 3D printing.

The ordinariness of all these objects belies the revolution taking place in the rest of the building—and, by extension, in America's manufacturing future. 3D printing, also referred to as additive manufacturing, may not be the most visible or exciting manifestation of "advanced manufacturing"—robotic factories likely get that distinction—but it may be the most impactful. In ways both large and small, additive manufacturing is poised to upend notions of what it means for America to "make things" again.

It is also a key component of a grand strategy to seize the vast opportunities of the coming revolution in resource productivity to build a robust and resilient American economy. In the process, we can demonstrate leadership to the world—that we can have the good life today without devouring our kids' future. And, in keeping with our theory of change, these necessary shifts can be led by business.

The ability to print things of all sizes, shapes, and materials is nothing short of revolutionary. Digitizing the instructions for creating both simple and intricate shapes, then printing them in materials as varied as carbon fiber and chocolate, allows for radically efficient manufacturing, saving time, waste, packaging, and transportation. 3D printing technology may well be as disruptive to today's Millennials as the Internet was to yesterday's Boomers: it won't merely transform the way things are done, but how we think about what's even possible.

3D printing and advanced manufacturing are part of a resource revolution that stands to revitalize the industrial capacity of the United States, especially in the Rust Belt, for which Youngstown may be the poster child. Youngstown, located in the northeast corner of Ohio halfway between Cleveland and Pittsburgh, has deep industrial roots and is named for John Young, who established the region's first sawmill and gristmill in the late 1700s, less than a quarter century after America's founding. The city's rise mirrored that of fossil fuels: the growing availability of coal contributed to the development of iron mills and, by the turn of the twentieth century, steel mills. By the 1920s, Youngstown was second only to Pittsburgh in terms of total steel production in the United States.

For the next 40 years, Youngstown tracked the growth of the postwar automotive industry, becoming a key industrial hub that housed the massive furnaces and foundries of such companies as Republic Steel and U.S. Steel. But the city never hedged its bets, diversifying its business base like Akron, Chicago, Cleveland, Pittsburgh, and other Midwest cities did. When U.S. automobile manufacturing plants began moving offshore during the 1970s, shuttering the steel mills that supplied them, the city found itself with little to fall back on. Youngstown fell into depression.

Things didn't pick up at the turn of the millennium. According to the 2010 decennial U.S. Census, Youngstown followed the trend of Ohio's other major cities—including Akron, Canton, Cincinnati, Cleveland, Columbus, Dayton, and Toledo—by losing residents between 2000 and 2010. Many of those who stayed suffered. In 2011, the Brookings Institution revealed that Youngstown had one of the highest percentages of residents living in concentrated poverty among America's top 100 metropolitan areas. In 2013, the Hampton Institute, a self-described "working-class think tank," dubbed Youngstown "America's fastest-shrinking city."

So it was economically, not to mention politically, strategic when President Obama announced, in August 2012, less than three months before a national election, the National Network for Manufacturing Innovation. It would be composed of 15 regional Institutes for Manufacturing Innovation, modeled after the Fraunhofer Institutes, a network spread throughout Germany that dates to the 1970s, each focusing on different fields of applied science, from machine tools to molecular biology. Obama sited the first such U.S. institute—the National Additive Manufacturing Innovation Institute—in Youngstown. The resulting entity, dual-branded as America Makes, opened its doors two months later, in October 2012, in a 12,000-square-foot facility that once housed a furniture factory—a potent symbol of the passage from Youngstown's manufacturing past to its manufacturing future.

BIG-M MANUFACTURING

America Makes's mission is "to help our nation's 3D printing industry become more globally competitive." Six federal agencies—the departments of Commerce, Education, Defense, and Energy, along with NASA and the National Science Foundation—came together to create the organization. They were joined by a network of more than 100 companies, nonprofit organizations, academic institutions, and government agencies. Members pay from $15,000 to $200,000 and get access to intellectual property, technical presentations, and workshops, as well as the use of America Makes facilities for R&D.

3D printing was born in the United States in the 1980s. Most histories credit a company called 3D Systems, founded in Southern California but now headquartered in Rock Hill, South Carolina, with developing the first commercial machines. Most printers work by using a laser or extruder that moves along an X, Y, and Z axis, guided by computer-aided design, or CAD, software to build an object in three dimensions, layer by layer, each only a few microns thick. The process yields almost no waste—there's nothing to sand, saw, drill, or cut. Those early models were used for what became known as rapid prototyping, enabling designers to create multiple iterations of engineered designs far more quickly and cheaply than before.

Today's 3D printers are used to make finished products from a wide range of materials. Like most technologies, the processes are getting faster, the equipment is getting cheaper, and materials are improving, including the ability to "print" metals and ceramics. 3D printers range from the size of a small microwave oven to that of a small automobile. Between 2010 and 2013 alone, prices dropped dramatically, with machines that sold for $20,000 in 2010 costing less than $1,000 three years later.

"It's a classic U.S. story," says Ed Morris, director of America Makes, as he sits in his second-floor office in Youngstown. "We invented the technology but lost the lead. The Europeans invested in it; we did not. We are still the dominant user of the technology, but the leadership in the equipment manufacturing and the materials is still in Europe, with a general sense of they're five years ahead of us. I'm trying to regain the lead for the United States. But while we're doing our investment, China is doubling down and heavily investing in the technology."

Morris, an affable 60-something, came to America Makes after a career in aerospace and defense. He spent more than 40 years in the industry, the last 21 with Lockheed Martin, where he was corporate director of mechanical engineering and manufacturing. It's hard to find someone more enthusiastic about the future of manufacturing.

He's out to change what people think about the word. "When Americans hear the word *manufacturing*, they are thinking 'dirty, dumb and dangerous,' which is very myopic," he says. Instead, Morris refers to what he calls "big-M" manufacturing—"everything you do to conceive, design, produce, inspect, test, field, and support an ultimately disposable product. If you're a manufacturing company, those are the things you do." Morris believes additive manufacturing will reenergize big-M manufacturing in the United States, bringing a wealth of new products and companies. America Makes's role is to work through the technical and business issues that come with any disruptive technology "to drive the bottom-line economy in the United States."

Morris points to Alexander Hamilton, the nation's first Treasury Secretary, as "the first federal bureaucrat to understand the value of a strong industrial base for the purpose of national defense." Hamilton noted in 1791 that an industrial policy should be interwoven with foreign policy, and to have a foreign policy that doesn't consider its own impact on manufacturing enterprises is useless. "'Tis for the United States to consider by what means they can render themselves least dependent" of other nation's manufactures, Hamilton wrote, "on the combinations, right or wrong, of foreign policy."

THE PROMISE OF PRODUCTIVITY

What's happening in Youngstown represents just one facet of what's come to be called the resource revolution, defined as the greatly improved efficiency of stuff: the amount of natural resources, energy, and other inputs needed to manufacture, grow, and build our physical world; the quality of the things we produce; and the amount of waste created at every step of the life cycle, from raw material extraction through manufacturing, use, and disposal. For the Midwest, it portends a midcentury population shift back to the geographic center of the United States, reversing a half-century exodus from the heartland to the coasts, which are closer to export markets and where residents are more likely to suffer increased storms, floods, and drought engendered by climate change. It heralds the diversification of the American economy, away from the service industries that now dominate, as the agility, versatility, and flexibility of 3D printing gives manufacturing itself a more service-like feel.

It is also, according to Stefan Heck and Matt Rogers, coauthors of the 2014 book *Resource Revolution*, "the biggest business opportunity in a century."

That may sound more than a bit hyperbolic, especially following a century that saw the birth of television, the personal computer, mobile phones, and the Internet. But if you do the numbers, it's more than justifiable.

Heck and Rogers begin with the assumption that we'll see 2.5 billion people climbing out of poverty and into the middle class between now and 2030 (other estimates put the number at 3 billion). Accommodating their needs will require building cities, roads, homes, and vehicles; growing food; and making clothing, furniture, smartphones, TVs, and whatever else these new consumers are willing and able to acquire. To put that into perspective, during the second industrial revolution, roughly between the Civil War and World War I, about 16 percent of the world's population industrialized for the first time. This time around, it's 37 percent of a global population that has more than tripled since 1920. The growth of GDP in emerging economies like China and India is faster than anything we've seen in human history.

It is also a resource nightmare. There simply are not enough metals, minerals, oil, gas, water, fertilizer, and other basic resources to go around. And the capacity of the planet's air, waterways, and soil to absorb the waste and pollution associated with this exploding global economy is wearing thin. The potential for resource wars between regions and nations over access to such things as fishing and mining rights, energy resources, and fresh water threatens the security of almost every national government. And climate change, which stands to alter weather patterns and shift growing regions on land and upend the food chain at sea, could lead to water and food shortages and further destruction of natural resources, according to the Pentagon's 2014 *Quadrennial Defense Review.*

Across the globe, the demand for commodities of all kinds has been steadily growing, with no end in sight. This isn't exactly new—natural resources have always been a critical input and a key driver (or constraint) of economic growth, and their use has been on a steady incline since the beginning of the industrial revolution. But the growth in consumption of nearly all natural resources has accelerated since the turn of the millennium. The challenges are most acute for water and minerals. At the global, regional, and local levels, natural resource supplies have often struggled to keep pace with accelerated demand, pushing prices upward. Real prices for nearly all commodities have increased significantly since 2000, according to the World Bank Commodity Price Data. Between 2000 and 2014, prices for energy more than doubled, and more than tripled for fertilizers. Prices for agricultural commodities overall grew 58 percent during that period.

The good news is that we are rapidly gaining the know-how to do so much more with so much less. The tools and technologies available to deliver higher-quality goods and services at scale using a fraction of the resources is growing by leaps and bounds. And the economics make sense: every $1.00 of manufacturing sector output creates $1.35 of ancillary economic activity, according to a report by the President's Council of Advisors on Science and Technology in 2012. (By comparison, retail returns 55 cents for every $1.00 of sector output while financial services returns 63 cents.) For America's economy, this represents a vast, largely untapped opportunity for boosting prosperity in a way that also enhances our security and sustainability.

That's why resource productivity is the third leg of the economic foundation of our grand strategy. By seizing this massive opportunity, we stand to simultaneously address five key challenges facing all of the world's economies, both developed and developing. And in doing so, we will regain our footing as a world leader in manufacturing. Addressing resource productivity will allow us to take on:

Decarbonization: reducing the greenhouse gas emissions associated with producing goods and services, as well as those needed to package, ship, and recycle or landfill many of them.

Detoxification: reducing the toxic ingredients of products that end up in the air, water, or soil and cause harm to both humans and the environment.

Planetary limits: living within the means of Earth's ability to provide the resources we use and absorb the wastes we create, thereby ensuring healthy and productive forests, fisheries, fresh water, and other ecosystems needed for a secure and vibrant economy.

Skills gap: producing the next era of high-wage, high-skilled jobs associated with advanced manufacturing and related industries.

Geopolitical tensions: de-escalating tensions and conflict between countries or regions over limited and declining natural resources.

The revolution in resource productivity is in some ways a forced market opportunity, not unlike what dropped in our laps as a result of World War II. By exceed planetary limits before achieving full economic inclusion, we have drifted so far that the return to safe operating parameters will take so long—and could be so disruptive—that we need the market to lead the transformation. To do this, American business needs only to live up to its best traditions and realign our markets toward this strategic imperative.

This shift is both necessary and lucrative. Of the major global economies, our per-capita environmental footprint is the largest—that is, the worst, according to the Global Footprint Network. "If everyone lived like a resident of the United States, we would need the resources of 4.5 planets," says the nonprofit research group. That makes resource efficiency necessary, but it also makes it potentially lucrative, as there are currently many off-the-shelf improvements that American firms can implement that will bring positive returns on investment within a very short time frame, in many cases under one year—"low-hanging fruit," as these opportunities are often called. Clearly, there is a lot of waste.

According to a study by the World Resources Institute, America entered the twenty-first century consuming 50 percent more resources to achieve the same or lower standard of living as western Europe.

This is, ironically, good news. In the midst of so many federal subsidies that support inefficiency, the solutions are obvious. Engaging both labor and capital in this revolution before attempting to get Congress or regulators to address their contribution to misaligned economic incentives will make the task far easier. Once we begin to achieve parity on resource intensity with Europe and Japan, we can begin to ensure that our policy house is in order.

BEYOND EFFICIENCY

The idea of promoting more efficient business practices is as old as business itself. Indeed, cutting costs to improve competitiveness and productivity is at the heart of a market-based capitalist economy. In theory, such markets foster competition and reward companies with the most efficient allocation of resources.

The reality, of course, is that subsidies, tax preferences, and consumer whims often roil capitalism's so-called rational markets. Simply put: actual human beings frequently don't behave as rationally as economic theory would have it. We buy things that give us pleasure or status, for example, often based on advertising or packaging highly tuned by marketers to fulfill our biological or psychological needs. We buy into a herd mentality or network effect; paradoxically, we exercise our individualism by fitting in.

So efficiency may have little to do with it. Since the Great Recession of 2008–11, there's a growing understanding that the economy is a complex, dynamic, open, and nonlinear system that has more in common with ecosystems than with the purely deterministic systems on which neoclassical economics is based. Efficiencies are great, but not to the extent that you have no depth or resilience in the systems should something go awry. Again, we return to our ecosystem model: the logic of ecosystems includes diversity and variety so that flexibility and agility are essential properties of participating subsystems—such as companies, value chains, economies, and nations.

The history of efficiency in business goes back more than a century. Management theorists like Frederick Taylor and Frank and Lillian

Gilbreth designed time-and-motion studies primarily to improve workers' efficiency. The past half century or so has seen steady growth in materials efficiency, bolstered by an array of management techniques: total quality management, lean manufacturing, just-in-time manufacturing, agile manufacturing, Six Sigma, and others. Each promises to squeeze efficiency and savings from manufacturing and production systems, all while improving quality and reliability.

One problem with most such systems is that efficiencies need to be purpose-driven. One can't mindlessly ride Moore's Law, improving the technical efficiencies of computer systems, without addressing the deleterious effects of mining, e-waste, toxic emissions, and energy use, among other things. Increasing the efficiencies of corrosive systems will only make them more efficiently corrosive.

Discerning what should become more efficient may be more easily determined if we look at Adam Smith's original notion of why economics is important: we make profits to fuel economies so that they serve the betterment of humans. Today's logic turns that on its head: people labor to keep the economy going so that we can make profits for shareholders. This isn't necessarily the system we need to make more efficient.

The combination of emerging resource shortages and global competition is upping the ante on efficiency, requiring businesses to look beyond incremental improvements to radically rethink products, processes, and business models. Seizing the promise of the resource revolution means upending old, linear models of production known as "take-make-waste," in which we extract resources to make things that eventually become unusable or unwanted, grist for landfills or incinerators. The vision of tomorrow's economy is circular, a closed-loop cycle of material flows that extracts ever more value from every molecule.

As the architect and designer William McDonough quips, playing off the phrase attributed to Ludwig Mies van der Rohe, one of the founders of modern architecture and a proponent of simplicity of style: "Endless is more."

THE INDUSTRIAL INTERNET

Resources may never truly be endless, of course, but thanks to digitization we are now able to stretch resources well beyond once-imagined limits. The Internet of Things, or IoT, represents a digitization of the physical world, a deeply interconnected network where just about everything is embedded with sensors, communications capabilities, and other wizardry that enable a given device—a car, a person, pretty much any object anywhere—to be continually tracked, monitored, and optimized: where it is, what it's doing, how well it's doing that, what kind of attention it needs, and even what it is likely to do next.

And it will bring great financial benefit. According to a 2015 study by McKinsey Global Institute, the IoT has a total potential economic impact of $3.9 trillion to $11.1 trillion a year by 2025, about 70 percent of it in business-to-business applications. Among the biggest applications, according to McKinsey, are factory operations and equipment optimization ($1.2 to $3.7 trillion); urban transportation and public health ($930 billion to $1.7 trillion); and logistics and navigation ($560 billion to $850 billion). That's *per year.*

But it's not simply a matter of wiring things up and getting them to talk to one another. That's fairly straightforward these days. All the necessary components for an IoT device—an accelerator; ambient light sensor; GPS; gyroscope; magnetometer compass; proximity sensor; sensors that measure temperature, humidity, and pressure; a microphone; a power source; and a machine-to-machine communications capability on a cellular or other network—can be embedded in something smaller than, well, a smartphone. Much of it will fit on a single chip. The magic comes when all of that intelligence can be analyzed so that decisions on how to optimize a machine or system are made automatically in real time.

When that technology is embedded in a large, energy-gulping machine, it offers the biggest opportunities yet to save money, materials, time, labor, and other resources.

Consider General Electric, the iconic American company founded in 1892 by Thomas Edison. Its history tracks the trajectory of energy development, from incandescent lamps to steam engines to the latest high-efficiency power plants and aircraft engines. In 2012, GE set a new focus on what it dubbed the Industrial Internet, "the convergence of the global industrial system with the power of advanced computing, analytics, low-cost sensing, and new levels of connectivity permitted by the Internet." It's about how "the deeper meshing of the digital world with the world of machines holds the potential to bring about profound transformation to global industry, and in turn to many aspects of daily life, including the way many of us do our jobs," according to the company. It's fundamentally about data and how it transforms and even revitalizes the dirty work of manufacturing, transportation, and energy production.

GE sees vast potential in "things that spin"—the millions of rotating machines around the world that are the workhorses of our industrial world: engines, turbines, compressors, pumps, fans, blowers, generators, rollers, conveyors, and more, from simple electric motors to the highly advanced computed tomography devices, better known as CT scanners, used in health care. Each of these assets is subject to temperature, pressure, vibration, and other variables, which can be monitored and manipulated to provide safety, enhanced productivity, and operational savings.

This is already happening, says GE, though it's early days: "Companies have been applying Internet-based technologies to industrial applications as they have become available over the last decade. However, we currently stand far below the possibility frontier: the full potential of Internet-based digital technology has yet to be fully realized across the global industry system. Intelligent devices, intelligent systems, and intelligent decisioning represent the primary ways in which the physical world of machines, facilities, fleets, and networks can more deeply merge with the connectivity, big data, and analytics of the digital world."

GE sees this convergence as a very big business opportunity: it estimates that connecting devices to the Industrial Internet could boost global GDP by $15 trillion by 2030. That's nearly the size of the entire U.S economy, which was about $18 trillion in 2015. The savings come from such things as lower fuel and energy costs, and better-performing and longer-lived airplanes, power plants, and other physical assets. The company claims that in the United States alone the Industrial Internet could boost average incomes by 25 to 40 percent over the next 20 years "and lift growth back to levels not seen since the late 1990s."

For example, says GE, achieving a 1 percent fuel savings across the entire global airline fleet would save $30 billion over the next 15 years. A similar 1 percent improvement in the efficiency of gas-fired power generation would save $66 billion over that same period. And a 1 percent improvement in railroad efficiency adds $27 billion to the total. Clearly, the potential for efficiency improvements is far greater than a mere 1 percent.

What GE also makes clear is that industrial companies are no longer just about manufacturing "big iron"—planes, trains, generators, and the like. Today, software, intelligence, connectivity, analytics, sensors, diagnostics, integration, user interface, and materials science are key parts of industrial companies' value chain. In the Industrial Internet, advances in software tools and analytic techniques provide the means to understand the massive quantities of data that are generated by intelligent devices, and the means to harness that data to achieve unprecedented efficiency.

One big challenge may be finding qualified applicants for the kind of jobs being created by GE and many other companies operating at the convergence of big data and manufacturing. According to the 2015 Manufacturing Institute and Deloitte Skills Gap Study, 84 percent of manufacturing executives agree there is a talent shortage in American manufacturing. Moreover, 6 in 10 execs indicate that skilled production positions often go unfilled due to a lack of qualified applicants, even when 80 percent of manufacturing companies are willing to pay more than the market wage. The study also projects that between 2015 and 2025, 3.4 million manufacturing jobs will need to be filled in the United States, the result of 2.7 million Baby Boomers retiring plus the creation of another 700,000 new jobs. They foresee an expected shortfall of 2 million jobs due to an advanced-manufacturing skills gap, which will limit the ability of the manufacturing sector to expand and restrict that sector's contribution to U.S. employment and economic gains.

MATERIAL WORLD

We'll need more than electrical and mechanical engineers to invent and run our resource-efficient world. We'll also need advanced-materials scientists—biologists, chemists, physicists, and others—to design the next generations of lightweight and sturdy materials that allow us to do more with less, and do some entirely new things altogether. The advanced-materials revolution has been under way since the 1930s and 1940s, when petrochemicals began replacing plant matter and other organic materials to make plastics. Polystyrene was among the earliest examples, pioneered in the 1930s by the German firm BASF and later produced by Dow Chemical in a foam format to create Styrofoam for building, packaging, and other purposes.

The 1980s saw the next generation of materials, as scientists manipulated molecules to derive materials with superior characteristics, such as toughness, hardness, elasticity, and durability. The past three decades have seen an explosion in such materials, ranging from aerogels (porous, solid materials, up to 99.98 percent air, with superinsulating characteristics) to zeolites (microporous minerals commonly used as commercial adsorbents and catalysts). In between are thousands of types of carbon fibers, graphite fibers, thermoplastics, ceramics, adhesives, foams, gels, nanomaterials, metals, alloys, polymers, and a cornucopia of composites made from any two or more of these.

The ability to combine materials is bringing newfound efficiencies—not just in materials, but in the energy and water it takes to produce them, the reduced or nontoxic chemicals used in their manufacture, and the efficiency of the end product itself. For example, the rotating blade for a modern wind turbine could be manufactured, based on computational modeling, to be made from sophisticated plastics reinforced with glass fibers or carbon filaments as well as carbon nanotubes specially tuned to optimize such qualities as strength, toughness, and fatigue resistance. Every molecule is optimized, individually and in concert, to do exactly the job it was created to do.

Not every new material is benign to manufacture, of course, and much of it can't be recycled or otherwise reclaimed, leading to a new generation of one-way materials that have no value at the end of their useful life. The chemical constituents contained in the "ink" used to make things via 3D printing, for example, are rarely discussed or disclosed, and there seems to be little heed paid to what toxic constituents, if any, are involved. Such is the price of progress, it seems. Eventually, one hopes, public (and activist) concerns will catch up to the technology.

But what if, in inventing the next generation of materials, we could design in qualities that not only minimize environmental impacts but actually help solve environmental challenges?

Consider the promise of materials that actually remove carbon dioxide from the atmosphere, potentially reversing climate change. For example, there's Newlight Technologies, which commercialized a carbon-capture technology that combines air with methane to produce a plastic material called AirCarbon that sequesters greenhouse gases instead of releasing them to the atmosphere. The company, based in Costa Mesa, California, essentially mimics what plants and microorganisms do: they use greenhouse gases to make useful materials, from carbon dioxide–capturing trees and coral reefs to methane–capturing hydrothermal vent ecosystems deep in oceans.

Newlight is manufacturing polyhydroxyalkanoates, or PHAs, linear polyesters produced in nature. The company combines a high-yield biocatalyst with air and captured methane-based greenhouse gas emissions to produce a thermoplastic material that it claims is cost competitive with petroleum-derived thermoplastics. Among the applications are films, caps and closures, furniture, electronics accessories, and bottles. Dell uses AirCarbon in the packaging for its Latitude notebook computers; Sprint is shaping it into cell phone cases for iPhones. In 2015, the company signed a contract with a privately held plastics and chemicals marketing and distribution company, Vinmar International, for 1 billion pounds of AirCarbon over 20 years, a huge vote of confidence.

The idea of mining the sky instead of the ground is a radical idea, to be sure, but Newlight isn't the only company pursuing it. There's Solidia Technologies, based in Piscataway, New Jersey, whose technology sequesters carbon dioxide by injecting it into concrete during the manufacturing process, transforming CO_2 from a pollutant into an ingredient that, the company claims, makes concrete that is stronger, more durable, more flexible, and costs less. A Canadian company, CarbonCure, has a similar technology. When CO_2 is added to concrete during mixing, the CO_2 reacts with water to form carbonate ions. The carbonate then quickly reacts with calcium ions released from the cement to form a limestone-like material. This mineral is created in the form of nanomaterials dispersed throughout the concrete mix. The conversion of carbon dioxide into solid carbonate minerals means that the carbon dioxide has become permanently bound within the concrete and will not be released back into the atmosphere. Liquid Light, based in Monmouth Junction, New Jersey, uses low-energy catalytic electrochemistry to convert carbon dioxide to multicarbon chemicals such as ethylene glycol, a raw material for plastic bottles, among other things. Still another company, Austin-based Skyonic, takes carbon dioxide emissions from power plants and industrial processes and turns it into "carbon-negative" materials for the manufacture of PVC pipes and glass, cattle feed, steel pickling, and other uses in the oil and gas industry.

The move to create advanced, carbon-sequestering materials isn't merely a good business opportunity; it also exemplifies the "feedstock shift" that we'll further detail in chapter 7, where oil and natural gas use are moved from combustion via fuels to bulk structural materials, like the kind Newlight and Skyonic are producing. It represents one of the prime roles of resource productivity in our grand strategy: to enable a radical transformation of our economy without upending trillions of dollars of investments.

The material revolution is just getting going. Automakers are developing porous polymers and new steel alloys that are stronger and lighter than steel. Green-minded entrepreneurs are growing mushroom-based packing materials to provide an alternative to polystyrene, derived from plants instead of petroleum. There are adhesives that mimic the gecko, a lizard that sticks to surfaces by weak intermolecular attraction called van der Waals forces, resulting in high tensile strength and nontoxic adhesives. The ability to wrangle molecules, or even atoms, to make a stronger, more resilient, and more efficient world is as unlimited as the materials themselves.

IF IT'S BROKE . . . FIX IT

The resource revolution is not just about big data, big iron, high-tech devices, or even advanced materials. It is also about rethinking business models and the relationship between companies and their customers. The Internet certainly has disrupted many of those—witness the myriad "freemium" business models—LinkedIn, Dropbox, Skype, Gmail, Flickr, and Spotify are great examples—where software or services are offered for free to all, with the hope that some portion of users will upgrade to a paid premium service with more features.

Freemium is just one example in business model innovation, though it may be the most ubiquitous; nearly everyone in business uses one or more of these services. As such, it has opened the doors wide for new thinking on how companies build customers and markets, and how quickly ideas spread from one sector to another. Each new idea and business model promises some higher level of efficiency by substituting digital code for energy and physical resources, or by allowing assets to be more fully utilized and profitable.

If you want proof of that, type the phrase "Uber for X" into a web browser and see what you come up with. Most likely, it will be a myriad of examples of companies leveraging the business model of Uber Technologies, the international transportation company whose mobile app allows you to summon a car and driver in more than 300 cities in more than 50 countries, from Baton Rouge to Bangkok to Beirut. Uber wasn't the first transportation company to enter the so-called sharing economy or collaborative economy, but its success and ubiquity have whetted entrepreneurs' and investors' appetites for on-demand services: food delivery, babysitting, pet care, dry cleaning, car repair, tailoring, moving, home buying, box shipping, home decorating, clothing rental, and more, all summoned via a smartphone or other device.

"The collaborative economy is fundamentally the most revolutionary change in the economy in a long, long time," says author and entrepreneur Paul Hawken. "It changes all the relationships between the players in the economy. It changes the incentives to scale. It then starts to go back to the village in a sense—your reputation, your character, whether you are or aren't trustworthy. It creates socialization. It's the opposite of the Internet, where you're online alone. It also has a huge impact on how much material we use. It shifts from the economy of stuff to the economy of information, transported and interchanged by people."

As Hawken notes, the collaborative economy transforms not just our relationships to our stuff, but to business, commerce, and one another. "In the new collaborative economy, sharing and networking assets, like platforms, car seats and bedrooms, will always deliver more value faster," says Robin Chase, cofounder of Zipcar and author of *Peers Inc: How People & Platforms Are Inventing the Collaborative Economy & Reinventing Capitalism*. "Think of the enormous loss of human potential bound up in patents, copyrights, trade secrets, certifications, and credentials. These hallmarks of the old capitalist economy harbor excess capacity just yearning to find the light of day. In the new collaborative economy, innovation is limitless. More minds working together will always be exponentially smarter, more experienced, and more well equipped than fewer ones who work inside a single company or government. In these big and well-organized networks, we can count on the right person—with the necessary skills, networks, insights, and location—to appear."

But the bigger, and largely untapped, potential for sharing underutilized assets is on the business-to-business side, and it's just beginning. Already, companies are providing services to share unused office space (LiquidSpace, WeWork, PivotDesk), farming machines (FarmLink), warehouse space (Flexe), available trucking capacity (Cargomatic), business equipment and services (Floow2, in the Netherlands), retail spaces available for pop-up shops (Storefront), and idle heavy equipment (Yard

Club). There's even a sharing platform for cities and other public agencies (MuniRent) to share heavy-duty equipment. All told, these companies and many others stand to disrupt how companies think about sales channels, supply chains, where to make things, how to make them—and whether to make them at all.

Adding to this is yet another emerging trend—we'll call it the "fixit economy." It's a simple, radical, back-to-the-future notion: that there's business value to be found in selling products that can be repaired and refurbished, thereby reducing disposal and waste by keeping things in service longer. So far, only a handful of consumer companies have dared to venture into this arena, notably Patagonia, the maverick outdoor clothing and equipment company. Its "Worn Wear" program encourages customers to bring broken or torn gear in for repairs; in 2015 the company even sent a truck on a California-to-Boston road trip with stops planned along the way in hipster coffee bars, surf shops, and Patagonia retail stores. At each stop, technicians managed a handful of on-site repairs, but the high-profile events are designed to promote the company's 45-person repair team in Reno, Nevada—the largest apparel repair facility in North America, claims the company. Repairs are done for free at both Worn Wear tour stops and by mail to the repair center.

It's a nascent movement, to be sure, but there are signs that the fixit economy may be stitching together a global network. Consider Repair Cafés, a company with 750 outlets in 18 countries, primarily in Europe but also in Australia, Brazil, and Japan; there are more than 20 Repair Cafés operating across the United States. Each offers free meeting places featuring tools and materials to help individuals make repairs to clothes, furniture, electrical appliances, bicycles, crockery, appliances, toys, and whatever else needs a little TLC. On-site repair specialists—electricians, seamstresses, carpenters, bicycle mechanics, and more—can help. The idea is to do it yourself, getting a little help from others when needed, offering it to others when you can.

None of this is likely to make much of a dent in retail sales of new stuff any time soon, but as a new generation of DIYers enters their prime earning years—the time of life when people traditionally acquire homes, cars, furniture, appliances, baby toys, and lots of other things—fixing what's broken will likely become second nature. So will an ethic of avoiding nonrepairable goods and shunning companies stuck in the cycle of cheap, disposable products. Brands whose goods are designed to be repaired or refurbished may find themselves winning market share from those whose aren't.

In many respects, the fixit economy is a subset of the maker movement, the umbrella term for a vast army of individual inventors, designers, and tinkerers. They bring together both digital technology—computers, laser cutters, 3D printers, and the like—and traditional artisan skills—welding, weaving, brewing, blacksmithing, gardening, glassblowing, and dozens of others. They attend a network of Maker Faires that extends from Nebraska to Nigeria and have their own bi-monthly magazine, *Make*.

"The Maker Movement has been described as the next Industrial Revolution, the outcome of a massive dialectic between an increasingly open internet and the real world," says Scott McLeod, an expert on K-12 technology leadership issues. "It is now possible for people to tinker, hack, design, code, prototype, and create in Makerspaces, Fablabs, and Hackerspaces with cutting-edge technologies, much like [Apple cofounders Steve] Jobs and [Steve] Wozniak did with circuit boards back in the legendary days of the Homebrew Computer Club. The real power of making—and why it is truly deemed a 'movement'—lies in the groundbreaking possibility of global and open collaboration on a scale and with tools never before available. What was once merely digital dreaming has become physical reality."

WHAT GOES AROUND

At its core, resource productivity is about reducing or eliminating waste in industrial systems. Waste has long been the bane of manufacturing; it represents inefficiency and lost profit. Much waste is considered "free" in that there is little or no cost to companies for disposing of it into the air, water, or soil. It's even incentivized in our tax system: you can waste for free, but your productivity is taxed.

But there are limits to how much waste can be excised from any given process. At some point, you stop cutting fat and begin cutting muscle and bone. That's leading a growing number of companies to think about their manufacturing processes not as assembly lines or value chains, but as continuous loops of material flows that need to be maintained ad infinitum.

Welcome to the "circular economy." Over the past few years, that term has gone from the margins to the mainstream, as companies as varied as Apple, Coca-Cola, HP Inc., Interface, and Steelcase seek ways to eliminate waste by designing for reuse and recovery, and by introducing new business models that extract more value from less stuff. Much of the action to date has taken place in Europe, where several dozen companies have worked with the U.K.-based Ellen MacArthur Foundation to create a framework for the circular economy. A 2012 report by the foundation, with analysis by McKinsey & Co., forecast an annual net material cost savings opportunity of up to $630 billion while "looking only at a subset of EU manufacturing sectors."

In a circular economy, "waste does not exist," the foundation points out. "Products are designed and optimized for a cycle of disassembly and reuse. These tight component and product cycles define the circular economy and set it apart from disposal and even recycling, where large amounts of embedded energy and labor are lost." Product components are made primarily from benign and nontoxic biological ingredients— "nutrients" that can be returned safely to soil or water or, in the case of more durable components, can be placed back into industrial cycles again and again. Toxic ingredients are not verboten; they can be used as needed in products or processes so long as they, too, are continuously cycled back into productive use and kept out of the waste stream. And, of course, as much of this as possible should be powered by renewable energy.

Sure, this may sound like some futuristic, utopian vision: factories with no smokestacks, drainpipes, or dumpsters, powered by the sun and wind, making products sourced benignly from nature, continuously recycled with no waste. And not long ago, it was, indeed, an unattainable ideal.

Then again, not long ago you could have said the same thing about "zero-waste" factories, where nothing goes into landfills. Now, they're commonplace.

If you want proof, take a trip to the Subaru plant in Lafayette, Indiana. There, off Route 38 about 10 miles southeast of Purdue University, is where some 4,000 employees have been cranking out the Subaru Legacy, Outback, Tribeca, and other vehicles since 1989—more than a quarter million a year.

The 4-million-square-foot facility, with more than 10 miles of production lines, first achieved zero-waste status in 2004 and has become an icon of industrial eco-efficiency. Scrap metal from the stamping shop is collected and sent off to become smaller car parts. Overspray from the paint shop is collected and turned into safety barricades for highways. Glass from used lightbulbs is turned into reflective road striping. The Styrofoam and plastic packaging used to ship parts to the factory is sent back to suppliers for reuse. In the body shop, weld slag is collected in large barrels and sent overseas to reclaim the copper. On top of all that, the company boasts that, thanks to a complex filtration system along with continuous reductions in water use, the water leaving the plant is cleaner than the water that enters it.

Incidentally, there hasn't been a single layoff at Subaru's Lafayette plant since the zero-waste program began in 2004, during which time the U.S. auto industry as a whole lost around 415,000 jobs. No one has credited the zero-waste status solely for that achievement, but clearly the plant is doing a lot of things right.

It's not just Subaru. More than 120 of General Motors's facilities worldwide have achieved zero waste, including both manufacturing and nonmanufacturing sites. In recent years, General Motors has generated nearly $1 billion in annual revenue by reusing and recycling its by-products. It avoided more than 10 million metric tons of greenhouse gas emissions in 2014 alone. All 23 of Nestlé's North American factories have achieved zero-waste status. The La-Z-Boy factory in Dayton, Tennessee, about 80 miles southwest of Knoxville, makes about 2,000 chairs a day but doesn't send an ounce of waste to landfills. In 2015, Unilever announced that it had eliminated nonhazardous waste from landfills across its global factory network—more than 240 factories in 67 countries. The company says it avoided more than $200 million in costs and created hundreds of jobs. And scores of other companies, from Boeing to Anheuser-Busch, have set their sights on zero-waste facilities and are on their way to reaching that goal.

However impressive, the circular economy is about much more than merely reducing and recycling waste. Its adherents are rethinking products altogether, designing in their reuse, repairability, and recyclability, and examining new business models that may not even involve selling products in the first place. In the circular economy, lighting companies sell lumens, not bulbs; carpet companies lease comfort and aesthetics instead of selling carpets; aircraft engine makers sell power services, not heavy equipment; car companies sell mobility, not cars and trucks. Some of these may seem like semantic gymnastics, but underlying them are profound changes in manufacturer-customer relationships and in how products are designed, manufactured, brought to market, and consumed. For example, the aircraft engine maker is financially incentivized to make the most efficient engines and keep them optimized and in service for as long as possible, then reclaim parts and materials to put back into production, whether as new engines or something else. These new models serve to eliminate the concept of waste that once had been considered business as usual and built into customer relationships.

There may be no better example of this transition than Ford Motor Company. In 2015, the iconic American manufacturer announced Ford Smart Mobility, a plan "to deliver the next level in connectivity, mobility, autonomous vehicles, the customer experience, and big data." The company launched the plan with 25 experiments aimed at better understanding consumers' mobility needs around the globe. As part of the plan, Ford is inviting more than 20,000 customers in six U.S. cities and London to sign up to rent their Ford-financed vehicles to prescreened drivers for short-term use, helping them offset monthly vehicle ownership costs.

The idea of dipping its corporate toe into offering "mobility services" is prompted as much by demographics as productivity: A third of U.S. Millennials are interested in renting out their cars and other belongings as a way to supplement their income, and more than half are open to sharing rides with others, often in lieu of buying a car of their own. Make no mistake: Ford plans to sell millions of vehicles for decades to come, but it is also offering new options in a topsy-turvy world where American youth no longer equate owning a car with "freedom."

The road from here to "zero" or "circular" can be long and bumpy, and few companies are traveling it alone. The journey requires new kinds of partnerships and alliances—with suppliers and customers, sometimes even competitors. In 2015, for example, 20 major companies with operations in the United States came together to form the National Materials Marketplace, a collaboration to identify ways to reuse or exchange undervalued materials via an online database and establish new circular supply chains. Participating companies include icons of American industry, such as GM, 3M, Dow Chemical, Eastman Chemical, Goodyear, and Nike.

"The increasing pressure on our natural resources sends a clear message: we need to find value in discarded materials," said Andrew Mangan, executive director of the U.S. Business Council for Sustainable Development, one of the marketplace's founding organizations, at the time of the launch. "Growing cross-industry collaboration for the efficient use of our resources is promising. This opens up new business opportunities while creating economic, environmental, and societal benefits." Adds John Bradburn, GM's global manager of waste reduction, the man behind the company's zero-waste initiative: "Material management is a business opportunity, not just a cost-reduction strategy. We have to reach the stage where by-products are viewed the same way we view product development—part of constant improvement and innovation."

This is serious stuff, and it's not about to go away. Indeed, the conversation about zero waste and the circular economy is just getting interesting. At the 2014 World Economic Forum Annual Meeting in Davos, Switzerland, a group of large companies launched Project MainStream, a multi-industry, CEO-led global initiative to help scale the circular economy. The World Economic Forum also hosts a "Meta-Council" on the circular economy that convenes business, policy, and civil-society leaders "to rethink and suggest redesign of policy ecosystems needed to allow systems-level change and widespread adoption of circular models."

It turns out that a "circular" economy may not even be the limit of what's possible. "The concept of the circular economy can certainly inspire us and point the way, but we have to remember it's still circular," says Bill McDonough, the architect and designer who has helped facilitate the Davos Meta-Council. "It's two-dimensional. It's flat. It's just the economy in a circle."

He continues: "What I am really excited about is how we'll build on circular economies and also move toward the next level: the spiral economy—an economy that's growing. You can't grow without income, and the only thing the planet has as income is solar energy. It doesn't have material income—the planet isn't raining phosphate. So the idea that we put these things in circles and cycles with new design science with effective business models, and then grow safe and healthy things and systems we can all share, is fabulous. We can start to talk about growth again."

REVIVING THE RUST BELT

The Industrial Internet. The collaboration economy. The fixit economy. The maker movement. Zero-waste factories. The circular economy. All of these represent advances in how we source, use, and dispose of the materials that flow through our industrial and commercial worlds. And as these innovations grow ever more mainstream, the potential of the productivity revolution moves closer to realization. These are still early days; we've barely begun to pluck the low-hanging fruit. There is almost no limit to what can be done.

Back in Youngstown, America Makes views this productivity revolution with anticipation and excitement. It's hard to overstate the potential of 3D printing to transform manufacturing and logistics—how we make and transport things—and its importance for U.S. competitiveness. 3D printing technology is rapidly becoming an essential tool in a wide range of industries. As costs continue to decline as quality and capabilities improve, 3D printing is finding uses in everything from dentistry to defense contractors. Now, spare parts for critical machines—think of a ship with a broken engine in midocean—can be manufactured on site in minutes or a few hours instead of waiting for it to be transported great distances. Prototypes for new products can be created and refined within minutes and at low cost, relative to machine tooling, dye-casting, and other traditional industrial processes. Parts for everything from car bodies to human bodies can be custom designed and individually fitted, quickly and economically.

All of which creates a long list of industries that stand to be disrupted by this manufacturing revolution: aerospace, biomedicine, construction, drug manufacturing, electronics, food processing, and on and on. True, the technology still has a ways to go: 3D printers are relatively slow, the materials are limited, and 3D-printed parts can be mechanically weak, limiting their applications. That will continue to improve as new entrants attempt to disrupt the state of the art, as we've seen with so many technologies over the past half century. For example, there's a Silicon Valley company called Carbon 3D, inspired—no kidding—by the 1991 movie *Terminator 2: Judgment Day,* in which the T-1000 robotic villain rises fully formed from a puddle of metallic goo. With Carbon 3D's technology, "you have an object arise out of a puddle, in essentially real time, with essentially no waste, to make a great object," says the company's CEO, Joseph DeSimone, who previously was a chemistry professor at the University of North Carolina at Chapel Hill. His process harnesses light, which can convert a liquid to a solid, and oxygen, which inhibits that growth, to grow parts continuously. "If you can control the process spatially, you can build things out of puddles," says DeSimone.

We'll need such out-there innovations to take manufacturing to new places. One of those is space, where long-distance voyagers will need to make the things they need over the course of their years-long journeys. The first-ever zero-G printer, designed by a Silicon Valley firm called, appropriately, Made in Space, was launched in 2014 and has become a test bed for understanding the long-term effects of microgravity on 3D printing and how it can enable the future of space exploration. (Talk about offshore manufacturing!) The ability of space travelers to manufacture things on demand will be critical if we are to extend our horizons to Mars and beyond. They'll need to carry with them the digital instructions for building their world, and the means to print them using locally available ingredients.

Meanwhile, back on terra firma, 3D printing already holds strategic importance to the United States and other countries. The technology allows sensitive components to be manufactured domestically, reducing the risk of the intellectual property (IP) theft or cheap knockoffs that have resulted from relying on factories in countries where weak IP laws result in production designs being stolen, copied, and distributed among competitors. That's one reason why defense contractors like Boeing, Lockheed Martin, Northrup Grumman, Raytheon, and United Technologies Corp. are among the charter members of America Makes.

But the bigger reason 3D printing could bring manufacturing back to U.S. shores is that its labor costs are low, eliminating the need to manufacture in low-wage countries and enabling manufacturers to choose factory locations based instead on distribution costs and speed of delivery.

"I see manufacturing taking a profound turn with additive technologies in the next five years," says S. Kent Rockwell, CEO of 3D printing firm ExOne, in a 2014 report from PwC. "We'll see elite job shops grow, and new start-ups grow. We'll also see blue-collar employees learn the technology and adapt and start wearing white shirts."

To get there, we'll have to raise the next generation of workers on 3D technology, the same way that Millennials were brought up on smartphones and wireless technology, and their parents on laser printers and the Internet. Already there are calls for mass adoption of 3D printers in K-12 schools across America. The cost wouldn't necessarily be prohibitive: putting a $1,000 machine in each of about 98,000 public schools would cost just under $100 million—real money, to be sure, but a pittance in federal and state budgetary terms. And that's before costs drop dramatically, which they are destined to do.

Making additive manufacturing part of basic education may no longer be optional. According to a 2015 report by 3DPrint.com, an industry website, the Chinese government intends to install a 3D printer in each of its approximately 400,000 elementary schools by 2017. Being fluent in additive manufacturing could soon become table stakes for young people matriculating into a competitive economy.

A RETURN TO YOUNGSTOWN

The resource productivity revolution is expanding at an exciting clip, but in the United States we're proceeding with one hand tied behind our collective backs. The demand for higher-efficiency products and services is so strong that American businesses are entering this market space *in spite* of policies that incentivize waste, not resource efficiency. This lack of vision has a real cost. America is strategically underperforming, missing out on the high-skill, high-wage jobs, investment returns, and geopolitical benefits that flow from making the goods that Americans—and the rest of the world—actually want to buy.

America knows how to generate an industrial awakening. One merely need look at the rapid expansion of the fracking industry, which, while environmentally problematic, demonstrates that even the nation's most staid and lucrative sectors can be rapidly overhauled in response to disruptive new technologies. Energy investment and employment have skyrocketed, creating new communities where there once was just a crossroads with a little bit of infrastructure.

By creating the opportunity to bring manufacturing back to the United States, resource-efficient manufacturing creates a virtuous cycle, bringing high-skill, high-wage jobs back to American communities, increasing household income, and further unlocking demand for the next

American dream. By diversifying our economy and creating redundancy in the global system, we're dramatically improving our own resilience while restoring America's prosperity.

All of this makes America Makes ground zero for America's industrial future. Obama pointed this out as he plugged America Makes in two consecutive State of the Union addresses, in 2013 and 2014. "A once-shuttered warehouse is now a state-of-the art lab where new workers are mastering the 3D printing that has the potential to revolutionize the way we make almost everything," the president said in his 2013 address, adding, "There's no reason this can't happen in other towns."

Youngstown is enjoying the boost America Makes is contributing to its still-recovering downtown. Cynthia Rogers, who runs a video production company in town, moved there from California with her husband and three sons in 2003—reluctantly, as she is quick to point out. "Everybody was so angry and negative" is how she described the locals upon her arrival. "When you'd explain that you just moved here, they would ask, 'Why would you come here?'"

The principal mind-set she found back then was that of returning Youngstown to its good old days. "When we moved here they still talked about the steel mills coming back because there was such a union mentality for generations and generations. Kids didn't go to college because they just went to work in the steel mills with their dads. There was automatically a job going to be available for them when they graduated high school so they never bothered with college."

That attitude eventually softened as alternatives like 3D printing showed promise. "People realized, 'Wait a minute, maybe we can do this here,'" says Rogers. And so the kids, who used to leave for Cleveland or Pittsburgh after graduation, are coming back, or are sticking around to attend Youngstown State University. They are adding to an increasingly vibrant downtown scene. There are new bars and restaurants opening, a renovated children's museum that is getting rave reviews, more out-of-town license plates, and a little more bustle along West Federal Street.

Rogers's oldest son left to attend college at the University of Toledo, but she hopes that he'll come back to Youngstown. "I can very well see that he will. And I wouldn't have said that five years ago."

PART III

FROM HERE TO SUSTAINABILITY

CHAPTER SEVEN

CAPITAL AND STRANDED ASSETS

AS WE LAID OUT IN CHAPTER 3, THE STRUCTURE OF THE NEW ECO-
nomic engine we envision is based on the formula *Demand + Capital –
Stranded Assets = New Growth Scenario*. And we've described the three
massive pools of demand that can be accessed in short order. It is now
time to assess the state of the other two parts of the equation: capital and
stranded assets. That will set the stage for our alternative growth scenario.

The good news is that, thanks to a massive amount of money sitting
on the sidelines of the economy, the future is very encouraging, though
far from certain.

Just after President Obama was reelected in 2012, Lloyd Blankfein,
CEO of Goldman Sachs, wrote an op-ed in the *Wall Street Journal* calling for the president and Congress to create the "certainty" that markets
need to invest. "There is more than a trillion dollars of cash that is sitting on the balance sheets of U.S. nonfinancial companies," he pointed
out. By 2015, that number had grown to $3.5 trillion, according to the
Federal Reserve. Hedge funds and private-equity cash holdings add another $10 trillion to the pile of idle capital. For Blankfein, certainty
meant clear policies on taxation, deficits, immigration, and energy. Deliver that, and companies will open their wallets. Even a small portion
of that $3.5 trillion could go a long way toward rebuilding America,
profitably and relatively quickly.

Why all this underutilized liquidity? There are many contributing factors. Productivity has increased dramatically while wages have

stagnated, meaning gains are captured by management and shareholders, not (most) employees. As Thomas Piketty wrote in his 2014 book *Capital in the Twenty-First Century,* the returns to invested capital are outpacing economic growth, concentrating wealth with the owners of capital. Contributing to this, U.S. corporate taxes are historically low, meaning profits are being retained and not going into government coffers. With the federal and state governments not spending much on infrastructure, asset managers are unable to find the bonds that would absorb a portion of this excess. As Blankfein noted, uncertainty is high, acting as a disincentive to spend cash that might be needed as a buffer against future economic downturns.

By the middle of 2015, the absence of sizeable investments by the private sector looked less like a problem of tax rates and more about management's reluctance to think beyond the next quarter or two. As Laurence D. Fink, CEO of BlackRock, the world's largest asset manager, with $4.5 trillion under management, wrote to the CEOs of the Fortune 500: "The effects of the short-termist phenomenon are troubling both to those seeking to save for long-term goals, such as retirement, and for our broader economy."

Short-termism is the relentless focus on quarterly business results. It also leads to actions that have little to do with investment and growth and everything to do with shoring up a company's stock price. Facing long-term uncertainty, significant cash reserves, compensation packages tied to stock performance, and shorter CEO tenures, companies increasingly are choosing to use their cash hoards to buy back their own stock. It's an easy quick-fix, temporarily boosting (or stabilizing) the share price instead of investing that money in the R&D or modern equipment that could lay the foundation for future innovations and more durable growth. In his letter, Fink urged CEOs to get a sound strategy for long-term growth, a move that could provide long-term investors like BlackRock with what they need to defend CEOs when they miss their quarterly targets.

Not only are there trillions of dollars of capital to invest in a new growth strategy, that money is getting organized. While the push may be fiduciary obligation, a major pull is coming from a range of hypotheses tied to sustainability. The prize is not trivial: according to a 2015 report from the campaign organization New Climate Economy, new spending in cities, agriculture, and energy will top $90 trillion over the next 15 years, and that transition needs to be financed.

The so-called sustainable and responsible investment segment now has $13.5 trillion under management globally, according to the World Economic Forum. The Investor Network on Climate Risk—a project of the nonprofit activist group Ceres, representing private-equity houses like KKR, asset managers like BlackRock, and giant pension funds like CalPERS—is also beginning to throw its weight around. For example, the group is demanding that publicly traded companies disclose their climate risks to investors, and it is working to get the Securities and Exchange Commission to put its regulatory muscle behind the request. But regulation may not even be necessary: the nonprofit Sustainability Accounting Standards Board, whose board of directors includes former New York City mayor Michael Bloomberg as its chair and former SEC head Mary Schapiro as its vice-chair, has developed standards for companies to report their climate risks. While SASB, too, would like SEC backing, it may not need that, as it can rely instead on shareholder activism to persuade companies to provide such transparency.

In a similar effort in September 2014, just before the United Nations Climate Summit, investors representing $24 trillion of assets called for an aggressive carbon-pricing policy to deliver the certainty needed to invest in the low-carbon economy at the scale and speed necessary to effect change. To the extent that money talks, it seems to be speaking increasingly loudly.

Another encouraging sign is the use of "green bonds"—fixed-income financial instruments used to raise funds dedicated to climate mitigation, adaptation, and other environmental projects. It is growing quickly: between 2012 and 2015, bond issues grew tenfold, from $3.1 billion to $36.9 billion. But that's just scratching the surface of what's possible. Supply is the only thing stopping green bonds from grabbing a larger share of the $80 trillion bond market. In fact, green bonds are frequently oversubscribed two to three times, with total volume nearly doubling during each of the last three years, according to EY and the Climate Bonds Initiative, as investors line up to add a wide range of sustainable projects to their portfolios, from clean-energy infrastructure to public transit systems to climate-adaptation measures along coasts and waterways. Such financing mechanisms had their moment in the spotlight at COP21, the 2015 United Nations climate summit in Paris. At the event, 27 global investors representing more than $11.2 trillion of total assets issued the "Paris Green Bonds Statement," calling for support of policies that drive the development of global markets in green bonds as part of financing solutions to climate change.

Along with major banks like HSBC, insurance companies like AXA, and reinsurance companies like Munich Re—all of which recognize the need to rapidly transition to a low-carbon economy—the financial sector is poised for a transformation. In 2015, Citi, the global banking giant, announced it would invest $100 billion over ten years for "lending, investing, and facilitating" activities focused on mitigating climate change and for other sustainability solutions. A few months later, Bank of America upped the ante, committing up to $125 billion in "low-carbon business" over the same period.

There's more like that, but the point is implicit, if not explicit: with tens of trillions of dollars sitting idle, underutilized, or deployed in unsustainable investments, we have the wherewithal to pump billions into clean energy, regenerative agriculture, resource productivity, smart cities, and other things that can rebuild America's economy while providing solid returns—without relying on Congress or the U.S. Treasury.

A NEW INVESTMENT HYPOTHESIS

It's not just the big investors who are sitting on their wallets. Amid today's economic uncertainty, many Americans simply don't know where to put their savings. Those in the middle of the economic spectrum— say, making between $55,000 and $100,000 a year—are probably paying off their credit cards, lines of credit, college debt, and mortgages instead of investing, and low wages and job uncertainty may be leading them to hold on to whatever they manage to save. Boomers and Millennials may be waiting for the kind of home they want, perhaps in a walkable neighborhood that is not yet available or affordable. Put it all together, and most Americans just aren't in a mood to spend or invest, at least at the levels we need to reinvigorate America's economy.

What's needed is a compelling new investment hypothesis.

An investment hypothesis is essentially a plan based on a particular goal and a particular investing style. It can be simple—say, putting one's money in a mutual fund or a family of mutual funds. It can be more complex—creating a diversified portfolio of stocks, bonds, cash, mutual funds, exchange-traded funds, or any of the dozen or so other investment vehicles that offer some mix of growth and security. Hypotheses change throughout life. Early on, an investor may be more willing to take a higher risk in order to grow a nest egg; later on, the goal may simply be to protect that nest egg, even if it means little or no additional upside. Whether all this is done actively or passively, it's nonetheless an investment hypothesis.

So, what is America's investment hypothesis? And who's determining it?

It's an open question. At one level, our elected leaders certainly have the power to reset the economic engine. But Congress is divided among committees that reflect the economic and strategic landscape of the last century. When Congress taxes or spends, it does so in categories and at levels that reflect where we've been more than where we're going. As we noted earlier, spending on highways, taxes on income, and especially interest on the national debt all reflect our old hypothesis.

Then there's the Federal Reserve. The Fed's mandate is twofold: keeping both inflation and employment in a happy place. It has a range of tools with which to achieve this goal and effectively acts as the economy's first responder, but at the end of the day, it really only has two pedals: a brake and an accelerator. Certainly, the Fed has some ability to pick what gets stimulus funding and what gets slowed down, as seen in the choice of assets purchased in the three rounds of quantitative easing, or in the other financial machinations during the late 2000s. But the Fed alone cannot alter America's investment hypothesis.

At the state and local levels, the outdated investment hypothesis of ever-expanding suburban consumerism gets embedded further, through zoning and other regulations that determine how the private sector invests—in single-family homes, dense apartment buildings, or strip malls, for example. Each decision—say, whether to preserve an open space or pave paradise and put up a parking lot—is part of an investment hypothesis, implicit or explicit.

There are a lot of players involved in all this: giant Wall Street banks and investment firms; pension funds and university endowments, which need to "park" millions or billions of dollars until they are needed; local developers and city planners, who influence, if not decide, what kinds of things get built; colleges and universities, the recipients of countless millions of dollars from both the public and private sectors, some of which is invested in research and product development; and others.

Amid all these players, and despite all the hundreds of billions of dollars they handle each year, one thing is clear: no one is looking at the long-term investment hypothesis for America.

That's a missed opportunity. As we've seen throughout our history, there are critical moments when a nation's leaders, both in government and business, aim their sights at the big challenges of the day. But when it comes to today's big challenge, global unsustainability, and the massive pools of demand we've already identified, no one is driving the ship. In fact, no one even seems to know where the ship is supposed to be going.

In chapter 8, we'll propose an investment hypothesis for America, and a concept for a private institution that can aggregate excess liquidity and deploy it to shift billions of dollars into creating a new, sustainable growth scenario—without public funds and without waiting on Washington. But before we look at the opportunity, let's address some of the barriers.

STRANDED ASSETS

A stranded asset is something—a piece of equipment or property, for example, or an individual's job skills—that once had value or produced income but no longer does, usually due to some kind of external change. While many asset owners watch over their holdings, some still get stranded. Changes in technology strand assets periodically. (Think about all those old computer devices or cables crammed into closets because they no longer work with the computer for which they were originally designed due to model changes or "upgrades." They are stranded assets.) When electricity started replacing oil and gas lamps for illuminating homes, lighting businesses suddenly found their gas or oil lamp inventory devalued; meanwhile, the whaling industry lost a key market for whale oil, leaving entire fleets idle. When the steel industry departed the United States for lower labor costs overseas, foundries, forges, smelters, and coking machines that could not be packed up and shipped abroad were stranded, along with many of the workers trained to use them.

Stranded assets are important to anticipate and manage as we consider a strategic shift. World War II absorbed the labor and industrial capacity stranded by the Great Depression. Then, as victory began to look inevitable, the prospect of the end of hostilities confronted our leaders with having to put to work 15 million unemployed veterans, excess agricultural capacity, and a substantial surplus of everything from weapons-making capacity to merchant marine tonnage. Had we failed to employ those returning vets, it's quite likely that we would have gone back into another depression.

As we head into the next economic era, we anticipate a new round of stranded assets. Some cannot be avoided. Coal, for instance, has few uses beyond combustion—the entire infrastructure network supporting coal-fired energy is already being written down or written off by companies as renewable energy, natural gas, and nuclear power outcompete coal on price per kilowatt-hour, with the added bonus that they contribute less (or not at all) to climate change. While the federal government could create a "bad bank"—a corporate structure designed to isolate and subsidize illiquid and high-risk investments—to take these assets off the books of their owners, it's hard to find a viable private-sector solution to coal.

But some assets are so systemically significant that they cannot simply be written off. These assets hold so much value or are so well distributed across the population that it is necessary to redeploy them productively in the new economy. It's important to understand where these are, as they create significant obstacles if unaddressed; if redeployed responsibly, they could greatly accelerate the economic transition.

Let's look at three key assets that are systemically important, including the challenges they present and a viable solution for each: unburnable hydrocarbons, underskilled labor, and capital equipment and real estate. Public infrastructure is a fourth category, which we'll deal with separately.

UNBURNABLE HYDROCARBONS

The International Energy Agency estimates that to stay within 2 degrees Celsius of atmospheric warming, the global economy will have to avoid emitting the carbon from roughly 80 percent of the world's proven oil and gas reserves. This is referred to by some as "unburnable carbon." John Fullerton, president of the Capital Institute, working with the Carbon Tracker Initiative and other data sources, estimated the approximate value of this unburnable carbon at roughly $20 trillion. To put that into perspective, that is slightly more than America's annual GDP.

Unburnable carbon is likely the single biggest obstacle to progress on climate change. To impose a cap on greenhouse gas emissions would mean destroying trillions of dollars of market value of publicly traded and state-owned fossil-fuel enterprises, most of which are woven deeply into the fabric of our retirement systems and global security calculations. Pretty much every retirement saver who has a 401(k) or a mutual fund holds some amount of unburnable carbon in their portfolio. The companies that own these assets—giant oil companies, energy utilities, and others—also wield extraordinary power because of their outsized earnings (and campaign contributions and lobbyists), giving them and their shareholders trillions of reasons to fight any proposed limits on burning the energy reserves they already own, never mind exploring for new ones.

This is described by some observers as an either/or situation: you can have a livable climate or you can have your oil and gas companies, but you cannot have both. We respectfully disagree. There is a way to get oil and gas out of combustion and preserve the lion's share of shareholders' asset valuation.

We call it a feedstock shift: instead of burning hydrocarbons, we build with them, leveraging the resource revolution we've already described in chapter 6. Oil and gas contain some of the most sophisticated polymers available in bulk, and our society has chosen to burn more than 80 percent of them, mostly to operate vehicles and heat buildings. With the rest, approximately 18 percent, we can make plastics, carbon fiber, 3D printing "ink," and advanced textiles—essential elements of our global economy for which demand will only increase.

However, given the industry's current business model and its ready market for fuels, the natural demographic increase in materials demand will not be sufficient to account for all the unburnable petroleum and gas products. To do that, we'll need to make a conscious, aggressive shift, not unlike the one Winston Churchill executed when he shifted the Royal Navy from coal to oil: Britain was not at risk of running out of coal; rather, oil offered strategically superior characteristics and important advantages that Britain wanted to exploit on its own terms and timetable.

Today, the United States and other major economies have a similar strategic opportunity, and an opportunity to dictate when and how it will happen. Executing a feedstock shift reduces the primary political obstacle to aggressively addressing climate change and minimizes the risk of market shocks from ramping down oil use, all while removing oil and gas as an Achilles' heel for the world's major economies. It needn't take an international incident that creates yet another roller coaster of energy prices to see how this reduces risk and uncertainty and improves national security. For nations like the United States, Japan, China, India, and those in Europe that are facing complex climate and energy security issues, this is practically a no-brainer.

A feedstock shift from combustion to bulk structural materials will reduce the amount of lumber, cement, aluminum, and steel used, substituting them with advanced, petro-based materials with superior characteristics. Each of these legacy materials is significantly more carbon intensive than its hydrocarbon-based alternative, and, in many cases, structurally inferior. For example, plastics reinforced by carbon fiber are now the premier material for high-performance vehicles and engineering applications. Thanks to such materials, BMW's leading-edge i3 electric vehicle uses no structural steel and has increased strength and dramatically reduced weight, reducing the size of the battery needed to move the car the same distance. It won't be that long before most vehicles are made this way. Boeing is using carbon fiber and advanced composites for half of the structural components of its 777 and 787 airframes, providing lighter weight and higher integrity. Similarly, plastic and composite wood products are commonly used in both structural and decorative applications for both exterior and interior architectural uses, exhibiting superior weathering and durability and requiring no special tools. As we said in chapter 6, cement, too, is in line for a transition, as it comprises fully 5 percent of worldwide carbon emissions. New polymer-and-sand composites are being developed that offer faster curing times and increased stability without compromising on ease of use or design flexibility, all while reducing greenhouse gas emissions.

Seem farfetched to move oil from Pontiacs to polymers? First, as we mentioned earlier, we're not starting from zero. Oil and gas already are the primary feedstocks for the plastics industry. So the question is, can we rapidly change the ratio of how petroleum is used, from mostly combustion to mostly materials? The good news is some oil and chemical companies already are preparing for a future in which advanced materials are a larger part of their business. Royal Dutch Shell, Saudi Aramco, and Dow Chemical have made strategic moves in this direction. Royal

Dutch Shell named Chad Holliday as nonexecutive chair of the board in 2015. Holliday, the former CEO of DuPont and former chair of the World Business Council for Sustainable Development, was brought on to lead the company's transition to a low-carbon business model. Our feedstock shift, he told us, is in line with his thinking.

Dow Chemical has already brought to market an array of building materials, from solar shingles to advanced insulation products, that will both generate and conserve energy while sequestering oil and gas safely as building materials. The Saudis have built an entire city devoted to advanced petrochemicals. Jubail Industrial City, the world's largest civil engineering project, is home to the headquarters for the Saudi Basic Industries Corporation, better known as SABIC, one of the largest petrochemicals producers in the world and tied closely to the kingdom's oil producer, Aramco. Closer to home, Doherty and Mykleby launched the Advanced Materials Development Group, an engineering research center at Case Western Reserve University, to help the 1,200 polymer-product companies in northeastern Ohio capture the North American lead in advanced materials.

Essentially, what we're proposing is sending hydrocarbons up the value chain in the form of high-value materials, products, and services, rather than up the smokestack in the form of polluting fuels. In the process, we can fulfill the commercial demand and personal aspirations of a growing global middle class while building an on-ramp to the next economy for oil and gas companies. It should be far easier, politically and economically, than trying to phase out oil and gas exploration and production. (Coal, for its part, is already winding down, an outmoded fuel that is no longer economically or environmentally viable.) In the end, we're looking to create a win-win-win situation for companies, consumers, and the planet.

UNDERSKILLED LABOR

For the past 30 years, Americans have been told to prepare for service-sector jobs—occupations like sales, hospitality, housekeeping, child care, teaching, and bookkeeping. Yet for America to succeed strategically, we will need to restore our manufacturing base. According to a 2015 report by Deloitte and the Manufacturing Institute, 3.5 million new manufacturing jobs will be created over the next decade, and 2 million of them will go unfilled, despite the millions of Americans still looking for work. And that's before executing the manufacturing-intensive strategy we're proposing. America's retail and hospitality sectors are experiencing high unemployment, with more than 2 million people out of work, compared to "only" 690,000 unemployed in the manufacturing sector. We cannot leave that many workers stranded without meaningful work.

Meanwhile, American farms are suffering from their own labor shortage—jobs traditionally held by recent immigrants—and food prices are rising partially as a result. The cause is pretty simple to understand. Contrary to what the inflamed public debate over illegal immigration suggests, the number of illegal immigrants has dropped significantly since the Great Recession. (As of late 2015, more Mexican immigrants have returned to Mexico from the United States than have migrated here since the end of the Great Recession, according to a Pew Research Center analysis.) The lack of available jobs made it harder for them to find work in America that would allow them to send money back home to their families. It's simply not worth the peril of attempting to cross the U.S. border if there's an uncertain economic payoff. The result is that some agricultural communities are scrambling to find workers willing and able to endure the tough tasks and low pay of harvesting and processing crops. Exacerbating this is the aging of America's farmers, as noted in chapter 5. That's further clouding agriculture's near-term future, let alone what's needed to transition to regenerative farming techniques, which tend to be more labor-intensive.

The workforce problem is quite real and cuts across other sectors, such as electric utilities, many of which are suffering what they darkly joke is a "silver tsunami"—a wave of retiring engineers, linemen, and others whom they are hard-pressed to replace with qualified applicants. The pathway to sustainable prosperity requires a significant increase in manufacturing and agricultural workers, jobs our current workforce is not prepared for. To reinvigorate America's economic engine, we will need to creatively redeploy a labor force prepared for a fundamentally different career path. As we succeed, our public school systems and vocational schools could require increased funding to train citizens for the careers awaiting them.

The saving grace of the American job market is mobility. Across the nation, 12 percent of Americans change homes annually. As the fracking boom illustrated, Americans will move and build new communities where there is work to be had for good pay—even to the far reaches of North Dakota.

Given that mobile workforce, we can see at least one pathway forward that can serve a significant percentage of the workers currently un- or underemployed, without waiting on Washington to act. The plan would involve concentrating initial investments in places where the opportunities for construction, manufacturing, and food-processing jobs are the greatest and where real estate prices are affordable. This profile matches the many interior cities of America, with their legacy manufacturing capacity and expansive agricultural belts. With a concentration of high-value-added employment, the heartland will be able to absorb a larger share of service and hospitality jobs, without the problem of high real estate prices forcing long commutes. The only new requirement is that we develop the capacity for a private institution to aggregate and invest capital in a concentrated way. We'll discuss how to do this in chapter 8.

CAPITAL EQUIPMENT AND REAL ESTATE

There are layers of capital equipment, private infrastructure, and land whose value is tied to the legacy economy that will need to be dealt with to build a new economy. Some of this value is already withering, reducing the scale of the problem but causing unnecessary pain. With the 2008 financial crisis, for example, suburban commercial real estate suffered a devastating hit and has yet to recover. If our demographic forecasts are correct, it never will. Meanwhile, oil and gas capital expenditure in the United States is $200 billion per year. The value of pumps, storage facilities, refineries, pipelines, gas stations, and trucking is enormous and is already devalued due to the overall drop in petroleum use; there will likely be further devaluation during the feedstock shift described earlier.

Rust Belt cities like Detroit, Flint, Gary, Toledo, Cleveland, Pittsburgh, and Buffalo know what happens to capital equipment when there is a sudden transition. So, too, do the textile mills of the Northeast and Southeast and the abandoned sawmill towns of the Pacific Northwest. The last job some local workers have at these plants is to pack up the machines and gear that can be economically shipped to a new location or retrofitted for a new purpose—then turn off the lights and lock the doors.

In a few cases, industry clusters can be repurposed. For example, Toledo's legacy capacity in automotive glass manufacturing is well positioned to become a hub for manufacturing solar-energy equipment, in particular windows embedded with solar collectors, enabling almost any building to generate some or all of its own power.

Housing developments in some areas are another stranded asset. The 2008 financial crisis left homebuilders in a massive lurch in places like Ft. Lauderdale, Florida, with partially built homes uncovered and rotting along with sizeable communities of finished but unsellable large-lot homes. On top of that were the homes abandoned once their owners' mortgages became "underwater"—that is, the home's value was smaller than the mortgage that covered it. It wasn't just Florida. As of the middle of 2015, there were still more than 12 million abandoned homes throughout the United States. Add to that another 4 million homes that, according to the website Zillow, are more than 20 percent underwater on their mortgages.

Like industrial clusters, suburban residential and commercial real estate can be upgraded and property values maintained and increased. Here's how that could work:

Out of most American cities are radial road arteries that extend from the city limits into the suburbs. As a thought exercise, imagine that every other such artery could be closed to autos and become a transit corridor, served by light rail, streetcars, and bus rapid transit systems. Intersecting these arteries every mile or so would be commercial centers containing a low-density configuration of strip malls, gas stations, and big-box retail. Those intersections contain enough surface area for a robust community of 3,000 to 5,000 people within a half-mile radius. By building these town centers around transit stops, we could repurpose low-value commercial real estate, increase the tax base for services, increase the use and utility of public transit, and increase the property values for the adjoining suburban neighborhoods. Because of the extraordinarily uniform pattern of postwar development in the United States, the opportunities for retrofitting can, to some extent, be rapidly standardized for investment purposes, while differentiated aesthetically by reviving local architectural traditions, harnessing the local topography, and working with the local climate.

RETHINKING PUBLIC INFRASTRUCTURE

America's extensive network of public infrastructure represents the fourth category. It, too, is at risk of being stranded in a world of walkable communities. We prefer to see this as an opportunity to rethink the kinds of infrastructure we'll need in the communities we'll be building during the coming decades.

Most of the highways, schools, ports, and airports built since World War II were designed around a logic that is about to change. As we transition from car-dependent to walkable communities, we will still need highways, of course, but intercity travel is more convenient and affordable by train when metro areas have developed a sufficient network of walkable places connected by light rail (including the suburban transit centers we just described). But remember: what makes intercity rail work is the walkability and transit orientation of a metro area, not the other way around. Building high-speed rail first, before local streetcar networks, runs the risk that rail projects will not bring reasonable returns on investment. Some stranding can be avoided by converting roads from highway to rail, a process that will generally return land to local authorities for privatization, which will yield additional development and revenue generation.

TRANSIT

As we build new transportation networks, the watchword must be *intermodal*. Mobility solutions need to be connected, allowing people and things to move rapidly to their destination by multiple modes of transportation—cars, buses, subways, light rail, and—for the last mile or so—bicycles, electric scooters, small neighborhood vehicles, and our feet moving along attractive walkways. Intercity high-speed rail needs to exist for both passengers and freight. Light rail must be able to deliver freight to retail outlets and distribution points in town centers, taking advantage of reduced passenger demand at night. In doing so, we'll be putting a necessary measure of redundancy and resilience back into our communities, as well as creating healthy competition among various modes of transportation. (Say goodbye to monopoly transit systems that have no market incentive to keep costs low and service levels high.) Ports and airports must be located on local and intercity rail lines, providing passengers and cargo with convenience and options. Short-haul shipping by tug and barge, with its focus on regional coastal trade and possessing unmatched energy efficiency relative to trucking, can restore the logic of our prewar cities and their ports while creating the kinds of lasting, well-paid port and warehouse jobs our communities need.

With regard to air travel, airports offer a challenge that can be addressed by the market. While connecting them to intermodal transportation networks is a minimum requirement, the emissions profile of modern air travel is problematic. Liquid jet fuel is so energy dense per unit of weight that battery and fuel cell technologies have a significant innovation hurdle to clear before they can power commercially viable aircraft systems. From our perspective, if there were one sector that ought to focus on converting away from fossil fuels, aviation is it. In addition, intercity high-speed rail is much more energy efficient and time efficient for most travelers, and as more nationally significant companies move their headquarters to the dynamic urban places served by high-speed rail, this efficiency will only improve. That leaves long-haul routes as the primary market for air travel, which will likely force consolidation, new business models, and new technology.

SCHOOLS

Where we locate our schools is another key issue, as it represents a powerful determinant of educational outcomes and community relations. As we create new communities with mixed-income and mixed-use characteristics, we'll need to make sure that families can thrive in these places, which requires strong daycare and elementary schools. Much of the gentrification that has occurred in American cities over the past 20 years has neglected schools, favoring housing for empty-nesters, young urban singles, or career couples without kids. If we are to arrest the "drive until you qualify" dynamic—where you drive increasingly farther from a city center in order to find a home for which you can afford a mortgage—which pushes new parents out of walkable places and into the suburbs, we need to ensure their kids can get a high-quality education wherever they live.

Elementary school students are the least independent of the K-12 population. They need the most parental involvement to establish a strong foundation on which to learn and grow. Having elementary schools within walking distance of homes and either work or a transit hub is critical in reducing commuting time and increasing parenting time. In addition, elementary education serves as a generator of heterogeneous social bonds, fomenting strong relationships across a community based on the randomness of children's friendships and classroom assignments, as opposed to the often homogeneous choices parents make for their children based on income levels or racial or ethnic identity.

The bottom line for all this is that the big challenges surrounding these various stranded assets—the challenges so often pointed to as reasons why we can't move forward even if we wanted to—are really just design challenges that have very real and profitable solutions. The solutions are very real because we also have the capital and the market forces available to fuel the work needed to actually begin the transition to a more sustainable economy. This is a classic case of private profit for public good at a scale we haven't seen since the end of World War II. All we really need at this point is a business plan to get ourselves organized to capture the historic opportunity that's staring us in the face.

We'll lay out that business plan in detail next.

CHAPTER EIGHT

A BUSINESS PLAN FOR AMERICA

WE'VE COME A LONG WAY IN THIS NEW AMERICAN NARRATIVE. LET'S recap.

Three billion people are pounding on the gates of the global economy. Climate change and ecosystem depletion are degrading Earth's carrying capacity and disrupting human communities, with the high potential for much greater disruption to come. We're only about halfway through the deleveraging behind America's shaky recovery. Americans want a new lifestyle that the suburban economy cannot deliver. And global infrastructure, systems, and supply chains are fragile, prone to shock and disruption. As we ricochet from crisis to crisis, the international order is unwinding and Americans are getting increasingly concerned, impatient, and angry.

Against this backdrop, we believe America needs a new grand strategy in which our economy does the heavy lifting to lead the global transition to sustainability.

Demographics and macroeconomics have aligned to present an economic engine that can address the nation's needs: a game-changing, $1.3 trillion annual opportunity. Americans overwhelmingly want a new American dream that could put people and capital back to work. Cities and suburbs are rethinking what constitutes "the good life" and building walkable communities that may rebuild the social fabric. America's farmers have the opportunity to restore the health of the planet's life-support system, and get paid better to boot. We are witnessing the beginning of a revolution in resource productivity that can rebuild middle-class lives and wages. Capital is ready for a new investment hypothesis in America, and we can articulate a new grand bargain on oil and gas that could massively accelerate the transition of the energy system, unlocking a multihundred-billion-dollar sector without contributing to climate change.

Seems like a no-brainer. Problem, meet solution. All we need is to implement.

And there's the rub. Who's got this? From our experience in the military, public policy, and the business world, the answer is both simple and bleak: no one.

As we mentioned briefly in chapter 7, no one is looking at the core investment hypothesis in America. More important, no one is really looking at strategy. It's a national blind spot. Only a year after he issued his call for big ideas, President Obama declared in a 2014 interview with the *New Yorker*'s David Remnick that he did not see the need for grand strategy, let alone a twenty-first-century version of George Kennan. It was a clear statement from the nation's chief executive that there is no one, inside or outside the Capital Beltway, who will be given the time and funding to examine, much less implement, a true strategic vision of America's future. Even if we were to get a receptive president, Congress is unlikely to provide the necessary legislative support. It seems our elected leadership is not the place to look for, well, leadership.

If the president and Congress are not able or willing to lead, we might look to groups with a broad membership across the economy—the U.S. Chamber of Commerce, for example. Unfortunately, the chamber is focused on serving the needs of existing businesses (and their current business models), not necessarily on the health and viability of the overall system of commerce. While the chamber did (belatedly) acknowledge climate change as a problem and the rise of Asia as an opportunity, its lobbying priorities have been focused on avoiding decisive legislative solutions while pushing incremental rule changes to benefit specific sectors or individual members. Few other groups have the same national profile or focus. The World Economic Forum, with its working groups on climate change, the circular economy, and new growth models, does have the vision and membership, but as a global organization it is unable to catalyze and lead what needs to be, ultimately, an American conversation.

WHAT WOULD BILL KNUDSEN DO?

Instead of bemoaning the lack of leadership in Washington, we need to remember the can-do spirit that allowed our parents and grandparents to prevail over the great existential challenges of the twentieth century. In fact, it is from that extraordinary twentieth-century experience that we can find the right question to help us get out of the leadership gap.

Here it is: What would Bill Knudsen do?

Knudsen, as we explained in chapter 2, was the immigrant former head of Chevrolet and General Motors who marshaled the private sector to enable America to become the arsenal of democracy during World War II. Knudsen convened American chieftains of industry and got down to business. This is where Knudsen shined: with little formal authority, he was able to get the right people in the room and place orders for new kinds of goods and services in order to get our industrial legs underneath us in advance of our entering World War II.

If Knudsen were around today, we believe he would gather American business leaders in a room and get to work designing a new industrial ecosystem that runs on twenty-first-century demand and is paid for by pent-up capital. Notice we did not say "lobby Congress" or "advise the president." We think business can design and launch this new industrial ecosystem without waiting on Washington. (Citizens have a role to play too. More on that in chapter 10.) What would such an industrial ecosystem look like? Strap yourself in; in this chapter we'll lay out a prototype.

FROM ANGER TO ACTION

Under business as usual, most of those polled by PwC for its annual Global CEO Survey do not see a significant value proposition in the concept of "sustainability." Indeed, that concept has hit a kind of glass ceiling. Sustainability has been accepted as a niche sector of the consumer marketplace; as a framework for reducing the cost of company operations, as in energy or water use; and as a right-to-operate issue, a component of brand and reputation management. (We submit that many of these CEOs aren't adequately viewing the risk of climate change to their operations and supply chains over the next few years.) Indeed, with economic policy still so skewed toward propping up the consumption and infrastructure priorities of last century's suburban lifestyle, boards of directors and senior management are finding little appetite for aggressive business model transformation of any kind. Ironically, they view taking on these issues as just too risky.

However, among a growing corps of corporate leaders, frustration with the absence of policy-led change is starting to reach a tipping point. In 2013, an Accenture survey of 1,000 global CEOs affiliated with the United Nations Global Compact reported that more than two-thirds saw sustainability as critical to their future strategy, but that the group is frustrated with the pace of adaptation. Rather than waiting on governments to act, 84 percent of CEOs believe that business has to execute a "step change in ambition and action" through "innovating new systems, markets, and structures."

Putting their money where their mouth is, some large companies are doing just that, moving capital and headcount into these new concepts. Here are a few significant examples:

- At the 2015 Consumer Electronics Show, Ford Motor Company CEO Mark Fields, wearing jeans on stage, announced a major strategy evolution for the storied automaker. Ford is going to attempt a "Xerox"—that is, transition out of the business of selling cars and into the business of selling "mobility services," much like Xerox did by leasing copiers instead of selling them, thus retaining ownership of the machines as assets it could refurbish and put back into service. This is no mere linguistic shift on Ford's part. As the vast majority of the world's citizens move into increasingly dense cities by 2050, the market for individually owned vehicles will be limited while the market for mobility services—moving people and things in a timely, sustainable, and affordable way—is unlimited. Could Ford Motor Company eventually become "Ford Mobility Company"? Stay tuned.
- Also in 2015, Royal Dutch Shell welcomed Chad Holliday as its new global chairman, the first American to hold that position in the Anglo-Dutch energy company. Holliday's job, as he told us, is to help Shell effectively leverage natural gas as a bridge into the next energy economy. In that new economy, Holliday sees Shell shifting from primarily using the hydrocarbons in oil for

combustion to using it for materials. Shell envisions that over time it will stop burning oil and start building with it.

- In 2014, Walmart began a project with its food supply chain in Iowa, Illinois, and Nebraska to reduce the agricultural runoff from farms that was poisoning the Mississippi River tributaries and ending up in the Gulf of Mexico. The reason: every ounce of nitrogen fertilizer that washes out of the soil isn't just pollution, it's wasted resources, making it harder for Walmart to deliver on its promise of the lowest possible prices. For Walmart, using the size and scale of its supply chain to help the world "live better" now also includes promoting more domestic manufacturing to keep jobs in America, creating jobs for potential Walmart shoppers; it also happens to reduce shipping costs and make it easier to sustainably produce products while reducing living costs for its customers.

Other companies—whether they are multibillion-dollar enterprises like Whole Foods Market, Tesla, and the Cleveland Clinic, or earlier-stage technology companies like Local Motors, Acclima, and Bloom Energy—were born with sustainability concerns in their DNA. They stand to take market share from their incumbent counterparts, even some of the Goliath companies named above. But their natural expansion may be limited so long as the economy at large retains the constraints and limited vision of Cold War economic strategy.

The fundamental changes roiling incumbent business models are occurring, in part, in response to the challenges, opportunities, and uncertainties we have outlined in this book, from stranded assets to consumer preferences to misaligned policy. But for an individual company to traverse the twenty-first-century economy in a way that avoids the worst impacts of the inevitable shocks and disruption, firm-level or sector-level coordination is not enough, even for a company as big as Shell or Walmart.

For boards of directors to exercise their rightful fiduciary obligations, we need to increase certainty across the economy. For example, for Ford to jump headfirst into mobility services requires clarity on urban planning, fuel prices, local regulations, and material availability, among other things. For Shell to commit to the feedstock shift requires knowing that customers will demand what it is selling. For Cisco to transform its production and deploy the kinds of sensor and communications networks needed in our smart, interconnected world, it will need to collaborate with other players across sectors and borders to ensure the kinds of standards and security that produce reliable and sustainable markets.

In the United States, the conventional path to increasing certainty is to ask Washington to provide it: regulations, standards, subsidies, tax breaks, price guarantees, import tariffs, and any number of tools available to Washington. Assuming you could get such changes through the incremental, partisan D.C. machinery, you'd be designing the economy backward, with politicians as the engineers. We didn't even attempt that level of government control during the existential test of World War II.

Despite the Founders' wise separation of Federal powers, congressional rules are designed so that insiders control Washington; seniority paves the path to power. They, in turn, are powerfully influenced by incumbent business interests that are organized, flush with cash, and willing to throw money into the political sphere and in the process achieve "regulatory capture," as it is known. Innovators and disrupters frequently run into this brick wall. Google, once it became the dominant online search engine—and beset by incumbents whose services were being displaced—set up what is now one of the most extensive government relations shops in the nation's capital.

This happens at the local level too. Uber, the transportation company, is a prime example, running up against taxi commissions happy to block its market-disrupting business model in favor of maintaining the status quo. There's a pattern driving this: industry regulators and overseers are frequently alumni of the industry they regulate, and just as frequently return when they have finished their public service. Their loyalty is bought and paid for by this revolving door. Yes, it may be legal, but it's still incestuous and incredibly corrosive. Legislators and presidential candidates are similarly beholden as they seek corporate support for their campaigns. As a result, policy makers seeking long-term careers in Washington have little interest in strategic adaptation—if they are even aware that it is necessary or possible.

Washington may be broken, but there is another option. Companies can create their own certainty, Knudsen-style. The volume of pent-up demand and scale of underutilized capital is, we believe, sufficient to overwhelm some of the key effects of current policy and initialize the new economic engine without waiting on Washington. We need only two things:

1. A critical mass of business leaders in the right sectors of the economy who share a common vision of the new economic ecosystem and begin building it.
2. The redirection of underutilized capital into the kinds of financing vehicles needed to unleash pent-up demand.

Meeting these two conditions would enable us to turn pent-up demand into real orders for real products and services. With enough orders distributed across sectors and geography, the roots of a new economic ecosystem can take hold. As they do, politicians, overseers, and regulators will sense the opportunity—and necessity—of supporting this new growth scenario, just as in 1960, when the two political parties and their presidential candidates, Kennedy and Nixon, accepted the new design of the postwar economy that took root under President Eisenhower. It was no longer a question of what our strategy would look like; it was a matter of how best to implement it.

AMERICA OS

Let's come back to the economic operating system metaphor we introduced in chapter 3. Picture an operating system like Apple's iOS or Google's Android or Chrome. Among other functions, they enable entrepreneurs and established businesses to build on them, creating countless apps that collectively become a dynamic, innovative ecosystem of commerce. And, along the way, they transform how we do things. The success of those operating systems relies on their ability to support core functionality well, provide a platform for established apps and new entrants to succeed, and be able to interact with other devices, including those that use different operating systems.

That's what our economy needs: an economic operating system that enables a sustainable twenty-first-century growth scenario, aligning demand and capital while minimizing stranded assets. We need that new economic operating system oriented toward the strategic challenges of the coming years and decades. It must be capable of frequent, low-friction, and predictably executed updates while supporting a vast number of continually innovating "apps"—businesses, investors, social enterprises, nonprofits, government institutions, community organizations, concerned citizens, and much more.

We believe we can extrapolate a new operating system from the bold strategic innovations and adaptations of companies like Ford and Tesla, Walmart and Whole Foods, and Shell and Bloom Energy. In all, we have identified ten sectors where large-scale opportunities exist for tapping into the pools of pent-up demand and putting capital back to work. In each sector, a new core business model is emerging, some led by business, others by investors, still others by state and local government. Frequently, it's a combination of all of these. If an operating system for a device is a platform made of code, a new economic operating system is a platform made of these strategically essential business models.

What's more, these ten business models are mutually reinforcing. Scaling in one drives more business—and more certainty—to the other nine. We estimate that a synchronized, business-led shift toward these models could leapfrog today's policy arguments, end America's deleveraging, put more Americans back to work in well-paying jobs, and lay the foundation for a new era of purpose-driven sustainable growth.

Add it up, and these ten business models comprise a powerful operating system for the new growth scenario and an exciting, prosperous, and secure economy.

- **Oil & Gas | Natural Gas Bridge & Advanced Materials**
  - From Burning to Building
- **Transportation | Multimodal Mobility Systems**
  - From Vehicles to Mobility
- **Real Estate & Infrastructure | Walkable Communities**
  - From Sprawl to Smart Growth
- **Farming | Regenerative Agriculture**
  - From Depletive to Regenerative
- **Natural Resources | Ecosystem Service Markets**
  - From Extraction to Stewardship
- **Electricity | Distributed Renewables**
  - From Centralized Combustion to Distributed Renewables
- **Telecom/Mobile | Gigabit Networks & Internet of Things**
  - From Megabits and Phones to Gigabits and Sensors
- **Retail | Small Footprint & e-Commerce**

- From Big Box to Bricks & Clicks
- **Manufacturing | Distributed Production**
  - From Outsourcing to Advanced Manufacturing
- **Health Care | Team-Based Wellness**
  - From Hospitalization to Primary Care

This new operating system offers a market-based framework to jump-start infrastructure spending, home construction, manufacturing orders, farm incomes, and technological innovation. Carbon emissions from combustion and agriculture would drop without stranding oil and gas. With job growth, reduced federal deficits, increased net exports, rising median household income, sustained consumer demand, and enhanced security, the American people will ensure the longevity of this new engine of the American dream. Sound too good to be true? It's not.

AN ALTERNATIVE GROWTH STRATEGY

We have mapped out scenarios for the profitable transformations of ten of America's largest business sectors, including the vision, the potential impact, who's already doing it, and what it would take to get to scale. Here is a snapshot.

1. OIL & GAS: FROM BURNING TO BUILDING

A feedstock shift in the primary end-use for oil and gas, from combustion to advanced materials. Instead of burning hydrocarbons, we will build with them, substituting them for concrete, steel, and other more carbon-intensive materials. Doing so means that "unburnable carbon"— oil and gas reserves that cannot be used for combustion without putting us past a tipping point on climate change—retains or even increases its value with minimal environmental impact.

Economic Opportunity: Preservation of at least $10 trillion in global hydrocarbon assets.

2. TRANSPORTATION: FROM VEHICLES TO MOBILITY

A shift in the business model of automakers from selling vehicles to providing mobility services. Instead of focusing solely on the production of vehicles for purchase by private owners, industry will focus on providing dynamic transportation solutions to consumers with changing preferences and needs. A wider range of vehicle types and business models will proliferate, from e-bikes and neighborhood electric vehicles to on-demand transportation services. Options like vehicle-sharing, self-driving cars, and multimodal transportation networks become the norm, not the exception.

Economic Opportunity: $897 billion in increased transportation-related U.S. GDP by 2025.

3. REAL ESTATE & INFRASTRUCTURE: FROM SPRAWL TO SMART GROWTH

A shift toward widespread building of walkable communities and dynamic shared spaces. Instead of enabling continued sprawl and a dispersed economy, building practices and plans will be targeted to smart urban growth, where economic development and infrastructure is optimized to meet growing demand while reducing environmental impact. Consumer choices and living options increase, from standalone houses to live-work spaces to co-housing arrangements.

Economic Opportunity: $231 billion in additional annual home sales.

4. FARMING: FROM DEPLETIVE TO REGENERATIVE

A shift from our current, depletive agricultural practices to a regenerative agriculture system. Instead of water-, chemical-, and land-intensive industrial agriculture, America's heartland will lead and feed the world through innovative practices that rebuild the soil and surrounding ecosystems while producing crop yields that can help to feed our growing global population through the relocalization of our food system.

Economic Opportunity: $193 billion increase in annual farm profits.

5. NATURAL RESOURCES: FROM EXTRACTION TO STEWARDSHIP

A business model shift where property owners generate revenue streams by increasing the stock of natural capital and the flow of ecosystem services from it. For example, owners of forestland would receive income from such things as carbon sequestration, flood control, and biodiversity; owners of farmland from carbon sequestration and water quality management; and owners of coastal wetlands from the value their property holds for fisheries and storm protection.

Economic Opportunity: $2.9 trillion expansion of the U.S. market.

6. ELECTRICITY: FROM CENTRALIZED TO DISTRIBUTED & RENEWABLE

A pathway for electricity generation to hit 100 percent renewable by 2050 through the mass deployment of renewable energy such as solar, wind, and geothermal systems in a variety of distributed configurations. To expedite the transition, dispatchable energy to anchor microgrid performance can come from distributed natural gas generation first through combustion, then through fuel cell systems that gradually convert to operate on renewable-produced hydrogen.

Economic Opportunity: Up to $657 billion in annual clean energy investment by 2050.

7. TELECOM/MOBILE: FROM MEGABITS TO GIGABITS

Upgrading our residential, commercial, industrial, transportation, energy, water, communications, and information systems provides the opportunity to build out the next generation 1/10/100 gigabit network at marginal cost, driving efficiency, productivity, and the network effect. New York City is already on this path, creating ultrafast citywide Wi-Fi, available at no charge to users.

Economic Opportunity: Boost to U.S. GDP between $897 billion and $2.5 trillion annually by 2025.

8. RETAIL: FROM BIG BOX TO BRICKS & CLICKS

Shift in retail distribution takes advantage of superior foot traffic in walkable communities, increasing sales from smaller-footprint brick-and-mortar shops and year-round farmers' markets. Revival of place-based retail encourages growth of businesses that can leverage local products, serve local tastes, provide a desired experience, or offer fresh, artisanal, or convenient goods, in many cases deliverable within a few hours of ordering online.

Economic Opportunity: Nearly $1 trillion increase in annual retail sales.

9. MANUFACTURING: FROM OUTSOURCING
TO ADVANCED MANUFACTURING

A shift to additive manufacturing, robotics, and the circular economy are among other advanced manufacturing strategies that transform our industrial processes. These will make the economics of outsourcing increasingly less favorable and return comparative advantage to the U.S. manufacturing sector.

Economic Opportunity: A boost of $7 trillion to the United States by 2030.

10. HEALTH CARE: FROM HOSPITALIZATION TO PRIMARY CARE

A shift in the way we provide primary health care that reduces reliance on high-cost hospitals and focuses on gathering a team of frequently used specialists under one roof in walkable communities, as well as using advanced technology solutions like "telemedicine" kiosks. This will decrease the cost of caring for high-utilization patients and create a more efficient business model with lower costs and healthier patients.

Economic Opportunity: Health-care savings of about $1.5 trillion per year in the United States.

GREATER THAN ITS PARTS

Ten sectors, ten alternative business models, three massive pools of demand. Even with each sector operating only in its own lane, the opportunity is extraordinary. The reality is that each of these sectors interacts with the others to create a self-reinforcing ecosystem that can deliver what could be the most dynamic, prosperous, and secure economy America has ever enjoyed.

It starts with housing. As we've noted, most Americans want their next home to anchor a smart-growth lifestyle. We think determining where to live is the decision that sets the pattern for much of the rest of the economy. Whether one rents or buys, housing is the largest expense in most household budgets. Second, the location of one's home, in relation to work, school, shopping, and other critical services and amenities, determines the amount, nature, and cost of the transportation a household needs—that is, whether one buys or leases a car, takes public transit, uses car sharing, bikes, or walks. Housing has additional influences, but let's stop here and examine the other sectors that intersect with the shift from sprawl to smart growth.

The key mobility factor for most dense neighborhoods, save for those adjacent to urban downtowns, is a transit hub. The key to walkability is to have residential housing within a half-mile radius of a transit hub that is a part of a network capable of taking riders to the majority of job centers in a region. That means a new pattern of infrastructure that requires a job- and investment-rich build-out—transit, water, electricity, communication, even delivery services—to serve communities efficiently. A growing prerequisite for local residents is a robust communications and energy network capable of providing distributed electricity generation and gigabit communications networks that facilitate renewable energy, home-based work, community-wide Wi-Fi, and other infrastructure services.

The migration from car-dependent suburbs to walkable places also sets the pattern for consumer behavior. When the daily walk to work and school passes grocers and farmers' markets, bakeries and butchers, individuals and families can buy fresher, healthier, local food. For those with busy schedules, even prepared food can become healthier, with fresh-made meals and restaurants readily accessible on the evening commute or a short walk from home. Either way, all that activity translates directly into to the volume of foot traffic stores need to thrive.

Health care is tied to location as well. In walkable American communities, team-based primary- and urgent-care walk-in facilities will flourish, able to treat common, low-intensity ailments like a cold or flu at no-appointment storefronts or kiosks. At each, a team of physicians, nurses, and other medical practitioners will be located under one roof to quickly diagnose, treat, and manage a wide range of health concerns— or refer serious cases for more intensive treatment.

Further, the growth and construction of new households will engender a new era of American manufacturing—locally made products and materials produced in waste-free facilities able to reclaim used goods and turn them back into new materials and products. Consider factory-built homes, also referred to as modular homes or precision-built homes. By whatever name, they are manufactured largely in factories, then assembled on site, making construction faster and cheaper, often with higher quality and with far less waste. Such homes needn't look "modular"—that is, they're not the double-wides on cinder blocks of yesterday's trailer parks. In fact, leading brands such as LivingHomes, Connect:Homes, and Blu Homes have entered the market from the luxury end, in a business model similar to Tesla's or Dell's: They can be customized in floor plan, design, and amenities for both single-family and multiple-unit structures. They look just like conventionally built homes. With the proper investment strategy (discussed in the next section), increased production—not just of homes, but furnishings, appliances, and many other things—will drive a new era of sustainable materials: lighter, cleaner, stronger, recyclable. The demand for such materials will simultaneously address the great political obstacle of stranded oil and gas by shifting petroleum use from fuels to materials.

Another big economic upgrade will be driven by putting an economic value on ecosystem services. Just as the transition from sprawl to smart growth will make our metropolitan regions more vibrant, the ability to invest in protecting and rebuilding natural capital—constructed wetlands, flood plains, barrier reefs, and other so-called green infrastructure—will be a boon both to cities and the suburban, rural, and coastal regions that surround them. Farming communities will see the creation of more jobs focused on land and water stewardship. Fishing communities will see more jobs in caring for river and ocean ecosystems. Mountain communities will see a sustained boom from improving forest ecosystem services, such as wildlife habitat and diversity, watershed services, carbon storage, and tourism. Research and the commercialization of new methods and technology will feed university communities and vocational schools with strong programs in understanding and maintaining the financial value of local habitats and watersheds.

As Americans join this great transition, our entertainment industry will pivot as well. Television studios long ago learned that Americans like to see the stuff of their daily lives reflected in their evening entertainment, providing both comic relief and the reassurance that the daily dramas associated with our changing lifestyle are not just ours, but are shared across the country. This storytelling has two effects. It creates the platform businesses need to advertise their products and services while also providing a narrative about societal norms: what's now, what's new, and what's next.

In the process of telling those emerging stories, we will work some American magic. American culture has long defined what it means to be modern—to define the good life and the good society—not just for ourselves but for others around the world. As we create the smart homes and cities, and the mobility solutions and lifestyles that work within them, these ideas and images will spread to other countries and continents, just as American culture and lifestyles always have. American manufacturing, primed by rebuilding the American dream, will be poised to export that dream. Competition will be stiff, no question, but at long last we'll be back in the game.

Add all that up and our platform for addressing the great challenges facing America is formidable. Prosperity and security through sustainability is not only possible, it's a compelling path forward.

A NEW INVESTMENT HYPOTHESIS

While these ten sectors are deeply aligned with twenty-first-century demand and are strongly self-reinforcing, they are not self-initiating. In the two great strategic eras of the twentieth century—World War II and the Cold War—government provided the initiating impulse. As we have discussed earlier, it is not likely today that Washington will rise to the occasion to deliver the scale and pace of economic change required.

It is also not necessary. To kick-start this new economic era we need a catalytic, long-term investment architecture to generate the orders for the goods, services, and infrastructure that, over time, will redesign and reinvigorate the economy. The good news is that pressure is building rapidly within the financial sector to find a new investment hypothesis. It needs to be focused and taken to the next level in the context of a coherent strategy.

FIDUCIARY FRIGHT

Sometimes, a signal cannot be clearer. And the stern letter excoriating "short-termism" that BlackRock chair and CEO Laurence Fink issued to Fortune 500 CEOs in February 2016 was one crystal-clear signal. In his letter, Fink criticized the CEOs for an overemphasis on quarterly performance, the proliferation of large-scale share buybacks, and, most critically, not investing profits for long-term growth. Fink's letter is part of a larger movement of investment leaders who are recognizing that the myopic approach of most investment analysts and business managers is compromising asset managers' fiduciary responsibility to provide for the secure retirements of their customers.

Meanwhile, those same corporations—along with hedge funds and private-equity firms—are facing the "problem" of too much cash, well over $13 trillion in 2015, according to the Federal Reserve. The companies' excuse? Uncertainty and risk. That is, they're holding on to their corporate wallets until there's less of both. Political risk and policy volatility in America today is enormous, particularly given the extraordinary ideological gap between the two dominant political parties, as we see every day but particularly every four years during presidential elections.

Macroeconomic risk is looming too. Unburnable oil and gas compose up to a third of the market capitalization in global stock markets— a macro time bomb. The Federal Reserve's interest-rate policy has been artificially stimulating production of suburban housing to such a point that bubble-like conditions in 14 housing markets are now visible across the United States, according to a 2015 study by Smithfield & Wainright, a real estate valuation company. Uncertainty in global markets, from China to Europe to the Middle East, is distracting and undermining company confidence. And then there are the disruptions to global value chains from the increased frequency and severity of floods, storms, and droughts attributed to climate change, along with the potential for horrific acts of terrorism any time or anywhere, from Palestine to Paris. Amid that range of challenges, it is understandable why holding on to one's cash can be an attractive investment strategy.

Back on Main Street, America's experiment with defined-contribution retirement accounts has failed the Boomers. At the heart of the 401(k) program is modern portfolio theory's near-religious belief in diversification as the key to risk management. But diversification is impossible in the presence of a dysfunctional economic strategy. While in a healthy economic engine, diversification is an important way to manage risk, diversifying insufficient retirement savings across a failed economic engine is like telling a Marine with a sucking chest wound to watch his cholesterol. Yet this is the experience of 401(k) investors across America, fully half of all Americans. For the investor lucky enough to have started investing in 1978, when the 401(k) program was enacted, the S&P 500 increased 292 percent by 1993, or just under 10 percent annually. For the 15 years from 2000 to 2015, total S&P return was less than 36 percent, or 2.1 percent annually. With average 401(k) account holdings less than $65,000 and 60 percent of 401(k) participants in their 50s and 60s, time has run out for business-as-usual investment advice; it's just not a path to retirement security for millions of Americans. Pressure is building for a change. The status quo is not meeting the fiduciary obligations of major players, and we're about to encounter a lot of anxious and angry Boomers as they look to retire.

It is time to bring our erstwhile hero Bill Knudsen back into focus.

What allowed Knudsen to work with his fellow industrialists to transform supply chains and product lines was the fact that there were actual orders to be filled, and profits to be made filling them. Knudsen was not just jawboning American business in the hopes that a massive coordinated shift would somehow produce all the machine guns, planes, and tanks America needed to succeed in World War II. Knudsen and industry worked together through the placement of real orders for real things with real specifications. It was those orders that drove the underlying logic that made us the arsenal of democracy. Similarly, we believe it will be orders for real things that will propel the transition to the next American dream.

Contracts are more powerful than regulation or even public-private partnerships. To cut to the chase, the whole ten-sector growth scenario needs to be activated by the systematic placement of orders. How? Bill Knudsen had the good fortune to be working with a government that gave him the tools he needed, during a time when America and the world had a critical need for war materiel. In our business-led scenario, we'll need that underutilized capital to organize itself in a purpose-built way and then make the investments that place the orders that ultimately ignite this new economic engine.

BANKING ON AMERICA

The idea of a financial institution created specifically to fund infrastructure improvements has been floated a number of times in America's history. Alexander Hamilton created the first one, in the form of the First Bank of the United States, which lasted from 1791 to 1811. The Second Bank of the United States existed from 1816 to 1836. With the founding of the Federal Reserve Bank in 1913, the infrastructure bank idea took a back seat. After the crash of 1929, the New Deal made infrastructure investment a matter of fiscal policy, an approach reinforced by Eisenhower with the Interstate Highway and Defense System.

By the 1990s, however, the midcentury, bipartisan consensus around advanced infrastructure had collapsed, gradually replaced by moderate and hawkish strains of fiscal conservatism. As a result, our infrastructure spending has remained in its previous patterns but dropped in inflation-adjusted terms. According to 2015 research by Moody's, real U.S. infrastructure spending per capita has hit the lowest level since 1950. Meanwhile, President Obama reported in his 2014 State of the Union address that more than 70,000 bridges are in need of repair. As we discussed earlier, the American Society of Civil Engineers estimates our current arrears in public infrastructure amounts to $3.6 trillion. To even spend that amount over a ten-year time frame, Congress would need to increase the entire federal budget by nearly 10 percent. That's not likely to happen.

Recognizing the conundrum, a wide range of policy makers has been trying to revive the infrastructure bank concept. Senators Christopher J. Dodd and Chuck Hagel proposed a National Infrastructure Reinvestment Bank in 2007. Barack Obama backed the proposed legislation in 2008 while a U.S. senator, and repeated his call in 2010 as president. Some version of an infrastructure bank has been introduced in every Congress since. In 2012, the liberal Center for American Progress called for a federally backed national infrastructure bank and a related infrastructure planning council. During the Great Recession, much work was done at the nonpartisan think tank New America. Recognizing that the stimulus effect of federal spending would offset the emerging crisis in financial markets, New America brought together bankers, economists, and business leaders to develop a range of viable public-private vehicles for spurring a new era of investment. And in 2015, Senator Deb Fischer of Nebraska, a Republican, proposed a national infrastructure bank to be funded by the federal government through repatriated corporate profits.

What was common to each proposal, from Secretary Hamilton's to Senator Fischer's, was the role of government in chartering and funding the infrastructure banks. Given Washington's inability to do so, we propose a rather significant modification: instead of a federally supported infrastructure bank, we propose a private, nongovernmental version—an Economic Improvements Group—to aggregate capital and drive this new growth scenario.

There is plenty of capital held by private and institutional investors to do this. As we've noted earlier, there is $3.5 trillion in corporate cash and $10 trillion in cash held by private equity and hedge funds, according to the Federal Reserve. Bank of America/Merrill Lynch estimates institutional investors are keeping a record 5.5 percent of their holdings in cash—an additional $2.5 trillion. Of course, the bank would be an ideal destination for a portion of the $24 trillion in American retirement savings. The Economic Improvements Group would both initialize the transition to a new economic engine and provide the long-term funding to keep that new economy diverse and prosperous over time.

THE ECONOMIC IMPROVEMENTS GROUP

A purpose-built, nongovernmental mechanism—to aggregate capital and direct it toward the kinds of strategic investments neither Wall Street nor Congress is willing to make—would fill a hole in the financial architecture of our market-based system of self-governance. And it makes sense. A private entity backed by patient capital would enjoy the right combination of agility and long-term perspective needed to underwrite a new investment hypothesis in America.

While there is more work to be done in thinking through how an Economic Improvements Group would operate and be governed, the major contours are readily discernable once we are clear about its mission. We propose that the mission of the group be to finance the infrastructure and mortgage systems necessary to launch and support a sustainable new economic engine, to promote retirement security, and to monitor the larger economy to support transparency and greater public awareness. At the end of the day, however, the job of the Economic Improvements Group would be to convert pent-up capital into the kinds of orders and contracts business leaders need to profitably and rapidly transition into the new economic ecosystem.

The Economic Improvements Group would have to consist of two distinct entities. The first would be an Economic Improvements Fund to aggregate long-term capital from institutional investors and individual retirement savers and then hold securities that produce a target long-term annualized return of, for instance, 3 to 5 percent. The second entity would be the Economic Improvements Bank, which would blend the Economic Improvements Fund's long-term capital with shorter-term funds from conventional capital markets and form that blended capital into specific investments.

Based on the Economic Improvements Group's mission, we could see a regionalized network of banks akin to the Federal Reserve System to ensure regional relevance and a headquarters in a city other than Washington or New York, so as to avoid groupthink and bureaucratic capture. We envision shareholders and accountholders providing the working capital for the bank, but with a governance system that ensures all stakeholders' interests are represented. As for investment priorities, we see at least three areas where infrastructure and mortgage products could accelerate the strategy and not compete with healthy private financial institutions: infrastructure build-outs for regional economies and global trade; a secondary market for smart growth mortgages; and transitions to regenerative agriculture.

PRICING NATURE AND ITS SERVICES

Redirecting financial capital into the new economic engine is half of the necessary financial architecture. The second half is a system to appropriately price natural capital and ecosystem services, or NCES.

The idea of natural capital—the limited stock of Earth's natural resources that humans depend on for our prosperity, security, and well-being—has been around a long time, since the 1973 publication of E. F. Schumacher's book *Small Is Beautiful*. (Even longer: FDR didn't use the exact term, but in 1937 he referred to "the fact that the natural resources of our land—our permanent capital—are being converted into . . . wealth at a faster rate than our real wealth is being replaced. . . . That is the unbalanced budget that is most serious.") Natural capital creates value through ecosystem services, the "free" deliverables provided to business and society by a healthy planet, including air and water filtration, pollination, recreation, habitat protection, soil formation, pest control, a livable climate, and other things we generally take for granted because we don't directly pay for them. In 2014 a team of researchers led by economist Robert Costanza estimated the annual economic value of 17 ecosystem services for the entire biosphere at $125 trillion, more than one-and-a-half times the annual global GDP of $74 trillion.

Of course, all that is pretty academic. Natural capital and ecosystems services rarely have been discussed inside companies or national accounting systems, let alone calculated in their financial statements or annual budgets. Why would they? They're free, after all.

In the absence of real prices on NCES, the economy relies on an incomplete and ineffective system of taxes and regulations to avoid excessive environmental destruction, policies developed by economists and negotiated by politicians and lobbyists. That system determines what is valued and how much, if any, cost we place on that value. Common sense would tell us that just because most natural capital and ecosystems services have no price in our tax and budget schemes, it doesn't mean they have no value. But the result is largely that: when there's no price for despoiling the air or water, or depleting resources faster than they can be replenished, they're considered largely "free." But as the ecologist Garrett Hardin pointed out in his classic 1968 article "The Tragedy of the Commons," nothing is for free when everyone's drawing from the same pool. Eventually, someone has to pay the bill or the whole system risks collapsing.

It's time for an approach that puts a price on ecosystem services based on data, demand, and actual value. To do that, we'll need a market, like the Chicago Commodities Exchange or the New York Stock Exchange, where investors can trade listed securities that provide pricing signals to value NCES.

While pricing some ecosystem services has been done in the past, we need to scale up and speed up efforts to build this market. The most common form of ecosystem service valuation is the conservation easement, in which development rights are purchased in perpetuity to preserve the character and quality of an area. At the global end of the spectrum, the Montreal Protocol established the first cap-and-trade system for environmental purposes, specifically the reduction of chemicals that destroy the stratospheric ozone layer. That market reached its goal—of phasing out the use of these destructive chemicals—in considerably less time and at lower cost than pretty much anyone anticipated.

Today, the European Union and several U.S. states and Canadian provinces operate cap-and-trade markets for carbon dioxide to reduce the emissions that cause climate change. Companies from Exxon to Microsoft have established internal prices for various environmental commodities, such as carbon emissions and water usage, that must be calculated into any return-on-investment calculation. Some ecosystem service valuations have even held up in court.

But NCES does not translate easily to financial capital. One promising approach is the Intrinsic Value Exchange, or IVE, whose mission is to transform intrinsic value into financial capital for natural and societal assets. The IVE team, led by Douglas Eger, is working through the thorny challenges of how to create an online natural asset stock exchange designed to value natural and societal assets. At the time of writing, the IVE, with a deal team that included the government of Suriname, the government of France, and McKinsey & Co., was preparing its first public offering of shares in the ecosystem services provided by the forests of Suriname, particularly freshwater production.

The approach we propose is based on creating a type of land trust, in this case a company whose purpose is to protect and grow the value of the NCES on a particular piece or portfolio of land. The land trust creates zero-cost-basis shares for its stakeholders, assesses the total asset and service value of the land, and then files an initial public offering, or IPO. Capital raised in the IPO is then directed at improving the trust's NCES portfolio. While the trust does not own the land, the land owner and the trust's interests are now aligned, with a real financial value placed on the land's NCES, allowing landowners to adjust commercial land uses with its NCES income and maximize financial return.

For investors buying shares of a land trust, the value proposition is twofold. First, for some land, its NCES will produce revenue flows to shareholders, for example from water withdrawals, carbon credits, or watershed management. Second, after the IPO, shares in the land trust will be tradable securities and will provide opportunities for financial upside as their price rises. The question is whether those shares will sell in the first place and whether they will appreciate.

This is where the incorporation of NCES valuation into a new economic operating system comes in. As a matter of policy, the Economic Improvements Bank could require the inventory, assessment, and valuation of natural capital as a component of any regional redevelopment strategy. The Regional Improvements Banks would then finance a revolving fund for the formation of land trusts within their service area. With NCES valuation built into the financing terms and the costs of land trust formation covered, we can anticipate a fairly orderly and rapid transition into a system where U.S. natural capital and ecosystem services are properly valued and therefore respected.

"OURSELVES AND OUR POSTERITY"

Since the Great Depression, America's greatness has been tied to our ability to find new pools of demand and harness them to our economic engine to achieve our national purpose. Beginning in the early 1990s, America has failed that most basic of tasks, instead choosing to defend and continually "recover" an economic engine designed for the Cold War. But demand has fled that design.

Today, three massive pools of demand are waiting for the United States. Ten new business models are poised to unleash it. A financial architecture that would solve two of America's greatest market failures is within reach. Washington need not lift a finger. The question is whether business can organize itself to imagine and then build a new economy.

We think the answer is, Yes, it can.

For those who think the task is too big, too complex, or simply not their responsibility, just look at what Steve Jobs was able to do at Apple. Jobs imagined a mobile operating system that provided enormous core functionality and the app ecosystem that would live on that OS. His imagination and willingness to pursue it would redefine how the world communicates, moves about, and learns. And the company that asked that core question—what do we want the world to look like?—is now the largest company in the world. Before Jobs, and after him, are other business leaders who had the vision, ambition, and moxie to do big things that changed the world.

It does not take a Steve Jobs. Our optimism is reflected in the Law of Accelerating Returns, promulgated by Ray Kurzweil, an American author, inventor, futurist, and a director of engineering at Google. It describes the notion that people tend to overestimate what can be achieved in the short term (because we conveniently tend to leave out necessary details and simplify complexity) but underestimate what can be achieved in the long term (because the effects of exponential growth of technology and ideas are misunderstood or overlooked).

Kurzweil's law can be seen in a number of sustainability-related inflection points, some of which took longer than expected but are now on steep upward trajectories. Consider renewable energy, long considered a niche technology—it is on a growth path many experts didn't see coming: 70 percent of new power generation capacity added globally between 2012 and 2030 will be from renewable technologies (including large hydro), according to Bloomberg New Energy Finance. Only 25 percent will be from coal, gas, or oil, with the remainder from nuclear. Solar installations are growing at 30 percent annually in the United States, and are on track to reach a million installations by 2016, generating the equivalent of more than 14 coal-fired power plants, according to GTM Research. Clearly, renewables are no longer niche. But it took decades for renewable energy to become an "overnight success."

Applying Kurzweil's law to the alternative growth scenario, we believe a business-led economic transition can, over time, yield unprecedented prosperity and security. It may take more time than we expect to bear fruit. But done with foresight, ambition, and determination, we can create enough fruit, metaphorically speaking, to feed the world.

Bill Knudsen wouldn't have it any other way.

CHAPTER NINE

WAITING ON WASHINGTON

AS WE SAID IN CHAPTER 2, GRAND STRATEGY, AMERICAN-STYLE, IS the alignment of America's economic engine, governing institutions, and foreign policy to meet the great challenge of the era. We've focused almost exclusively on the economic engine so far in this book, outlining how demand and capital are poised to ignite a prosperous, secure, and sustainable economic boom and how business can kick-start it. Despite the deeply rooted partisanship and legacy government institutions that are holding us back, we also believe that once our economy gets in gear America will once again have a strategic keel. Then, and only then, will Washington be able to turn to the critical business of adapting and aligning America's foreign policy and governing institutions.

Today's complex and dynamic world simply demands that we get our foreign policy right. And to do that we need the right kind of institutions, ones that can execute in a coherent, flexible, and agile manner both at home and abroad. That means focusing on organizational design at a national level. It means new authorities and relationships. It means rewriting United States Code, the general and permanent laws of the nation that, among other things, dictate the functional responsibilities of our federal governing institutions. It means big, challenging government work done with a sense of urgency and a disciplined pragmatism that Washington has sorely lacked for more than 60 years.

Given the level of dysfunction that defines today's politics, how in the world could such a transformation ever happen? The good news is that we don't have to start from scratch. There have been a lot of smart people doing a lot of smart work for a number of years, some with government sponsorship and some without, laying the foundation. Some have pleaded with leadership to move past the Cold War era and join the twenty-first century. Some have done the hard work of figuring out real, workable structural reforms to systemic problems—the National Commission on Fiscal Responsibility and Reform, also known as Simpson-Bowles, and the Project on National Security Reform (PNSR), a congressionally mandated nonprofit charged with recommending improvements to the U.S. national security system, are two good examples.

We don't pretend to have all the answers, or that anyone else does. Far from it. What we'll offer in this chapter is a basic conceptual framework for foreign policy and the institutions that enable such a policy to complete our new U.S. grand strategy for the twenty-first century. We have tried to do this in a way that addresses our current and emerging realities without being ideologically partisan or beholden to legacy constructs.

A MISSED WAKE-UP CALL

In 1987, Dr. David Manker Abshire, the U.S. ambassador to NATO, was recalled to Washington, D.C., from Brussels to serve as special counselor to President Ronald Reagan, just as the Iran-Contra affair was unfolding. His mission: spearhead a thorough, transparent investigation of the burgeoning scandal and, in so doing, restore the nation's confidence in the Reagan presidency.

Abshire was born in Chattanooga, Tennessee, in 1926. He graduated from West Point, served in the Korean War as a company commander, earned a doctorate in history from Georgetown University, and, in 1962, established, along with Admiral Arleigh Burke, an influential Washington think tank, the Center for Strategic and International Studies, or CSIS. Among other public and private positions, he served as Assistant Secretary of State for Congressional Relations, chairman of the U.S. Board of International Broadcasting, the head of President-elect Reagan's National Security Group, and, ultimately, the U.S. ambassador to NATO from 1983 to 1987.

Abshire had a gifted, strategic mind, one that stood out all the more given the paucity of strategic thinking in our nation's capital. In 1996, while the president of CSIS, Abshire wrote a prescient article for the *Washington Quarterly* titled "U.S. Global Policy: Toward an Agile Strategy." In it, Abshire lamented Washington's absolute lack of strategic awareness, let alone any sense of strategic urgency, in the aftermath of the Soviet Union's collapse in 1991. He observed, "The United States has not enunciated a truly coherent strategic framework for the post–Cold War era. Its absence can be felt powerfully in places like Korea, Bosnia, and Haiti, where debates on foreign policy priorities have taken place in an almost eerie vacuum of larger thinking about the U.S. role in the world and the strategies required to serve it."

Abshire intended the article to be a sharp wake-up call for America to shake off the post–Cold War lethargy that he described as a "strategic interregnum." Abshire argued for a new grand strategic approach to a post–Cold War world, which he saw as "a far more complex, multipolar, interdependent world order operating under the novel influence of information, business, and financial revolutions" that made the "Cold War's simple focus on military and defense issues . . . a thing of the past." He added, "A single-minded linear strategy like containment [is] no longer appropriate."

In Abshire's mind, what America needed was an "agile strategy," a strategic reset that demanded a new flexibility and nimbleness, including the ability to move quickly to take advantage of new opportunities or head off rapidly emerging dangers. And guiding it all, a keen long-range vision that would enable America to shape rather than react to world events, and to leverage our domestic strength to be "prepared for whatever new era, whether it be primarily competitive or cooperative, emerges from the strategic interregnum."

At the time, this was a big departure from the still-thriving Cold War perspective that myopically focused on "over there" security concerns and the conflicting interests of antagonist nations. Abshire's brilliance was in his recognition that a great power like the United States doesn't need to have a major threat to have a grand strategy; it just needs interests. And early on, he pointed out that the Cold War system of containment was not well suited to pursuing our national interests in the new world in which we found ourselves.

It's important to note that Abshire wasn't discounting threats and risks. On the contrary, his approach was purely realist in its nature in that it recognized that "world politics remains a modified form of anarchy in which power and influence are at stake. Therefore, conflicting national interests are a permanent and inevitable aspect of international relations." That said, he went on to underscore the importance of pursuing the opportunities provided by the converging interests—particularly economic interests—of global actors and the role our domestic condition plays in that realm: "An agile strategy must therefore provide the United States with the ability to operate in a world where military conflict is always possible and economic competition is inevitable. The economic competition, however, becomes constructive rather than destructive the more markets are not mercantilistic but mutually open, thus providing a win-win situation."

Abshire's advice was smart, timely stuff. Unfortunately, no one listened—or, if they did, no one did anything. Today, Abshire's insights are just as relevant as they were in the aftermath of the Soviet collapse.

OUT WITH CONTAINMENT, IN WITH SUSTAINABILITY

The focus on agility, flexibility, domestic strength, converging interests, influence, and doctrine-free pragmatism guided toward idealistic goals is particularly relevant to the grand strategic framework we propose. In their paper *A National Strategic Narrative*, Porter and Mykleby were aligned with Abshire's functional strategic sensibilities outlined above. But they also recognized that there had to be a coalescing strategic concept—a systems logic—to contextualize a new American strategy if it was to have the essential attributes of agility and flexibility in both the domestic and foreign policy realms. Just calling a new national strategy an "agile strategy" was not enough.

That's why they proposed sustainability as the coalescing strategic American concept for the coming decades. As we've explained earlier, not only does sustainability map to our enduring national interests of prosperity and security in the twenty-first century, it moves strategy formulation beyond the linear and deterministic "ends-ways-means" paradigm that is, in its core conception, wholly inadequate to the complex, ecology-like post–Cold War world we live in.

Getting away from the ends-ways-means construct is a key point. A grand strategy of sustainability recognizes that we're never going to get to a magic point in time—an end state—where we can proclaim, "We're now sustainable!" It is a condition for which we must constantly strive. Sustainability requires us to be open to adaptation and evolution over the long term, just as it will require us to be flexible and agile in the near term. This requires a strategic framework that is based on systems theory and complexity theory and the acceptance that we can't control global dynamics ad infinitum; a framework that focuses on our ability to be the best competitor in and the best contributor to the global strategic ecology. Charles Darwin would have loved it.

By understanding that our great global project is to lead the transition to an inclusive and sustainable global order, we have the kind of central strategic concept around which we can design a new national strategy and, in the process, create the conditions in which tensions among great powers over resources and ecosystems are reduced. Of course, as Abshire pointed out, "the agile strategy is not a panacea. It is not a comprehensive geopolitical road map to guide the United States through the next century. It is not a coherent theory of international relations. But the fact that it is not all these things is its strength: It deliberately avoids rigid doctrines that create mindsets that destroy agility." In other words, an agile strategy allows us to adapt and evolve as the strategic milieu ebbs and flows over time.

Our grand strategy—in which our enduring national interests of prosperity and security are addressed through the integration of our smart growth at home with our smart power abroad—does just that. It offers a coherent, purpose-driven strategic framework that will enable flexibility and agility so that our domestic and foreign affairs are fundamentally integrated, leveraging off one another to pursue our interests over the long haul in a complex and uncertain world. And in so doing, America will be able to learn, adapt, evolve, and, most important, thrive going forward.

Lest anyone think this is trendy postmodern wonkery, consider this: George Kennan, the consummate realist, highlighted the relationship between our national domestic condition and our ability to effectively engage and lead on the global stage as early as 1954, in a collection of lectures entitled "Realities of American Foreign Policy":

"Blighted areas, filthy streets, community demoralization, juvenile de-
linquency, chaotic traffic conditions, utter disregard for esthetic and rec-
reational values in urban development, and an obviously unsatisfactory
geographic distribution of various facilities for home life and work and
recreation and shopping and worship: These things may not mark all
our urban communities in conspicuous degree, but they mark enough of
them to put a definite imprint on the image of our life that is carried to
the world around us, and this is an imprint that leads others to feel that
we are not really the masters of our own fate, that our society is not really
under control, that we are being helplessly carried along by forces we do
not have the courage or the vitality to master. . . . Peoples of the world are
not going to be inclined to accept leadership from a country which they
feel is drifting in its own internal development and drifting into bad and
dangerous waters."

We are indeed adrift. Today, because we're still beholden to old
ideological mind-sets and institutions, we're simply not effectively engaging with the rest of the world, let alone leading it. Whether it's our
slow pace of addressing climate change, our lack of participation in the
International Criminal Court, Congress's rejection of the Convention
on the Law of the Sea, our obstructive approach to the nascent Asian
Infrastructure Investment Bank, or our vacillation around free trade,
we're seemingly unplugged from what is going on in the rest of the
world—and the rest of the world is taking note.

We seem to be an analog country in a digital world. We appear
relieved when Russia heads into Ukraine or when North Korea launches
another missile, just so we can use and validate our old Cold War operating system, which requires an enemy to function. But this system can't
keep pace with twenty-first-century dynamics such as globalization,
economic interdependence, climate change, and violent extremism. In
the end, our slavish adherence to our traditional tools has left us peren-
nially reactive to world events.

Instead, if we overtly focused on *converging* interests, while at the
same time accepting diverging interests (as is often the case with our
European friends) or being prepared—diplomatically, militarily, and economically—to deal with conflicting interests (as in the case of China,
Iran, and Russia), we could create much-needed flexibility by creating
options. By redesigning our institutions to foster agility, we could create

capacity to rapidly and proactively move from one option to another and exploit situations as they invariably shift and alter.

If we get this right, we will show the world that we have the courage and vitality to master our own destiny and, in the process, provide the steady, consistent leadership needed in the world today.

FROM CONCEPT TO POLICY

Today the United States' approach to foreign policy can, at best, be described as random acts of engagement; at worst, negligent ineptitude. There is no discernable framework, let alone overarching logic or purpose, to what we do or how we do it. Consider the Arab Spring, a relatively consistent region-wide phenomenon. From Libya to Egypt, Syria to Bahrain, we handled each situation as a separate, disconnected event: military intervention in Libya, a wait-and-see approach in Egypt, a "red line" for Syria (which we weren't prepared to enforce), a hands-off approach to Bahrain. The net result left the world scratching its collective head.

Even when we try to do big things, no one can trust that we'll do what we say. Fareed Zakaria, former editor of *Foreign Affairs* and now a CNN host, observed this in an April 2015 piece for the *Washington Post*. In 2010, the Obama administration announced a "pivot to Asia," but nothing really happened. Our focus remained on the Middle East, the president's own party fought against the Trans-Pacific Partnership, and the administration actively lobbied against the creation of the Asia Infrastructure Investment Bank, only to find we were out of step with the region's development needs, as well as our closest allies like Great Britain and Australia. Zakaria noted that Congress wouldn't even pass legislation to increase China's voting share in the International Monetary Fund despite the fact that its current share is equivalent to that of the Netherlands though it possesses the world's second-largest economy—and soon to become the largest.

In the end, our foreign policy, and the institutions charged with its implementation, are working at cross-purposes. At best, they have devolved into what James R. Locher III, the former head of the PNSR, describes as a system of "daily issue management." Daily issue management traps us in linear, myopic actions that rapidly become isolated and ineffective. We have no direction, and no flexibility. And absent a comprehensive understanding of our strategic context, our foreign policy will continue to be a series of reactive "one-offs," neither shaping the environment to our advantage nor providing the kind of international leadership the world needs.

What to do? We should start by taking the advice George Marshall offered George Kennan in 1947 as he sent him off to figure out the Marshall Plan: "Avoid trivia." Rather than attempting to control every geopolitical and geo-economic issue of the day, we should step back and look at a foreign policy framework that is appropriate to global strategic conditions, that synergistically integrates with domestic policy, and actually advances our national interests of prosperity and security as they relate to other global actors.

This means focusing on the four converging challenges of rapid economic inclusion, ecological depletion, contained depression, and the resilience deficit. To boil it all down: we need to transition to an economic order that is sustainable and inclusive. It's also what all the other major economies need, whether that's China, Japan, India, or Europe. The transition to a sustainable and inclusive economic system is in everyone's best interest. America's role? To catalyze that transition.

To do this, we must first lead by example, implementing our own decisive transition to sustainability and leveraging the global reach of our economy. We need America's $17 trillion economy to do the heavy lifting and address the four strategic antagonists, thereby reducing the high-speed, low-mass drivers of geopolitical conflict. In comparison, America's national security budget is in the neighborhood of only $1.2 trillion and is a wholly owned subsidiary of the national economy. We need the economy to be a wind at our backs, propelling our nation through the space our national security apparatus should be creating and capturing the opportunities our foreign policy ought to be developing.

Second, we must shape the international order to enable sustainable inclusion and recognize the diverse starting conditions around the world. While we recognize that the demand signals of walkable communities, regenerative agriculture, and resource productivity will take various forms around the world (for example, there is an extraordinary difference between where Japan is starting from compared to, say, the Democratic Republic of Congo), there will be common themes across every society given the trend lines of global economics, urbanization, climate change, and resource limitations.

Probably the best example of this is China, which is seeing huge rates of urbanization. Right now, China is about 56 percent urban. In the next 20 years, it needs to add an additional 292 million people to its urban environment. To do this, China's energy generation will have to double in 20 years, which will demand 65 percent more water, yet it only has 6 percent of the world's freshwater supplies (98 percent of China's surface water supply is recharged through precipitation, so droughts associated with climate change will exacerbate the problem), and the majority of China's coal reserves are in its driest regions. On top of this, two-thirds of China's 669 cities already have water shortages and 40 percent of its rivers are severely polluted. China has a huge, vexing, systemic problem on its hands when it comes to urbanization, energy, and water. The designs and technologies that we develop here in America to tackle our big problems not only become a great economic opportunity for American companies to do business in China, but they also provide us an opportunity to engage China around converging interests. It's a fundamental opportunity to reshape our foreign policy approach to China, not just contain them while wishing they would become good democrats and capitalists. At the end of the day, we need China to succeed. Such is the nature of our hyperconnected, intertwined, and globalized world.

In the sections that follow, we illustrate what this might look like. Specifically, we see the need to work in a new global partnership to develop robust regional economic blocs and to secure minimally sufficient space for making that transition. To do these things, we must, in turn, transform our own governing institutions to gain and maintain the necessary strategic flexibility and agility to act and lead in the world to come.

REGIONAL ECONOMIES

If we are to consider reshaping the international order, we must understand four things. First, no major economy is sustainable; the United States, China, Europe, India, Japan—all operate well past planetary boundaries, though in distinct ways. Similarly, no economy is self-sufficient—whether we're talking about food, water, materials, energy, or markets for exports, we are living in a fully interdependent world. Consider: more than 20 percent of American jobs are tied to exports, China cannot feed itself, Japan is resource-poor, and all major economies are emitting too much carbon dioxide.

Second, great disparities exist among nations, both in terms of power and access. The major economies, though still interdependent, can more easily shape their own fate. Some smaller countries have found their economies caught between these giants, becoming dangerously dependent upon them and drained of their resources, wealth, or human capital. Africa is the poster child, as seen in places like Nigeria (oil), the Congo (minerals), and Ethiopia (agriculture). Without the advantage of scale and access, most of these countries have little practical chance of achieving the kinds of economic growth that will meet the expectations of their smartphone-enabled citizens. This inadequate, two-tier design only exacerbates global unsustainability.

Third, we must recognize that the world is going regional. Regional-scale economies, such as North America, China, India, and Europe, are the primary actors in today's global economy. The post–Cold War dream of a single, rules-based globalized economy characterized by free trade and fair play is not materializing outside of the old Western bloc because it's not the urgent priority of the developing world, where the majority of humanity lives.

For example, following the EU model, the members of the Association of South East Asian Nations, ASEAN, sandwiched between the massive economies of India and China, have used regional economic cooperation to aggregate their economic clout and provide a constructive framework for continued U.S. and Japanese engagement in the region. The Shanghai Cooperation Organization, established in 2001 to settle border disputes among China, Russia, and several former Soviet republics, has expanded into a regional economic organization with a potential security cooperation role as well. It is also opening its membership to other countries. Meanwhile, trade between Russia and China reached $95.3 billion in 2014 and is expected to double to $200 billion by 2020.

Finally, we need to take note of what is happening as major economic regions develop stronger currencies. Presently, because the U.S. dollar is the dominant global currency, the United States has the luxury of being able to print money to bludgeon its way through economic difficulties without suffering the penalty of runaway inflation. That's why the Federal Reserve can inject $4 trillion at the same time we have a cumulative national debt of $18.6 trillion (as of mid-2015, not including unfunded liabilities such as Social Security and Medicare), slightly more than our entire $17.8 trillion GDP—and not suffer runaway inflation. If this were not the case, our experiment in "quantitative easing"—the Fed's effort to stimulate the economy during the Great Recession by buying financial assets from commercial banks and other financial institutions—could have sent us down the hyperinflation road of the Weimar Republic or Zimbabwe, where it takes a bag full of money just to buy a same-sized bag of groceries. With China's yuan becoming an International Monetary Fund reserve currency in late 2015, the future of the dollar's dominance is no longer an academic question.

Given these four dynamics, some countries, notably China, have questioned the utility and legitimacy of international rules they did not have a say in writing. If our shared global purpose is to accelerate the transition to sustainability, it is time to think about the shape of the global economy but without losing hard-fought gains in human rights and free trade. For members of the ASEAN, or the nations of Latin America and Africa, whose experience with global institutions like the World Bank or IMF have been checkered at best, regional blocs have the best potential to provide the benefits of increased free trade, finance, and security, without the faint scent of imperialism that comes from the U.S.-dominated World Bank and the Euro-centric IMF.

Indeed, it makes no sense to fight this trend. The underlying compromise in the WTO allows for countries with large populations of impoverished citizens to opt out of any trade rules they don't like, regardless of free-trade agreements. It makes far more sense to leverage trends and begin to shape the situation and ourselves so we are best positioned to address our interests. This means we need to establish a new framework for the global transition to sustainability based on regional economic blocs, establish regional economic strategies, and create and encourage access and participation for regional players, developed and developing alike.

A new global design made up of several regional blocs would provide the mechanism needed to accelerate the transition to sustainability. Each bloc would embark on a decisive economic strategy that places sustainability at its center, focusing on a mode of development that results in prosperity, security, and sustainability for its citizens. Just like in the United States, the universal global demand for housing, agriculture, and resource productivity will drive sustainable economic development, producing jobs, investment, and government revenue.

Within countries, the issue of individual access and participation will have to be addressed if we are to address our strategic antagonists before time runs out. Most of the world's population still does not have access to the formal sector of its local market and therefore cannot participate in this great global project. A whopping 4 billion citizens—more than half of humanity—do not have access to basic market tools, like identity papers, title to property, or access to courts, banks, credit, or insurance, according to the development economist Hernando de Soto. Until they get the economic franchise, we will be unable to realize the goals of global prosperity and security, let alone sustainability. As an illustration, 96 percent of Egypt's real estate is held outside of the formal legal system, meaning there is no functioning market for property and housing, the most fundamental of markets in any capitalistic economy.

With a bit of boldness and demonstrated commitment, America can lead the partnership of major economies to refashion the global economic system around regional economic blocs, each boasting the scale necessary to support mature industrial ecosystems. This means promoting and strengthening existing organizations such as the Association of Southeast Asian Nations, the Union of South American Nations, the African Union, the Commonwealth of Independent States, and the Organization of Islamic Cooperation.

At the same time, we need to get our own economic house in order so that we can be the best competitor in this new system and be prepared should the global financial architecture actually move away from the centrality of the dollar. In other words, we need to begin building flexibility in our national economic system and its interactions with the emerging international system so that we have "first-in advantage" and don't become the odd man out in a transforming global economic system. If the dollar remains the key global currency, all the better. Our economy will be that much stronger, more resilient, and more prosperous for the effort. If the world economy moves away from the dollar, we'll be prepared. At the end of the day, it's all about flexibility and having options.

SECURITY POLICY

Concomitant with a redesign of our foreign policy approach to the global economy, we also need to adjust our approach to security and recognize that the great threat to American security in the coming decades of the twenty-first century stems from the unsustainability of the international order.

Although addressing this threat is primarily an economic and geo-political exercise, the U.S. national security establishment must ensure that economic and political actors have sufficient space and time to adapt the system at home and, in partnership, abroad. The mission of America's national security establishment in this new era must be to maintain and extend that space while providing, to friend and foe alike, a credible assurance that America is committed to, and will actively pro-mote, a rules-based international order. And the first step in establishing security and providing that credible assurance is for the United States to demonstrate consistent strategic behavior at home and abroad.

The Old English epic poem *Beowulf* had it right: "Behavior that is admired is the path to power among people everywhere." Right now, our strategic behavior is not so admired mostly because it is so disjointed that no one can discern where the United States is going, let alone what it stands for beyond preserving the status quo. As such, our friends are forced into hedging strategies, making sure they have viable options in case their relationship with the United States turns into a strategic li-ability rather than an asset. A great case in point is Australia, which has developed greater bilateral government relations with China, having signed a free trade agreement with the Chinese in 2015 as well as joining the Asian Infrastructure Investment Bank, all because the Australians can't count on America to act in a predictable manner that is aligned with Australian strategic interests. For our great-power "frenemies," like Russia and China, our lack of consistent strategic behavior looks like the opportunity for them to create new relationships and gain influence by pointing to American unreliability.

What would consistent strategic behavior look like? It would start with us taking care of business at home, specifically by adopting a new economic operating system designed for the twenty-first century. That means we'd stop wasting our time kibitzing about emotionally and ideologically charged wedge issues. We would craft meaningful policy to support and accelerate the new economic ecosystem we have pro-posed; make R&D investments to solve our generation's big techni-cal and scientific challenges; and develop skills training to move our workforce from its current service orientation to a long-term production orientation to capture burgeoning global market demand in a responsible, profitable, and sustainable manner. We'd take on, in a very real way, the big, meaty, and truly critical fiscal issues staring us in the face, like our expanding public debt and chronic budget deficits. (Updating and implementing the recommendations of the 2010 Simpson-Bowles Commission in light of this new economic strategy would be a great place to start.) We'd establish coherent and integrated policies and legislation around energy, transportation, infrastructure, and agriculture. And we'd fashion a comprehensive and pragmatic approach to update and integrate education, public health, social service, and immigration policies so we can develop our national human capital to compete and lead in the global economy.

Using George Kennan's words again, this is how we show the rest of the world we have "the courage" and "vitality to master" our own condition. As our population becomes more prosperous and secure because of that new economy, the risk of our changing course will dissipate, providing an enormous source of stability in the world. We'll have the confidence and the resources to support predictable political and economic transitions and provide clarity of purpose that others can rely on and leverage as they pursue their own national interests.

This bears underscoring. Beyond our own borders, we'll have to demonstrate consistent strategic behavior, especially across party lines. Today's chasm between right and left is in itself a major security challenge. Many nations don't understand what America is doing today, and they are pretty sure that whenever we get a new president, that behavior will change once again. Consistency is not as hard as it sounds (though it's pretty hard to imagine these days), and once a successful new economic engine takes root in the United States, policy makers will be hard-pressed to mess with what's working.

As we reestablish consistency, we should work multilaterally when possible, unilaterally if necessary, to ensure that all countries respect borders, global commons, and basic standards of human rights. As David Abshire stressed, we must be pragmatic in the short term if we are to achieve our idealistic long-term goals. That means engagement rather than obstruction or isolation. The world is too intertwined to think we can go it alone or manipulate things from afar, let alone rely on ideological theories to carry the day.

Today, virtual presence is actual absence. You have to be at the table to play. And being at the table means building and maintaining effective regional security partnerships, a framework that mirrors our approach to regional economies. If the United States is going to lead the global transition to sustainability, we'll have to recognize that it will be a complex and dynamic undertaking. Its political impact will be unprecedented. Borders, many set during colonial rule, will come under strain. That is currently the case for the Kurds, a nation of more than 30 million people seeking geopolitical recognition as a new state with established borders, much to the chagrin of Turkey, Syria, Iraq, and Iran, since it is their borders that would have to be adjusted to make a Kurd state a reality. America will need to work with a wide array of partners to ensure that any borders that may be changed are done so by mutual consent and self-determination, not by violence or coercion. At the same time, we will need to stand firm on our right of access to the global commons as much as we honor the responsibility to respect them and protect them as a sustainable platform for navigation, commerce, and ecosystem services.

The good news is that we have a solid framework for developing and expanding regional security partnerships. Presently, the United States has seven established collective security arrangements—some bilateral, some multilateral—with more than 50 nations across the globe. (In contrast, China has just one, with North Korea.) The goal of American security policy abroad should be to leverage converging interests of regional actors and reduce global demand, over time, for U.S. military intervention. By building upon existing relationships, and creating new relationships as required, with capable regional security partners, we can foster a far more effective, cooperative, and affordable global security framework to handle the myriad of challenges that promise to emerge.

This isn't just some idealistic wish list. We are already doing this sort of thing to great effect. In 2006, the United States, along with 19 other nations, ranging from our best friends—like Australia, the United Kingdom, Denmark, Norway, Japan, and the Republic of Korea—to some less-than-best friends—like China, Laos, and Myanmar—became "contracting parties" to the Regional Cooperation Agreement on Combating Piracy and Armed Robbery against Ships in Asia (ReCAAP) and the ReCAAP Information Sharing Center. The whole point of ReCAAP is to set up a regional security framework to ensure the unfettered flow of trade and commodities through the most heavily trafficked sea lanes in the world, in particular the Straits of Malacca, which sees 25 percent of global trade pass through its waters, including 60 percent of China's oil.

There's also Combined Task Force (CTF) 151, established in 2009 between the United States and 14 other countries to combat piracy off the Horn of Africa. While its most famous mission was the rescue of Captain Richard Phillips (later dramatized for Hollywood by Tom Hanks), CTF-151's real impact has been to radically reduce the instances of piracy across the region, from a peak of 182 incidents in 2010 to practically none today. It is important to note that CTF-151 isn't a U.S.-run operation; command of the task force passes from country to country. Along with the United States, command has been shared among Thailand, Denmark, Republic of Korea, Pakistan, Turkey, Japan, and others. The model also works on the other side of Africa in the form of the Africa Partnership Station, established in 2007 between the United States and several European nations and other international partners, to coordinate maritime security and partnership building around the strategically important Gulf of Guinea region.

These are real, functioning, operationally effective regional security mechanisms designed to pragmatically address the converging interests of numerous nations, and they have been implemented without relinquishing our own national sovereignty or control of our military to an international body. While these types of regional partnerships won't fit every situation and will never be 100 percent effective, they offer a more flexible and less expensive approach to vexing security issues as well as providing the opportunity to engage a wide array of actors around converging interests and, perhaps, avoid situations of conflicting interest. At the very least, we will have foundations in place that are based on established relationships and shared experience so we can lead with our diplomatic chin should tensions arise.

Strategic flexibility—that is, having options—once again raises its beautiful head.

NEW INSTITUTIONS

Done well, our foreign policy will foster strategic flexibility. But if we want our foreign and domestic policies to converge around our enduring interests of prosperity and security, we'll need the right kind of organizational design, with the right kind of authorities structure, to implement foreign and domestic policy in an agile, coherent, and synergistic manner. Former Secretary of Defense Robert Gates nailed it in 2007 when he said, "If we are to meet the myriad challenges around the world in the coming decades, this country must strengthen other important elements of national power, both institutionally and financially, and create the capability to integrate and apply all of the elements of national power to problems and challenges. . . . New institutions are needed for the twenty-first century, new organizations with a twenty-first-century mindset."

Today's foreign policy institutions were largely designed to support the country through the Cold War, and they are misaligned with the requirements of the twenty-first century. These institutions can barely see the challenges of today, let alone predict the crises of tomorrow (and capturing opportunity is at best an afterthought). America's domestic departments are designed to support an economic strategy that worked for a time after World War II and through most of the Cold War, but that is now based on the borrowed money of China and the borrowed time of our kids. Congress is supposed to oversee this system, but it can't seem to rise above the noise, mostly because it is locked into a committee structure that works within very narrow lanes. (Example: according to a 2014 report from the Bipartisan Policy Center, authored by former members of the 9/11 Commission, the Department of Homeland Security reports to no fewer than 92 congressional committees and subcommittees, up from 88 a decade earlier.) The White House, meanwhile, has not possessed a robust strategic planning capacity since Eisenhower left office in 1961.

We're at a time when we must move beyond the basic organizational framework of the National Security Act of 1947, a framework oriented toward defense that set up the structures and functions of the executive departments and legislative committees to deal with the Cold War, but now requires a new design to foster the congruity, complementarity, and synergy in our domestic and foreign policies necessary to achieve our smart growth at home and smart power abroad.

Specifically, in their 2011 *National Strategic Narrative,* Porter and Mykleby called for the creation of a National Prosperity and Security Act that would establish a new design for both the executive and legislative branches with new authorities structures to be reflected in the

United States Code. It also called for more fungibility in funding across executive agencies, both foreign and domestic, to integrate the tools of development, diplomacy, and defense through the use of public-, private-, and civil-sector resources. Currently, because these functions are viewed through an organizational lens—"Who is responsible for what and where's my turf?"—the effectiveness of the functions becomes a victim to organizational equities that invariably lead to animosity and intramural backstabbing over budgets, authorities, staffing, and programs. The result is a system that can't capture emerging opportunities or effectively handle new crises since it lacks agility and is, at its core, sclerotic.

RE-ARCHITECTING THE BUSINESS OF GOVERNING

Given how dysfunctional the politics are, to think about reforming the bureaucracy seems a step too far. But there's good news. The lion's share of the work required for our foreign policy community to be more agile has already been worked out. In 2006, Jim Locher was appointed to lead the PNSR, a nonpartisan effort funded by Congress to identify and recommend a comprehensive reform of our national security system so that it could move beyond the Cold War and start addressing the realities of our twenty-first-century world.

Locher, now living in California, is no stranger to doing big reforms in Washington. He was the principal architect of and lead congressional staff member for the Goldwater-Nichols Act of 1986, which fundamentally reformed America's armed forces into the modern joint military system it is today, the most lethal and professional military the world has ever seen. When he took on the challenge of reforming the entire national security system, he knew the scale of this challenge would eclipse his previous challenge of "merely" reforming the military. As such, he assembled an impressive corps of national security and foreign policy professionals that eventually included more than 300 experts from think tanks, universities, federal agencies, law firms, and corporations as well as some heavy-hitting leadership that included (among others): David Abshire (again), General Jim Jones (former Commandant of the Marine Corps, soon-to-become National Security Advisor to the Obama administration), Admiral Dennis Blair (soon-to-be Director of National Intelligence for the Obama administration), Newt Gingrich (former

Speaker of the House), Brent Scowcroft (former National Security Advisor to Presidents Ford and George H. W. Bush), General Wesley Clark (former Supreme Allied Commander, Europe), and Joseph Nye (Distinguished Service Professor at Harvard's JFK School of Government). An impressive bench, indeed.

The work of PNSR was eventually captured in its final report, *Forging a New Shield*, released in 2008, to date the most comprehensive review of the American national security architecture in its modern form. It provided a thorough description of the nature and historical background of the current system, including a no-holds-barred assessment of the current system's performance and an in-depth problem analysis of why the system wasn't (and still isn't) working. It concluded with three distinct and viable options for reform in terms of architecture and authorities.

It just so happens that the second option PNSR proposed aligns remarkably well with the global economic regional framework we have proposed. PNSR's "Option Two" called for "Integrated Regional Centers" (IRCs) that would shift "the national security system's emphasis from the White House's control of interagency committees to issue management and integration at the regional level." The IRCs would be headed by civilian regional directors who would be granted the appropriate cross-agency authorities to leverage command authority over diplomatic, development, and defense resources within their regions. Among the key features of the IRC design:

- A President's Security Council would replace the National Security Council. It would be comprised of cabinet members and IRC directors and would be convened based on issues, not statutory membership.
- The National Security Advisor and a small staff would focus on the development and execution of a comprehensive national strategy and overall system management, because the IRCs would directly manage issues. (In other words, we'd actually have institutional capacity to do grand strategy.)
- IRCs would be given appropriate authorities to manage issues in a decentralized manner (an absolutely essential attribute for fostering strategic agility).

- Various departments and agencies would support the IRCs (similar in concept to the current relationship between the military services and the Defense Department's Geographic Combatant Commands, or GCCs, and Functional Combatant Commands, or FCCs).

Not only would this design foster greater flexibility and agility in execution, it would also bring our instruments of foreign policy back into balance. Presently, there is no organizational coherency between our diplomatic and military resources. For the most part, the State Department is still structured and funded to operate via embassies along bilateral, nation-to-nation lines, whereas our military is structured and funded to operate at a regional scale through its GCCs (Central Command, European Command, Southern Command, Africa Command, Pacific Command, etc.). The IRC concept would provide a comprehensive and balanced framework to make integrated decisions regarding priorities, resources, and operations. It is a tailor-fitted foreign policy governing institution design for our grand strategy of sustainability.

It is also important to note that the PNSR report, beyond laying out the institutional reforms needed to deal with twenty-first-century dynamics abroad, asserted that organizational reform had to be viewed more broadly than just as an issue of foreign policy and national security; it needed to include domestic issues of education, energy, public health, infrastructure, environment, and others. As such, just as our institutions and instruments of foreign policy need to be integrated more effectively, our institutions and instruments of domestic policy must follow the same design. That means taking a fundamental look at how the executive departments and agencies—of energy, commerce, health, education, transportation, agriculture, environment, et cetera—relate, integrate, and leverage one another; how their authorities can be applied with agility to address existing and emerging issues; and, most important, how resources can flow across organizational lines rather than being trapped by bureaucratic silos.

It also means that Congress has to move beyond its current committee system. Presently, Congress is organized into a cumbersome array of 49 committees—in the form of standing, special and select, or joint committees as well as commissions and caucuses—plus 170 or so subcommittees—all looking at sometimes separate but oftentimes similar issues, programs, and oversight responsibilities. The end result is that a lot of energy is expended in the process of running committees and subcommittees, but not much really gets accomplished in terms of meaningful legislation, resourcing decisions, the granting of authorities, helpful oversight, or communication across the branches and departments of government.

This is mostly because the committee system as it stands today is a product of the early days of the Cold War, just like our national security apparatus. The system of today came from the Legislative Reorganization Act of 1946, the last real, ambitious attempt to restructure how Congress operates (though another less ambitious attempt was made in 1993 with the Joint Committee on the Reorganization of Congress, but it only resulted in some minor adjustments to subcommittee formation rules in the House of Representatives and not much else). The complexity of today's world, both at home and abroad, is far greater than it was 70 years ago, and it's probably time for Congress to catch up organizationally to deal with that complexity.

Congress needs to be organized more simply along general functional lines, similar to how the executive is organized in terms of treasury, transportation, education, commerce, defense, state, national security, and so on. Additionally, Congress must develop the organizational processes to dynamically draw upon and focus functional area expertise in order to design approaches to the vast array of issues that continue to emerge around us and that can't be conveniently pigeonholed into a static organizational framework. The military calls it "task organization," in which functional components converge around a complex and novel situation to contribute their functional expertise to rapidly, efficiently, and effectively develop unique approaches to the situation. For Congress, a similar approach would create the capacity to meet recurring legislation requirements (transportation, agriculture, energy, maybe even the budget); deal with emergent issues and crises; and fulfill its oversight responsibilities in terms of resource allocation and authorities implementation. It would also provide some organizational balance and clearer lines of communication between the executive and legislative branches of government, which are sorely lacking today and have become a key element of our federal dysfunction.

IT TAKES A NATION

At the end of the day, the PNSR effort was brilliant work. It also went nowhere. By the end of 2009, PNSR had to shut down due to lack of funding and congressional disinterest. Similar to Simpson-Bowles, Washington just couldn't or wouldn't take on a practical, viable fix for a big problem, even when the plan was completely laid out for them. When we asked Jim Locher why PNSR died on the vine, his comments were as predictable as they were disheartening.

"The biggest obstacle that we had was the toxic political environment in Washington," he began. "The White House was very reluctant to take on an issue like this. They felt that they'd be quite criticized by the Republicans on Capitol Hill."

He continued: "And then when we shifted our focus to the Congress to try to get something started there, there was really no basis for a bipartisan effort in a major way. The parties were just too separate. I had probably briefed 35 senators and 85 or 90 congressmen, and all but two or three of them completely agreed with what we were doing but said they didn't know 'how we can help you—my committee doesn't have a broad enough scope and I don't have anybody on the other side that I could work with on this.'"

Moreover, he said, Washington is 30 or 40 years out of date in terms of organizational arrangements. The national security business has changed tremendously since the mid-1980s, and there's almost nobody in Washington who really understands modern organizational concepts and their great potential. "I have always said that Washington is a policy town, it's not an organization town," Locher noted. "If the policy doesn't work, it develops another policy. It doesn't look at the organizational problems that may have undermined the policy that had been formulated previously."

He continued: "Washington is focused on the components, not the whole national security system. And, if you think about it, you don't have any system-wide owners on Capitol Hill, because they're all focused on the committee system, and the committees oversee just components. There's no National Security Council or the National Security Council system on Capitol Hill. It's part of the Executive Office of the President, and so there's no jurisdiction over it. And in the executive branch, the only system-wide owners that you have are the president, the vice president, and the national security advisor. Everybody else is in charge of a component, and the components are where all the resources are and where the linkage to the power on Capitol Hill is.

"The system-wide owners don't have any money, and they don't have any time. Senior leaders are just completely overwhelmed with doing the business of today and tomorrow. So their bandwidth was extremely limited. We often went to the National Security Council to talk to them, but they didn't have any capacity to work on these issues because there were so many demands on them already."

When it comes to making the necessary changes, concluded Locher, there are lots of things the president could do unilaterally. But the big changes, or even sustaining smaller initiatives that the president would take, would require Congress to change the law. "So it does come back to Washington. There's no way of changing the national security system without involving both the legislative and the executive branches," said Locher.

Yes, it does come right back to Washington, as frustrating and deflating as that may sound. And while we've illustrated the problem using the national security community as an example, domestic departments, agencies, and congressional committees are equally dysfunctional.

But we, as citizens, have the capacity and the capability to force these very necessary changes. The Founding Fathers gave us the institutional gift—and mandate—to change things when necessary. It's time for us to get engaged.

Quoting Locher one more time: "If it takes a village to raise a child, it takes a nation to fix a government."

CHAPTER TEN

NOT WAITING ON WASHINGTON

IF IT TAKES A NATION TO FIX A GOVERNMENT, WE MIGHT BE WISE TO start on Main Street.

To begin with, there's plenty of enlightened leadership at local levels. City halls and county courthouses are where the action is, where stuff gets done in the short term, where there's a vision that extends beyond the next election cycle. In some cases, there's even a multigenerational view. Main Street is where people are more focused on what they stand *for*, and not so much about what they're against.

As we've shown throughout this book, innovative things are happening across America. They are being done by mayors, city and county councils, town managers, business executives, and citizens every day as they make pragmatic, effective decisions to ensure that their communities work, not just today but in the future. It is from these experiments in local governance that we get our inspiration and optimism about America's future.

Why are things different at the local level? The biggest difference between local and "higher" levels of government is that, in the former, public officials have no choice but to be pragmatic and deliver results, mostly because they live where they govern and have to look the people they serve in the eye nearly every day. They walk the streets, ride local transit, get stuck in traffic, traverse the potholes. They can't hide behind the false faith of ideology and the distant walls of a statehouse or Capitol Hill.

Ideology doesn't get the job done at the local level; decisions that prioritize and optimize limited resources do. So, just as we see the private sector as being the change agent at the national level, we see lo-cal government, in close partnership with the private and civil sectors, as the change agents from the bottom up—mostly by helping citizens do what they do best: be citizens. As we're seeing throughout America, such local partnerships represent the potent change agents so many of us are seeking.

This shouldn't surprise anyone, because it isn't new. Indeed, it's part of our cultural DNA, born at the beginning of our republic. In 1831, a 26-year-old Frenchman named Alexis de Tocqueville stumbled around a youthful United States, marveling at how well things worked in America. He spent nine months traveling the states and collecting information on American society, including its religious, political, and economic character. He captured his experiences and observations in a classic two-volume work, *Democracy in America*. One of his starkest and most compelling observations was that Americans act as individ-ual, contributing citizens. They don't wait around for someone to tell them what to do; they see what's needed and just get on with it. In Tocqueville's words:

> Every individual is always supposed to be as well informed, as virtuous, and as strong as any of his fellow-citizens. He obeys the government, not because he is inferior to those who conduct it, or because he is less capable than any other of governing himself; but because he acknowledges the utility of an association with his fellow-men, and he knows that no such association can exist without a regulating force. He is a subject in all that concerns the duties of citizens to each other; he is free, and responsible to God alone, for all that concerns himself. Hence rises the maxim, that every one is the best and sole judge of his own private interest, and that society has no right to control a man's actions, unless they are prejudicial to the common weal, or unless the common weal demands his help. This doctrine is universally admitted in the United States.

He went on to observe that the same thing held true when it came to local government:

> The township, taken as a whole, and in relation to the central govern-ment, is only an individual, like any other to whom the theory I have just described is applicable. Municipal independence in the United States, is

therefore, a natural consequence of this very principle of the sovereignty of the people.

This should be as powerful and heady stuff today as it was when Tocqueville penned these words in 1835. We merely need to listen to him to rediscover our unique DNA and begin directing our collective wits and energies toward a purpose-driven design that will deliver the prosperity and security we seek for ourselves, our families, and our collective future. Today, "the common weal" demands that all of us pitch in and engage, but we can't afford to have our efforts be minimized by rudderless, disconnected activities.

FULL-SPECTRUM SUSTAINABILITY

This is where sustainability comes in. As a purpose driver, sustainability gives us the rudder we need. It possesses the coherence and systems logic necessary to inform our actions on Main Street in the face of some pretty big and vexing national and global challenges. By taking a clear-eyed systems view, the logic of sustainability helps to avoid the common mistake of fixing something broken but, along the way, unwittingly causing harm both upstream (to the environment) and downstream (to future generations). Done right, it's about viewing our communities as systems and designing them so that their component functional subsystems—food, water, energy, industry, buildings and infrastructure, transportation, education, and the like—synergistically converge with, reinforce, and leverage the others. The result should be that the impact in terms of the prosperity and security of the whole vastly outweighs the individual impacts of each subsystem. As David Orr puts it, sustainability creates the conditions where "two plus two equals 22."

We use the term "Full-Spectrum Sustainability" to effectively describe what we're talking about. Beyond integrating society's functional systems, Full-Spectrum Sustainability is about how we integrate the resources of the public, private, and civil sectors (which include nonprofits, health care, and academic institutions) toward a common purpose: the creation of prosperous, secure, and sustainable communities.

It is also important to note that we're not framing sustainability with what has become its usual definition: as an environmental issue that demands fundamentally changing the current human condition in order to save the planet. Bluntly stated, this approach has failed because it speaks only to, at best, about half the population—usually the more liberal, Democratic Party half—and in the end becomes a never-ending "in-house" conversation. The other half—the conservative, Republican half and, let's face it, probably even some from the first half—just isn't buying this false choice.

With good reason: The "old" concept of sustainability as "green" is problematic. Most Americans tune out the environmental movement's notion of sacrifice in the name of Mother Earth, in large part because our present society reinforces a culture of *Homo economicus*—economic man. As Adam Smith described in *The Wealth of Nations*, *Homo economicus* is a self-interested being, seeking to consume the most at the least cost and to produce the most for the most profit. We have a tough time considering externalities in time and space beyond our current condition—things like the atmosphere we cannot see or future generations we haven't yet met. As a result, it's just too hard to change our behavior.

Yet America was not founded on the assumption that mankind's basic nature was limited to, or even dominated by, *Homo economicus*. For the philosopher-founders gathered in Philadelphia, the "pursuit of happiness" meant pursuing a life of virtue and just actions. Indeed, Adam Smith's view of mankind wasn't limited to his notion of *Homo economicus*, either. Before he wrote *The Wealth of Nations*, he wrote another book, *The Theory of Moral Sentiments*, in which he fundamentally, although not overtly, established the case for *Homo reciprocans*—reciprocal man—where we feel compelled to improve society and are motivated by a desire to engage collectively with our fellow citizens. After all, if we can improve the world around us, we can improve ourselves, too. "Enlightened self-interest," as it's known in economic circles.

When viewed in a functional sense, Full-Spectrum Sustainability can be our new system default setting that converges our *Homo economicus* and *Homo reciprocans* selves to get the best out of both. The task at hand is to translate the ethereal and conceptual elements of sustainability into real, pragmatic, actionable tools that *Homo economicus* can use for *Homo reciprocans* purposes. Sustainability has to take on a pragmatic, action-oriented voice, a voice that clearly and functionally articulates how it can be implemented in the way we live our lives, how we earn our living, and how our communities operate. It's about how our immediate self-interests of personal well-being can align with our long-term interests of generational and environmental well-being. As such, sustainability is far more than swapping out light bulbs, recycling stuff we don't want, or walking instead of driving.

THE NEW URBANISM

It turns out that a lot of the thinking about sustainable and walkable communities was done long ago by an Englishman, Sir Ebenezer Howard.

In 1898, inspired by the observations of Walt Whitman and Ralph Waldo Emerson that industrial society wasn't serving the human condition, Howard published *To-Morrow: A Peaceful Path to Real Reform* (republished in 1902 as *Garden Cities of Tomorrow*) in which he laid out a new type of community design, where people live in harmony with nature in a way that balances urban and rural commercial, social, environmental, and human needs. Howard intended to balance the needs of community with the needs of the individual in a way that fit within a capitalist system and wouldn't undermine it.

Specifically, Howard's intention was to design and create a "Group of Smokeless Slumless Cities" that would provide "wages of higher purchasing power" and "healthier surroundings and more regular employment" for both "mechanicians" and "agriculturists." The goal, he said, was "to raise the standard of health and comfort of all true workers of whatever grade—the means by which these objects are to be achieved being a healthy, natural, and economic combination of town and country life."

Howard was talking about Full-Spectrum Sustainability, even though he did not use that term. His was a hard-nosed, pragmatic systems design that addressed economic, environmental, social, and political concerns. His ideas were first put into action in England at the turn of the twentieth century, in a place called Letchworth Garden City, the founding of which kicked off what became known as the garden city movement. It spread across Great Britain and around the world. In the United States, the movement has been associated with the work of Frederick Law Olmsted Jr. and the proliferation of such highly livable (and well-heeled) communities as Forest Hills, New York; Chevy

Chase, Maryland; Shaker Heights, Ohio; and St. Petersburg, Florida, along with lesser-known (and less-affluent) verdant-named towns such as Greendale, Wisconsin; Greenhills, Ohio; and Greenbelt, Maryland.

Since the 1980s, we've seen a resurgence of Howard's ideas in the form of the "new urbanist" movement. That term has been trending within the planning community as developers and architects advocate a return to traditional neighborhoods to curb sprawl, encourage sustainability, and restore function and stability to communities.

In a sense, new urbanism aims to reverse the system of development that began after World War II, which rigorously separated the built environment into discrete and disconnected uses—housing, shopping, offices, factories, parks. The new movement calls for a return to mixed-use urban areas, with good pedestrian connections, a mix of independent businesses, and access to lots of green space, often knitted into a "town center" that vaguely resembles the citizen hubs of yesteryear and is not dependent on the prosthetic of a car to be viable. America's first new urbanism town, Seaside, Florida, was built in 1981 on an 80-acre parcel of land in northwest Florida. In 1993, a group of architects and planners created the Congress for New Urbanism, formalizing the concept as a true urban design movement. Since then, new urbanist towns and communities have sprouted up around the United States. There's Serenbe in the Chattahoochee Hill Country outside Atlanta; Kentlands in Montgomery County, Maryland; Laurel in Yuma, Arizona; Fairbourne Station in West Valley City, Utah; and many others. One of the newest, Stapleton, Colorado, is just outside Denver and is one of the largest, with 4,700 acres, 7,000 current residents, and full build-out not expected until 2020.

New urbanism is also fostering a new breed of developer. One example is Robert Turner, president of Habersham Land Company in Beaufort, South Carolina, near the southern tip of the state. Beaufort, which is frequently ranked in magazine stories as among "America's best small towns"—in 2013, it was ranked number 1 among "America's Happiest Seaside Towns" by readers of *Coastal Living*—boasts a historic downtown with remnants of the town's original English colonial settlement. (Beaufort is also the hometown of Mark Mykleby.)

Turner moved from Florida to Beaufort in 1990 after working on commercial building projects there. After renovating several historic homes in Beaufort, he quickly noticed the rising demand for housing within the classic American town setting—specifically the kind of town that had higher density and was walkable. It seemed like a market in the making. Looking at the innovative projects in Seaside and Kentlands— still in their infancy, they were not yet called new urbanism, they were referred to as TND, for traditional neighborhood development—he saw an opportunity. Turner spent two weeks going up and down the East Coast "looking at traditional old towns and what made them so great, why they were surviving a lot of economic booms and busts."

What Turner learned from that road trip eventually led him to begin developing traditional neighborhoods in the early 1990s. In 1998, he decided to build an entire community: Habersham, situated on the Broad River just outside Beaufort. The 285-acre project, based on the architectural charm reminiscent of nearby historic cities like Charleston and Savannah, features oak-lined streets, parks, southern architecture, and gracious porches. The town's marketplace features shops, service businesses, and restaurants along with a community waterfront pool, river retreat, and boat dock. Habersham homes sit along tree-lined streets and feature apartments, lofts, and single-family homes, with prices ranging from the $200,000s for lofts to the $400,000s for cottage homes to more than $1 million for the larger houses. Residents even have the option of owning a storefront on the street level and living in a loft above it, "just like our grandparents did," as Habersham's website notes. There were just over 750 lots sold and 400 homes built as of mid-2015, with more on the way.

Having built Habersham, Turner does not plan to go back to conventional residential development. "Higher density is always going to be better land use, generally less impact, less infrastructure, and less impact on the municipalities, such as the cost of operations and maintenance of roads," he told us. "It's not always less cost to develop because we spend more money on the public realm versus the conventional. We include parks, sidewalks, street trees, and civic structures to make the public spaces better."

One unanticipated benefit of building mixed-use developments like this, Turner found, is the ability to be flexible when markets shift, such as during the late 2000s, when housing values tanked. "When we hit the slow time in the market, the beauty of what we're doing is we just shifted to a lower-price point." With people looking for less-expensive housing and Habersham's mixed-use plan, Turner simply shifted to building apartments, townhomes, and smaller homes to meet the new market. Such a shift is virtually impossible in conventional development models, which tend to be segregated by price and square footage. Try dropping a 1,200-square-foot home into a suburban neighborhood of McMansions and see how the neighbors react.

Suburban inflexibility is only one of the many challenges Turner has faced while building communities that buck the conventional model of sprawling developments. "Things like mixed use, where you can have your office on the first floor and live upstairs, had ratios that FHA wouldn't finance. Our mixed use building is one-third commercial and two-thirds residential. FHA's ratio had to be no more than 25 percent commercial before they would finance it. So there were financing challenges at a federal level."

There are also building standards, some set at the state or federal level, that can get in the way of new urbanism communities like Habersham. Consider something as mundane as the width of roadways. New urbanism communities opt for narrower roads with wider sidewalks, making it more pleasing and safer for humans to interact, rather than convenient for cars to pass through—a hallmark of walkability.

But that doesn't always jibe with local code. For example, there are standards set by local fire marshals that say roads must be a minimum width to enable fire trucks to zoom quickly down a residential street, Turner explained. Toward that end, narrow streets and sharp turns are verboten, making it harder to create quiet, meandering streets. "The firemen get together at the federal level and pass policy that prevents getting smaller fire trucks or just sending first responders. Instead, they insist on sending a huge fire truck to every call," he laments. "They're designing roads for bigger and bigger fire trucks. That's being driven by the insurance industry, which is requiring that all this gear be loaded onto every fire truck for insurance ratings. And now we're building bigger fire trucks which make it harder to build more walkable streets. And when you build wider roads, people drive faster and more people get hit by cars. Fire has always been a challenge for new urbanist projects because you're building at a human scale, not for a fire truck."

Still, new urbanism towns like Habersham are finding their way through the thicket of federal, state, and local challenges, from financing to fire truck routes. For early adopters like Bob Turner it means investing more time educating banks, tax assessors, city councils, zoning boards, and the local citizenry in order to get the waivers, variances, and permits needed to buck convention.

AMERICA'S URBAN LABORATORIES

Habersham is just one of many examples of Americans getting it done, Tocqueville-style. Beyond the new urbanist examples, there are plenty of other communities taking matters into their own hands in any number of ways.

America's big cities are leading the charge, going well beyond creating walkable places. New York City under Mayor Michael Bloomberg, for example, instituted a range of policies, from congestion charges to requirements for new building projects to provide their own power generation, that have broken new ground among American cities. Los Angeles under Mayor Eric Garcetti worked with the consultancy PwC to integrate sustainability principles across the entire $8 billion city enterprise. Chicago under Mayor Rahm Emanuel created the Chicago Infrastructure Trust to direct public and private investment in a more strategic and sustainable way, reducing city government energy consumption by 20 percent and extending wireless broadband service throughout the subway system to increase ridership. Chattanooga mayor Andy Berke has presided over lightning-fast municipal Internet speeds—and a resulting tech boom—when the electricity utility decided to build a smart grid to increase the reliability of the power system. There are examples in towns both big and small.

One of the best examples is in one of America's most forlorn cities. Detroit's Eastern Market is one of the nation's most ambitious urban revitalization efforts. The market, located on the city's east side about a mile northeast of downtown, was founded in 1841 and has been located at its current site since 1891. In 2006, it was transferred from city management and now operates through a public-private partnership with the Eastern Market Corp., whose mission is to mobilize leadership and resources to make the Eastern Market the undisputed center for fresh and nutritious food in the region. Already, Eastern Market is the largest historic public market district in the United States, and its farmers' distribution center is the nation's largest open-air flowerbed market, with more than 150 foods and specialty businesses. On a typical Saturday, about 45,000 people find their way to the 43-acre site.

Dan Carmody, president of Eastern Market Corp., holds the vision. Carmody, who previously headed the Downtown Improvement District in Fort Wayne, Indiana, has taken on the role of promoting economic development for the Eastern Market neighborhood. It's a good fit. In addition to his background in city planning, Carmody once worked in a Kraft Foods factory. As he likes to quip, "I worked my way through University of Illinois making Parkay Squeeze and Miracle Whip."

But Carmody is serious when it comes to the potential for Eastern Market to engender economic and workforce development, food security, business incubation, and other benefits to the region. It's a vast, untapped opportunity. "Michigan ranks somewhere between second and fifth in terms of crop diversity, but somewhere around twenty-fifth in terms of value-added food processing," he explains. Carmody wants to change that by incubating and accelerating new food companies, and by doing a better job of retaining and attracting larger ones. "The market provides a clarion call to organize a modified form of food and agriculture that's more locally based, more entrepreneurial, with a greater spread of wealth—and trying, by using microproduction methods, to increase awareness of food in general, so that it also begins to impact on health."

Carmody is quick to point out this isn't just about urban agriculture. "We've found that people start paying a lot more attention to food when they're more familiar with where it comes from, and so urban agriculture sometimes is the default description of what we're trying to do, which is to strengthen regional food systems. But that's just the growing part. We think there's more wealth creation in the processing, distribution, and retailing of food. The growing part is where we can really help connect people to better diets, and we can collectively build a stronger food culture that kind of is a reinforcing, self-supporting cycle between food entrepreneurship and better health."

On a tour of the market in 2015, Carmody offered a detailed vision of the market as "the most inclusive, resilient food hub in America," and addressed food access, nutrition education, economic development, workforce training, job creation, community development, and more. It's a multilayered, multigenerational view of the urban food movement and how it could become one of Detroit's next big industries. The plan is already taking shape. Late-night food trucks servicing Eastern Market compete with nearby art galleries, loft apartments, craft breweries, restaurants, and other local businesses. Under Carmody's watch, more than $80 million is slated to be invested by the end of 2016, including new sidewalks, sheds, streets, parking lots and garages, and new kitchens for food start-ups to test and create their wares—the recipe for the kind of entrepreneurial endeavor he dubs "small food."

"We want to be a place where big food and small food come together," says Carmody. "We can't feed ourselves without both being here. We can't change our system without healthy conditions for small food."

NOT-SO-URBAN LABORATORIES

In dozens of communities, colleges and universities are becoming hubs for a more integrated approach to regional sustainability and resilience efforts. It makes perfect sense: institutions of higher learning are, or should be, learning labs for innovative solutions and, ideally, systems thinking. Moreover, colleges and universities are often economic engines in their communities, especially those in smaller college towns. The power of their purchasing can support the local economy and send a demand signal about sustainable production and manufacturing practices. And when academic institutions throw their weight into something substantive, it can be transformative.

There's no better example of this than in Oberlin, in north-central Ohio, about half an hour's drive southwest of Cleveland. The town—founded in 1833 by two Presbyterian ministers and named after Jean-Frédéric Oberlin, an Alsatian minister who inspired them—played a key role in the abolitionist movement in the United States. During the Civil War, for example, the town of Oberlin was an active station on the Underground Railroad, with thousands of blacks passing through it on the road to freedom. The town is also home to Oberlin College, itself a touchstone in civil rights history. It was the first college in the United States to regularly admit African American students, beginning in 1835. Its first black graduate, George B. Vashon, matriculated in 1844 and went on to become one of the founding professors at Howard University and the first black lawyer admitted to the New York State Bar.

The town of Oberlin, like others in the Rust Belt, hasn't fared well economically, and while its unemployment rate tracks closely with the national average, its growth prospects are dim. Outside of its namesake college, there's little to draw people to the area. The town of Oberlin has a 28 percent poverty rate, about twice the national rate of 14.5 percent.

David Orr set out to change that by transforming the town into a beacon of sustainability and hope. In 2009, he helped form the Oberlin Project, a partnership between Oberlin the college and Oberlin the city, along with private-sector and other partners. Orr, a celebrated academic in sustainability circles, is the Paul Sears Distinguished Professor of Environmental Studies and Politics, and special assistant to the president of Oberlin College. His long career as a scholar, teacher, writer, speaker, and entrepreneur has focused on a wide range of environment topics. Among his many accomplishments, Orr organized, in 1987, studies of the use of energy, water, and materials on several college campuses that helped to launch the green campus movement. Two years later, he organized the first ever conference on the effects of impending climate change on the banking industry.

The Oberlin Project's goals include building an example of "a sustainable economy powered by renewable energy in the heart of the U.S. Rust Belt," as he puts it, and moving an entire city to being sustainable while "creating employment and long-term business development in the energy sector." And, in the process, he hopes to create a replicable model for transforming other cities, colleges, companies, military bases, and more.

That may sound ambitiously daunting to some, but Orr has already proven his ability to take on challenging projects. In 1998 he spearheaded an effort to design, fund, and build the Adam Joseph Lewis Center for Environmental Studies, named by the American Institute of Architects as "the most important green building of the past 30 years" and as "one of 30 milestone buildings of the twentieth century" by the U.S. Department of Energy. It boasts innovations that these days are more commonplace but were unheard of in 2000, when the building opened. For example, a "Living Machine" on the main floor—what looks like a series of plants, potted in soil that runs more than 30 feet underground—merges elements of conventional wastewater technology with the purification processes of wetland ecosystems to treat and recycle the building's wastewater—all of it. In 2006, the building and surrounding site became a net energy exporter, producing 30 percent more energy than it needs to operate and sharing the excess with the community. Even today, relatively few buildings have achieved that.

The Oberlin Project takes the lessons of the Lewis Center to a town scale. Its plans include an art library, classrooms, a hotel and conference center, and new retail space. The whole project is designed to be "climate positive," meaning that it will sequester more carbon dioxide than it produces, resulting in a net removal of greenhouse gases from the atmosphere.

But the Oberlin Project is about more than green design and construction. It's about how a small group of people in a community can work at various scales—a building, a neighborhood, a city, a region— and view their work through the lens of Full-Spectrum Sustainability. In Oberlin, that means creating jobs, economic development, energy security, housing security, food security, educational opportunity, economic inclusion, and other desirable attributes.

This isn't just academic. For Orr, the ripples created by the Lewis Center embody the way transformation happens in communities, regions, even nations. "This was a small change leading to a slightly bigger change, and then to bigger change, a cascade effect," says Orr, sitting in a light-filled Lewis Center conference room. The creation of the center arguably changed the college, attracting students, donors, and international acclaim. It led to the Oberlin Project, which itself is garnering attention from other regions around Lake Erie and beyond. "What we're trying to think of in the Lake Erie Crescent is how to take that model up one more scale. Can we use the model of bundled buying power and begin to improve cities at the regional scale?" The collateral benefits, he says, are lowered crime, increased prosperity, nicer cities, lower police costs, better public health, and reduced carbon emissions.

Orr likes to talk about a "black swan" world, where events of low or unknown probability but with high, long-lived, and often global impacts roil the status quo—things like extreme weather, terrorism, economic calamities, and health epidemics. As such events unfold, it will be up to communities as much as national governments to build resilience and get things back to "normal" as quickly as possible.

"No government on its own can protect its people in a black swan world or from the growing impacts of climate destabilization and the turmoil likely to accompany the transition to a post–fossil fuel world," says Orr. "Citizens, neighborhoods, communities, towns, cities, regions, and corporations will have to do far more to ensure reliable access to food, energy, clean water, shelter, and economic development in the decades ahead." With the Oberlin Project, Orr intends to model how communities can embrace that future.

THE CLUSTERING OF AMERICA

Habersham, Oberlin, Detroit, and so many other towns and cities focused on sustainability, regional resilience, and new urbanism principles share a common philosophy and common design principles, but not much else. They are not connected and, as such, their positive effects aren't amplified and replicated as widely as they could be. The lessons they offer—economically, environmentally, or socially—go largely untold beyond a small circle of developers, planners, and happy residents. These efforts need to be placed into a larger framework so that investment capital, both private and public, can start colliding with the market forces we've already described at a scale necessary to become a driving force for a new American grand strategy.

That's where clusters come in. While at the Pentagon, Puck Mykleby and Wayne Porter assessed ways to animate the ideas articulated in the *National Strategic Narrative*. That led them to the concept of regional clusters and the work of Michael Porter, the Bishop William Lawrence University Professor at the Institute for Strategy and Competitiveness at the Harvard Business School.

According to Professor Porter, U.S. competitiveness is defined by and built upon regional economies that, in turn, are defined by concentrations of related industries in a specific geographic location. The U.S. Cluster Mapping Project, a joint effort of the U.S. Economic Development Administration and Harvard Business School, is used by governments, economic developers, and businesses to understand and shape the competitive landscape for a range of industries. The idea is that regional clusters, which would become hubs of innovation, provide the nation with the ability to produce high-value products and services.

According to the Cluster Mapping Project, "Clusters enhance productivity and spur innovation by bringing together technology, information, specialized talent, competing companies, academic institutions, and other organizations. Close proximity, and the accompanying tight linkages, yield better market insights, more refined research agendas, larger pools of specialized talent, and faster deployment of new knowledge."

Porter identifies two types of clusters:

- **Traded clusters** tend to be groups of related industries that serve as the core of regional economies, engaging markets beyond the region they operate in and, as such, are exposed to competition from other regions. According to the U.S. Cluster Mapping Project, it is virtually impossible for a region to reach high levels of overall economic performance without strong traded clusters. Examples of traded clusters include financial services in New York City, information technology in Silicon Valley, the automotive industry in Detroit, and video and film production and distribution in Los Angeles.
- **Local clusters**, in contrast, are groups of businesses that serve the local market. They exist in every region of the country, regardless of the competitive advantages of a particular location. The majority of a region's employment comes from jobs in local clusters, and since local clusters are tied to the regions in which they are located, they are not directly sensitive to competition from other regions. Examples include entertainment such as movie theaters and playhouses, health services such as drugstores and hospitals, and commercial services such as dry cleaners and hair salons.

Porter's cluster mapping, however, misses a vitally important level of economic organization in the United States. Researchers call this the "megaregion"—clusters of clusters, if you will, whose traded clusters are interrelated. The old Rust Belt modeled this notion. Iron ore was mined in Duluth and shipped to the steel plants in Cleveland en route to Detroit to make cars. Akron made the tires and Toledo made the glass. Thousands of other suppliers across this geographic region were part of this megaregional system.

America 2050, a project of the Regional Plan Association, has identified America's distinct megaregions—the places where most of America's population growth and a larger share of our economic expansion is expected to take place. Megaregions, according to America 2050, are:

defined by layers of relationships that together define a common interest; this common interest, in turn, forms the basis for policy decisions. The five major categories of relationships that define megaregions are:

- Environmental systems and topography (for example, the San Francisco Bay Area or Mississippi Delta)
- Infrastructure systems (the Northeast Corridor connected by efficient intercity rail)
- Economic linkages (the auto industry across the Great Lakes region)
- Settlement patterns and land use (the low-density lifestyle of Southern California)
- Shared culture and history (the South, or the state of Texas)

Megaregions are important because that's where global direct investment happens. When multinational companies are looking at where to place production facilities or regional headquarters, they look to see what metropolitan region can attract the right kind of talent and can deliver the full range of skills, logistics, components, and resources. These are the places in America that have the population and capacity to compete with Shanghai, Mumbai, and Hamburg. The Regional Plan Association identified 11 U.S. megaregions: Arizona Sun Corridor, Cascadia, Florida, Front Range, Great Lakes, Gulf Coast, Northeast, Northern California, Piedmont Atlantic, Southern California, and the Texas Triangle.

It's at the metropolitan or the megaregion level that Full-Spectrum Sustainability has the ability to drive self-financing and self-sustaining economic growth. While Oberlin can transform its building stock on its own, it needs to work in partnership with other, larger players in the region to address its transportation and agricultural challenges. Salt Lake City's process had to include 80 percent of the state in order to get the scale right so that it had the population, resources, and investment levels to make their numbers work. Los Angeles needed to work with 180-odd other regional governments in Southern California to get the incentives necessary to move away from sprawl as its primary growth pattern. It's a far more rational unit of planning than states, whose borders were drawn without much thought to economic flows.

SUSTAINABILITY AT THE CENTER

Put it all together, and the blueprint for a new self-organizing system begins to take shape. When we know where the demand is coming from, where the finance is to be found, what our strategic parameters are, and, finally, where America's comparative advantages are located and how they are organized, entrepreneurs from mom-and-pops to multinationals can make the kinds of decisions and forge the private-public partnerships that will launch America's revival, putting people and capital to work even before official Washington deigns to act.

What does all this have to do with Full-Spectrum Sustainability? Let's return to our earlier definition: Full-Spectrum Sustainability is the focused, purpose-driven application of public-, private-, and civil-sector resources to functionally integrate the various subsystems that constitute our society today—food, water, energy, industry, buildings and infrastructure, transportation, education, et cetera—so that they synergistically converge with, reinforce, and leverage one another in a manner that makes our communities prosperous, secure, and sustainable.

Integrating Full-Spectrum Sustainability with regional and mega-regional cluster design makes a lot of sense. Rather than focusing on the efficiencies around keystone industries designed for the last economic engine, we should put sustainability at the center of our regional framework, as per Michael Porter's original concept, and focus on unlocking the demand for walkable communities, regenerative agriculture, and resource productivity. In other words, we should focus on applying the alternative growth scenario in each region or megaregion. Why? Because the challenges we face won't be solved by making our current economic system more efficient. Again, given what we know about systems theory and feedback loops, making a system that produces undesirable effects more efficient will only make it more efficient at being undesirable.

The trick is recognizing that America's exceptionalism is not rooted in the myth of the rugged individual but in what Tocqueville actually observed nearly 200 years ago: that we are special because, while we cherish our individual liberty, we also recognize the utility of association in the preservation of those liberties. In other words, we do not shun the concept of collective action to solve shared problems. We embrace it.

In a nation where more than 80 percent of Americans already live in metropolitan regions and only 1 percent work on farms, the embracing of self-organized, bottom-up collective action is more important than ever. As regions and megaregions reorient around where twenty-first-century demand is, business models will fall into line to create new opportunities. By expanding the opportunity space to rethink the broadest array of functional sectors (food, water, energy, transportation, built environment, education), we will necessarily bring American businesses, local governments, and academic institutions back into the kinds of pragmatic and principled partnerships that have been lacking in our society in recent decades. A new generation of leaders will, we believe, emerge from this rich stew.

By converging diverse sector leaders and resources in a manner appropriate for regional conditions and circumstances, while at the same time aligning with America's long-term strategic goals, a regional cluster can provide long-term investment opportunities as well as living laboratories in which to integrate, synergize, and refine the various systems that constitute our society today. This is the essence of Full-Spectrum Sustainability.

And when various regional clusters are established across America that orient their economies toward the macro demand signals of walkable communities, regenerative agriculture, and resource productivity—and take on climate change at a meaningful scale with a sense of urgency—remarkable opportunities will emerge to rebuild the economy and social fabric of the nation. It also serves to show that grand strategy is real and that, at the end of the day, it is just as relevant on Main Street as it is on Pennsylvania Avenue or Wall Street.

Think of it as "trickle-up" economics: scaling and replicating local successes will inevitably engender state and federal leadership. It would definitely be a parade politicians would be proud to jump to the front of.

There are several key things that need to happen in order to make Full-Spectrum Sustainability a reality:

- **Import Substitution.** Instead of sending dollars out of the region to buy goods or services, many, particularly food, can be produced at home. This can help maximize potential synergies among the three pools of demand. These are similar to "import-replacement," proposed by Jane Jacobs in her 1984 book, *Cities* *and the Wealth of Nations: Principles of Economic Life.* The desired effect is to retain dollars in the regional economy longer, taking advantage of economic multipliers and, in so doing, fostering greater economic depth, value, and competitiveness at a national and global scale.

- **Coordinated Investment.** Develop regional-level investment strategies to deploy capital purposefully and systemically for maximum benefit throughout the region. A financing mechanism like the Economic Improvements Group is part of the answer, but so is coordinating regional sources of funding. The problem today isn't a lack of money. In 2014, total giving in the United States to charitable organizations alone was almost $360 billion, which equates to approximately 2 percent of U.S. GDP. That's a lot of dollars being thrown at any number of issues or initiatives—and it doesn't even include money from government grants or private-sector investments. This is the problem: there typically are no cross-cutting strategies to deal with problems and capture opportunities in a coherent, integrated manner, mostly because we are organized to deal with our local world geographically (within state, county, and city lines) and on an issue-by-issue basis (crime, education, air quality, the arts, etc.) rather than systemically. As a result, a lot of money is lost in the din of servicing one-offs. We tend to do things because we can (or think we can), not because they actually matter.

- **Collaboration Across Jurisdictions.** It's essential to promote collaboration throughout any given region across political and economic silos. There are scores of regional organizations out there, many at the state level—the Regional Council of Mayors in Minnesota, New York State's Regional Economic Development Councils, California's Local Government Commission, and others. These are important players, but they need to get organized beyond themselves and focus on breaking down policy and shortsighted equity barriers in order to foster regional environments of sustainable opportunity.

- **Think Strategically, Act Regionally.** Eventually, to have national impact, established regions will need to partner with other cities and regions in a wider American grand strategy. This is how we establish an almost tribal identity and action-based momentum that shows we know where we're going as a nation, that we have the courage and vitality to chart our course in the future, and that we have our swagger back.

LESSONS FROM THE FIELD

Mykleby, Doherty, and Orr have been leveraging their relationships across America to launch several regional cluster projects since 2013. The most advanced of these initiatives is in the heart of the Rust Belt, what Orr referred to earlier as the Lake Erie Crescent—LEC for short—a region stretching more than 200 miles, roughly from Detroit to Youngstown, Ohio. A new, integrated, globally competitive economy is within reach across this region. The Rust Belt rose as a regional economy, collapsed as a regional economy, and can be revitalized as a regional economy—if only it can redirect its collective energies, resources, and investments toward a new design. For the cities of the LEC, the value proposition is clear: by strategically capturing the burgeoning market demand around walkable communities, regenerative agriculture, and resource productivity, the region will be able to compete and lead on a global scale and, in the process, provide the prosperity and security that seems so elusive to its citizenry today. And do so without Washington's help.

The project is taking lessons learned from the Cleveland Foundation's Evergreen Project and the Oberlin Project to the regional scale, which includes the industrial cities along the western Erie shore. The goal is to help redirect investments and purchases of major regional institutions and organizations to support more rapid deployment of regionally produced renewable energy, a local foods economy, green building, and advanced manufacturing and materials.

To do this, the LEC project is working to establish a collaborative, long-term systems-level approach to harnessing regional public, private, civil, and academic sector spending and investment in order to catalyze and power sustainable development along Lake Erie. The cities throughout the crescent were once the heart of the national economy and we believe that they can again become an economic engine designed to be resilient in a turbulent global economy. The foundation for that transformation exists in the region's many assets in manufacturing, education, research, advanced technology, and, not least, its diverse and capable people. By serving as a catalyst for organization and coordination on a regional scale, the LEC as a regional initiative intends to create a new era of jobs, investment, and sustainable growth that can serve as a model for the rest of America to follow.

And, with all due apologies to Frank Sinatra, if we can make it there, we can make it anywhere.

Consider the opportunities for Cleveland alone. The city has tremendous assets: one of the largest freshwater resources in the world, abundant and affordable land, underutilized industrial capacity, world-renowned academic institutions, and a competitive workforce infused with a midwestern pragmatism and an ability to get things done. As such, Cleveland has enormous economic potential and can serve as the launch pad and linchpin for the LEC, with the potential to be both replicated and scaled across the Great Lakes region.

To demonstrate this potential, we are working with Cleveland's businesses, local government, and civil society on four separate but integrated, and mutually supporting, endeavors:

Advanced Materials Development Group. As we've already discussed, the specter of climate change makes it impossible to burn all the hydrocarbons we have at our disposal, but we can't afford to wipe them off the balance sheets, either. The opportunity is to preserve the economic value of hydrocarbons from oil and natural gas by moving them up the value chain as materials and products, rather than up the smokestack (or out the tailpipe) as greenhouse gas emissions. To capture this opportunity, the AMDG has been established at Case Western Reserve University with the goal of partnering with regional engineering colleges—at Ohio State University, the University of Cincinnati, and the University of Akron—as well as regional industrial partners such as Fairmount-Santrol, Lubrizol, PolyOne, Sherwin-Williams, Nottingham Spirk, and Ford Motor Company. The goal is to creatively integrate and leverage the region's academic, industrial, technical, intellectual, and human capital resources to create economically viable businesses that can transform America's stranded hydrocarbon assets into an economic opportunity by developing and commercializing advanced material products, technologies, and services.

Affordable Passive Housing Initiative. Much of the demand for advanced materials will come from the housing market. The good news is that across the entire region there is a need to develop affordable, energy-efficient, and healthy homes in mixed-use, mixed-income, walkable neighborhoods. The Cleveland Museum of Natural History's PNC SmartHome Cleveland project proved that it is possible, even in the cold climate of northeastern Ohio, to build a high-quality, good-looking house that meets both market needs and the Passive House energy standard, the world's most rigorous residential energy-performance standard. However, the relatively high per-unit cost of these homes (roughly 30 percent higher than a conventional home) is an affordability issue, despite the fact that these investments are repaid many times over through energy savings. The added expense is primarily due to the costs of using imported advanced materials to meet efficiency standards. (For example, windows had to be imported from Germany.) Integrating the AMDG with the Affordable Passive Housing Initiative can reduce costs, both by increasing the volume of available passive homes on the market and by using locally produced advanced materials, technologies, and services. In the process, the region will build new businesses and create new jobs that are aligned toward its future reality, not to mention future growth.

Clean Energy Finance Hub. Infusing these initiatives with capital will be key. Recognizing this, Cuyahoga County executive Armond Budish provided the kind of political leadership we seem to find only at the local level these days and announced in 2015 the creation of the Cuyahoga County Clean Energy Financing Hub. Its purpose is to assist businesses, institutions, local governments, and eventually homeowners in cutting energy costs as well as purchasing new clean-energy retrofits and renewable-power supplies. By leveraging a mere $225,000 of county resources to contract out for private-sector predevelopment work and planning, the hub will make up to $120 million of private-sector capital available for low-cost financing for purchasing more efficient homes, office buildings, and infrastructure, along with component systems such as HVAC equipment, motors, and solar energy systems. As the hub matures, it can expand to include a wide array of products and services, such as anaerobic digesters that leverage local and urban agriculture by-products, microgrid and smart-grid systems and technologies, and advanced energy-storage technologies.

Institutional Purchasing Power. By redirecting the purchasing and investment power of key regional institutions (such as community foundations, major universities, professional sports teams, banks, and hospitals) back into the region—initially toward the economic sectors of renewable energy and energy efficiency, local regenerative agriculture, and building and infrastructure development—the capital needed to fund a sustainable regional economy can be readily available. The LEC seeks to redirect an initial $1 billion of the collective purchasing power of Cleveland institutions to catalyze a regional purchasing and investment framework that leverages the increasing demand we have identified, viewed through the lens of sustainability.

BACK HOME AGAIN IN INDIANA

Just to the west and slightly south of Cleveland (and outside the LEC) sits Indiana, in the heart of a region that a century ago was among America's most vibrant farming and industrial centers. Today, of course, it is part of the Rust Belt. Unlike Cleveland, which is a decidedly Democratic big city, Indiana hails from the other side of the political aisle. As such, it represents a compelling counterpoint to Cleveland (and Detroit) from the perspective of thinking about Full-Spectrum Sustainability as the organizing logic for a regional revival. It's bound to be a tougher sell. For much of this region, environmental issues are nonstarters, politically speaking, and "sustainability" typically means simply staying economically viable.

Beginning in 2012, a small corps of business and community leaders from across this region began working to create a Mid-America Prosperity and Security (MAPS) Cluster, spurred by leaders at several colleges and universities. The group, including Puck Mykleby, met at Purdue University in the fall of 2013, and again in Bloomington in early 2014. It represents another example of what can happen when disparate groups come together to view the opportunities before them in a larger context than just their own town or industrial sector.

"We'd spent a lot of time talking to the choir and not getting the movers and shakers in the room," recalls Bill Brown, director of sustainability at Indiana University in Bloomington, who helped organize both meetings. "So this seemed like such a dramatic way to get everyone to the table to reframe the conversation around prosperity and security."

At first blush, Indiana seems an unlikely spawning ground for this kind of economic innovation. It is a solidly red state, where Republicans hold supermajorities in both chambers of the general assembly. Its

Republican governor, Mike Pence, believes that the science behind climate change "is very mixed," as he told *Hardball*'s Chris Matthews in 2012, and in 2015 he declared that his state would not abide by the EPA's plan to battle climate change by requiring reductions in emissions from coal-fired power plants. (Indiana joined 23 other states in suing the EPA to block the plan.) There's a good political reason for this: 95 percent of Indiana's electricity comes from coal, second highest in the United States after West Virginia. In 2014, the Indiana legislature ended the state's popular energy efficiency program, which, though costing residents only about $2 a month per household, was seen as a financial burden that did not provide useful benefits. Suffice to say, the state is hardly a progressive stronghold.

And yet there is a movement afoot in the Hoosier State to harness sustainability as a means of revitalizing its economy and communities. "There was something being birthed in that room," recalls Michael Gulich, director of university sustainability at Purdue University, who attended the MAPS organizing meeting. "There was almost a giddiness about it. Even though we didn't know exactly what we were doing, there was a sense that we could alter the course of our community and our state."

It turns out that there already is a lot going on in Indiana that could alter its course. For example, there's an emerging hub of battery and electric vehicle (EV) technology companies. EnerDel in Greenfield makes an advanced lithium-ion battery for use in EVs and as backup power for the electric grid. Energy Systems Network in Indianapolis is building an energy ecosystem that connects partner companies and institutions—in Indiana, across the United States, and around the world—to create microgrids, battery charging systems, and other so-called smart-grid solutions. There's a Battery Innovation Center in Newberry, a collaborative of universities, government agencies, and commercial enterprises focused on bringing next-gen energy storage systems to market for defense and commercial customers. IER Group, the French entity that runs Autolib, the highly regarded Paris vehicle-sharing program, established its U.S. presence in Indianapolis. That city's Republican mayor from 2008 until he termed out in 2016, Greg Ballard, a retired Marine Corps lieutenant colonel with 23 years of active-duty service, shifted the city's vehicle fleet to hybrid and plug-in electric and oversaw the installation of more than 100 EV charging stations, among the most of any U.S.

city. Ballard, who views EVs as a route to energy independence, unveiled in 2014 a "Freedom Fleet"—425 plug-in sedans that are expected to save the city 2.2 million gallons of gas over a decade. Terrorists, he says, "have looked at our situation and realized they can use oil against us." As mayor, Ballard was hell-bent on removing that option.

Energy storage is just one piece of the puzzle. There's also Ancilla College, in the small northern Indiana town of Plymouth (population 10,000), a two-year liberal arts college run by the Congregation of the Poor Handmaids of Jesus Christ, a religious order of Catholic women. Ancilla is the scene of an unlikely and unexpected project aimed not only at making the school more self-sufficient, but at helping to revive the region.

The college boasts an organic farm, a cooking school, a nursing home, a wind turbine, and a small geothermal installation. It aims to weave these together to create a "green hub," providing education, tourism, and, not insignificantly, jobs in an economically depressed area. "The nuns want this to be a part of their legacy," says Anita Joglekar, a technology consultant who has helped with the effort. "They want this to create an impact in the neighborhood and in the neighboring communities. They're calling it a green initiative, but it's really just a sensible initiative."

The idea of food security is just beginning to enter the consciousness of Hoosiers. At the organizing meeting of MAPS, some of the conversation focused on the fact that about 95 percent of the roughly $17 billion spent annually for food in Indiana comes from outside its borders. "Those of us who have grown up here in Indiana still think of this as a farm state and agricultural state, but that's not really the case anymore," says Bill Brown. That represents a massive opportunity for Indiana's farmers, along with the entire food value chain: processors, packers, wholesalers, grocers, restaurants, and others. Says Brown: "Indiana probably could produce a lot more of its own food if we scaled up some of these great ideas. People have already figured out how to make money doing it. A great door swings open when we start talking about the outcomes we're trying to get to."

MAPS is a clear-eyed effort by regional leaders who have decided that they cannot wait on Washington or even statehouses before tapping into the vast opportunities that have emerged for their region. These clusters are allowing citizens and politicians across America to kick the tires of a new economy at the Main Street level. In Indiana, they're see-ing the potential in making that economy come back to life.

JUST. GET. STARTED.

We need to be equally clear-eyed about all of this. First of all, there are no templates. Creating a regional cluster, with or without Full-Spectrum Sustainability at its center, isn't a paint-by-numbers exercise. At its core, this sort of thing has to be based on local context, local re-sources, and local actors, all converging on a regional design that is still emerging and that isn't officially recognized or possessing formal au-thority. These things go in fits and starts—from lots of activity to dead silence, from sprints of progress to spinning your wheels. It's more than merely building an airplane while you're flying it; you're also designing it and learning how to fly it, all the while booking, ticketing, and seating new passengers of varying worldviews, political perspectives, financial wherewithal, and expectations.

Second, the protectors of the status quo are alive and well and do-ing a great job of defending against almost anything new and different (never mind that it bears the suspicious moniker of sustainability). It's not that they're evil or misguided. They just view the risk of change and the unknown as being far more daunting than the knowledge that the current system will either evolve of its own accord or, perhaps, grind to a halt at some undefined time in the future. It's an unfortunate human characteristic to focus more on getting your own when the getting is good—or simply sticking with "the devil you know"—than to risk the seeming certainty of today in favor of the unknowable tomorrow.

At the end of the day, however, our experience in launching several regional cluster initiatives has been that people get it, they want it to succeed, and they want to be part of it—whatever "it" turns out to be. For us, "it" is creating a future that is worthy of our kids and grandkids. It requires time, energy, patience, and, most important, grit to make it work. It also takes a willingness to dive into the future based on our faith in logic, science, and the American capacity to do big things. You just have to believe that America can still create something better than the status quo.

This is the American way. If it wasn't, Thomas Jefferson, Meri-wether Lewis, and William Clark might still be standing on the east bank of the Mississippi River, looking west, their hands on their hips, asking one another, "Whaddaya think is over there?" Lucky for us, they didn't worry about knowing exactly what they had to do or even if they were right about a western passage through the Continental Divide. They just got started.

That's what this generation needs to do. Let's stop worrying about doing the next thing right; let's get on with doing the next right thing. It's time to just get started.

CHAPTER ELEVEN

WE THE PEOPLE

"WHENEVER I RUN INTO A PROBLEM I CAN'T SOLVE, I ALWAYS MAKE it bigger," General Dwight Eisenhower remarked when asked about his success in winning World War II.

That may be the most succinct articulation of what we've proposed in this book.

The economy, the nation, and the world are all facing a set of circumstances whose component parts are individually massive and collectively daunting: inclusion, depletion, depression, lack of resilience. To truly solve any one requires also solving for the others. If we want to keep the American experiment going, we'll have to confront this thorny, seemingly unsolvable knot.

The urgency is real. As we write this book, the symptoms of our out-of-date operating system are dominating the headlines. Climate, conflict, and corruption have spurred a massive migration out of the Middle East and North Africa that is disrupting Europe and testing the core principles upon which the European Union stands. Dependence on oil and gas for energy and some leftover twentieth-century animosities are enabling dangerous geopolitical skirmishes in Eastern Europe, the Persian Gulf, and the South China Sea. Continued deleveraging by American consumers has kept demand low, contributing to China's slowing economy as well as a major shakeout of its stock markets, which, in turn, has rattled American markets. Can anyone say "interdependency"?

This increased uncertainty hits at a time when the United States, perhaps more than ever, needs to expand the prosperity of our middle

class, close the wealth gap, provide stable returns for investors, preserve
the environment, and be a force for principled action in global affairs.
The Baby Boom generation is struggling with how to retire despite having insufficient savings and pensions. They face the disturbing reality
that they will have to work longer, their homes will need to preserve
their value, and their health-care costs will need to decline at a time
when their health-care needs will likely rise. Millennials will need an
economic operating system that allows them to invent technologies,
launch enterprises, and find jobs that will contribute to solving our strategic challenges while advancing the American dream, whatever that
means to them as they reach their prime earning years. Unlike the generations that preceded them, the sum of their work must enhance, not
degrade, America's enduring and inspiring purpose.

None of that is happening. Instead, we're sitting idle. At best, we're
playing Whack-A-Mole as crises multiply, complexity escalates, and
politicians dither.

We cannot hope to navigate the future without a flexible and coherent strategy—one that allows business, civil society, and government to
adapt rapidly, in a collective, purpose-driven way. To do that, we need a
new consensus backed not by ideology but by facts and reason, the kind
Alexis de Tocqueville admired way back when. And we need business,
with its seemingly unlimited capacity to innovate and scale, to design
and implement that consensus.

A HISTORIC OPPORTUNITY

Fortunately, the prospects for America's economy have never looked better. Since the dawn of the twentieth century, the great macroeconomic
question for America has been how to rebuild demand. When demand
goes missing or plateaus—the Depression of the 1930s, the stagflation
of the 1970s, or the deleveraging of 2008, for example—bad things happen. Based on our reading of the record, the one consistent source of demand is time-of-life demographics—specifically, an increase in people
buying homes. Today, America is facing more pent-up housing demand
than ever. It's a historic opportunity.

We believe homes are the broad foundation of the pyramid of demand, demonstrated by the power of new housing starts as an indicator of national economic health. Mortgages for those homes, in turn,
create a strong foundation for the financial sector. Transportation

needs are determined by where one lives and works. Filling that new home with stuff adds greatly to the mix. All in all, consumption is the building block of the American economy. It can be a positive force if done in the right way. Reviving the real estate sector will be the key to our success. But it, too, must be done in the right way: smart growth, not sprawl.

It doesn't stop there. We've shown that demand for food is rising and that we can increase farmers' profits per acre while healing the land and feeding the world. The requirement for a revolution in resource productivity offers American business the innovation and production platform to compete on the global stage. With high-wage, high-skill jobs growing at home and exports rising, our middle class will thrive once again and our trade balance will flip from red to black.

It all adds up to an unprecedented investment hypothesis for America. And that kind of opportunity and certainty is exactly what investors at home and abroad need. Today, America's annual rate of investment is at or near an all-time low, while China's rate of investment is far exceeding its capacity to consume. Now is the perfect time to rebalance these financial flows and attract investment to American shores, while China develops its consumer economy, and both nations strive to bring consumption within the limits of Mother Nature. Best of all, we can do this without running that money through the U.S. Treasury, or the capricious political apparatus that controls it.

It's a truly exciting time. Yes, the challenges are historic and America is late to the party. But it's a party we can't afford to miss. The opportunities are simply too massive to ignore, and we can now see a viable course of action that is scaled to the challenges we face but also, more important, to the opportunities that are available. It will be a marathon, not a sprint, but it will feel good to get our endurance back so that we can go the distance, mostly because we can do the quintessentially American thing of doing well while doing good. Finance can once again be a force for social progress and not just a catalyst for shareholder returns. America can once again be the strong, principled leader the world has come to expect, not the curmudgeonly obstructionist we've become.

OUR COLLECTIVE RESPONSIBILITY

To do these things, we'll need to be honest about where we currently are and, equally important, about the hard work that's needed to shape our future. America remains the greatest power the world has ever seen—politically, economically, militarily—and with great power comes great responsibility. Yet individually and collectively, we too often neglect our responsibilities as democracy's owners while demanding the entitlements of renters. In doing so, we focus on increasingly narrow, self-absorbing issues until we lose sight of the big picture.

A quarter century after the end of the Cold War, our last big national challenge, Americans have stopped asking big questions, and our politicians have stopped working on them.

Corporations, too, have a responsibility. Today, the further away an issue is from a company's core operations, the less likely it will be substantively addressed. Yet ever since the Supreme Court equated corporations with citizens and money with speech, the weight of corporate responsibility has only increased. We see a few American business leaders stepping up—Jeffrey Immelt, Chad Holliday, Tim Cook, and Indra Nooyi come to mind—but generally, corporate chieftains are not looking at the big picture; they're driven more by the tyranny of the quarterly report than an obligation to improve the human condition.

As a result, strategy and the big picture have become "somebody else's problem." The real problem is that there is no one else. If we don't do it, it won't get done.

It's time to grow up. Shaping the system is a hallmark of being a superpower. Many people assume that America's lack of effort toward reshaping the system is, therefore, intentional. We think the real answer is less calculated and more deeply concerning: Americans don't care enough and are distracted. In some areas, like trade, it has been possible to mobilize enough companies and citizens to forge a national consensus, but ultimately, today's trade deals are creatures of the twentieth century, artifacts of a system left on autopilot for too long. Zombies.

But we're not the walking dead. Far from it. We're citizens of the United States of America, a "government of the people, by the people, for the people," as Abraham Lincoln put it at Gettysburg, and if we don't want to see this great republic "perish from this earth," we, as citizens, whether on Wall Street or Main Street, need to get it on however we can. The future of our kids, our country, and our species isn't something we can afford to outsource, particularly to a body of folks who can't see past the next election.

Today, without waiting on Washington or the next existential crisis, this generation must begin taking responsibility for the whole thing, the big picture.

Along the way we'll have to learn about the world as it is—not as it was or as our ideologies tell us it should be, but how it actually is. And while we learn, we will need to make choices based on some concept, strategy, or plan. As General George Marshall understood, the value of strategy lies not so much in the plans as in the planning. By strengthening our strategic muscles we will once again be able to think at the scale of our problems and build and test new solutions, and in so doing, turn crises into opportunities. Just what you'd expect from the Land of Opportunity.

This is squarely on our shoulders. Previous generations could plausibly claim ignorance of the current system's global impact. The next generation will be locked into the infrastructure and decisions we make today. It's on us.

AMERICA THE BEAUTIFUL

We know what we've presented in this book is big and audacious, but this nation has done so many big, audacious things before just by tapping into what makes us Americans: a thirst for opportunity, a spirit of innovation, a stubborn grit, and an irrepressible belief that nothing is beyond our grasp. We can do it again.

That's what we've learned in writing this book and in talking to people across this nation. We're convinced more than ever that there is a way for America to get its mojo back. That citizens can actually shape our world today and build the world we want for tomorrow. That our small-minded politics needn't stop our high-minded ideals.

We've also learned that, in our history, the big ideas that have transformed the American experiment have come mostly from outside of Washington, as groups of patriotic citizens took charge and worked to fix the system and shape the future: the conference on Jekyll Island in 1910 that designed the Federal Reserve System; the arsenal of democracy, built and run by our hero Bill Knudsen and his corporate colleagues; the Southern Christian Leadership Conference, which coalesced and empowered the civil rights movement; the incredible resilience of the citizens of Greensburg, Detroit, and New Orleans to rebuild their devastated communities. Private action for the public good has consistently made big things happen. That is a defining characteristic of the American way. To succeed in the twenty-first century, with all its great problems and promise, we'll need to do that again, big time.

It's not that complicated. At the end of the day, our operating system is merely the sum of all the things that get done every day by people working to do a little better for themselves and their families. It's not just us 320 million Americans—it's all 7 billion of us, all at the same time, all on this one planet.

We have an opportunity to be the next Greatest Generation. Our best isn't behind us. We have much more "best" to discover and deliver. It's time to get to work. It's time to make some history. It is nothing less than the cause of all mankind.

ACKNOWLEDGMENTS

THIS BOOK REPRESENTS THE CONVERGENCE OF THREE INDIVIDUALS AND careers, along with a vast supporting cast who, individually and collectively, contributed ideas, inspiration, feedback, and support.

Grateful appreciation to Gail Ross of the Ross Yoon Agency, for believing in this book and shepherding it every step of the way. And to the dedicated team at St. Martin's Press: Emily Carleton, Donna Cherry, Laura Apperson, Annabella Hochschild, and others.

Thanks to Michael Martin of Effect Partners, who introduced Mark Mykleby and Joel Makower. To Dr. David Orr at Oberlin College, a visionary strategist for sustainability and sustainable communities, who has become a valued friend and thought partner for our work.

We owe a debt of gratitude to Chuck and Char Fowler for the generous financial support and their steadfast backing without which this book would not have been possible. And to Kate Wolford and the Board of the McKnight Foundation for allowing us to get version 1.0 into President Obama's "big ideas" binder.

There are many people who have supported the Strategic Innovation Lab (SIL) within the Fowler Center at Case Western Reserve University's Weatherhead School of Management, whose work is deeply intertwined with this book. Thanks to Dr. David Cooperrider for coming up with the idea of bringing the grand strategy work to Cleveland and introducing our work to Chuck Fowler. Also, thanks to Case Western's leadership, namely, Barbara Snyder, president of Case Western Reserve University; Rob Widing, dean of the Weatherhead School; Roger Saillant, director of the Fowler Center; and the Fowler Center Advisory Board members (Jacqueline Cambata, Lyell Clarke, Harry Halloran, Michele Hunt, Marcela Kanfer Rolnick, Peter Senge, Fred Tsao, and Nadya Zhexembayeva). Thanks to those in the university administration as well as faculty and staff across the campus that have been so supportive and involved in making the SIL a success.

And very special thanks to the SIL team: Dylan Beach, Nicole Brownell, Morgan Bulger, Jib Ellison, Sue Helper, Sara Gilbertson, Martin Goebel, Michael Kleeman, Molly McGuigan, Rick Miller, Bill Reilly, Lila Robinson, David Sherman, Steve Swartz, John Whalen, and Larry Wilkerson.

Many others provided insight and support, and they deserve recognition and thanks: Deb Amos, Tom Ashbrook, Ravi Agrawal, Amjad Atallah, Caroline Atkinson, Kenny Ausubel, Mallory Baches, Peter Bakker, Joe Bankoff, Jake Bartolomei, Bill Becker, John Berg, Bob Berkebile, McKenzie Beverage, Perminder Bindra, Phyllis Bleiweis, Arnauld de Borchgrave, Matt Bogoshian, Julian Boxenbaum, Kristin Brethova, Brodie Broland, Bill Brown, Garrett Budds, Dan Bubacz, AMB Nick Burns, Dan Chamby, Ben Cohen, Joel Cohen, Chip Comins, Marion Conlin, Ben Cross, Steve Cross, Michael Crow, Trammell Crow, Jr., Caren Dewar, Louise Diamond, Vince Dibianca, Michael DiVirgilio, Annie Donovan, Carol Dumaine, Chris Duston, Alyssa Dwyer, Jim Dwyer, Rick Edwards, Douglas Eger, Jeff Eggers, Richard Eidlin, Michael Ellis, PM Mike Eman, Margaret Evans, Steven Feldstein, Eric Faurot, Dave Feldman, Gordon Feller, Frank Femia, Leonard Ferrari, Bud Ferillo, Brian Fisher, Tom Fisher, Joe Fiksel, Mike Foley, Rosemarie Forsythe, Madilyn Fletcher, Rick Foster, Nena Fox, LTG Ben Freakley, Gil Friend, Matthew Freedman, Marc Frey, John Fullerton, Tom Gallagher, Bill Gannon, Anne Gibbon, Paul Glastris, John Glenn, Kathy Gockel, Mary Beth Goodman, Jamie Green, the entire GreenBiz team, Jonathan Greenblatt, Janet Gresham, Michael Gulich, Katherine Gullett, Rahul Gupta, Fred Haberman, Ray Haller, Paul Hamill, Heather Hamilton, Adam Happel, Fran Harris, Mark Harrison, Senator Gary Hart, Chip Hauss, Brian Helmuth, James Holbrook, Chad Holliday, Charles Holmes, Elliot Hoffman, Suzanne Hunt, AMB Robert Hunter, Jerri Husch, Former Congressman Bob Inglis, Dick Jackson, John Juhasz, Brian Kaiser, Richard Kauffman, Nasser Kazeminy and the National Ethnic Coalition of Organizations, Lorelei Kelly, Billy Keyserling, Richard Kidd, Meg King, Dan Kinkead, Avery Kintner, Brennan Klose, Stefano Kotsonis, Bud Krogh, Anita Joglekar, Kristen Joiner, John Lang, Roberta Lang, Annie Leahy, Eleanor LeCain, Chris Leinberger, Jeremy Lenz, David Levine, Fred Leyda, Peter Liljegren, Stephen Linaweaver, Michael Lind, Danielle Camner Linholm, Paulina Lis, Jim Locher, AMB Bob Loftis, Chris Lohmann, Phil Longman, Kristin Lord, Blaine Lotz, Amory Lovins, Irwin Lowenstein, Beth Lowery, Jim Ludes, Barry Lynn, Michele Malvesti, Andy Mangan, Steve Mann, Spider Marks, Dana Martin, Jim Matlack, Melissa Matlins, Susan Maybaumwisniewski, Tom McDermott, AMB John McDonald, Jessica McGlyn, Terrance McNally, Kate Meis, David Milliband, Alanna Mitchell, Matt Moran, Tom Morely, Chris Murray, Reese Neader, Deb Nelson, Jane Nelson, Uri Neren, Craig Newmark, Rolf Nordstrom, Senator Sam Nunn, Steve and Marie Nygren, Jared O'Connell, John O'Connor, Chris O'Keefe,

Dick O'Neill, Patrick O'Shea, Olofundeyi Olaitan, Noel Perry, Michael Peters, Dale Marie Pfeifer, Leslie Platt, Jonathan Powers, Jim Poyser, Alysson Pumphrey, Matt Purushotham, Tom Rautenberg, Sue Raftery, Anne Ralte, Celina Realuyo, Mayor Robert Reichert, Robert Ricigliano, Ben Riley, Greg Riley, Mayor Joe Riley, Mark Ritchie, Niel Ritchie, Joe Robertson, Ted Rolfvondenbaumen, Elliot Ross, Stewart Rowan, Caroline Savage, Patrick Schmidt, Brian Schupper, George Schwab, Tom Sebastian, Kabir Sehgal, Pam Sellers, Kahlil Seren, Jigar Shah, Andrew Shapiro, David Sherman, Nick Shufro, Sunny Simon, James and Marilyn Simons, Sarah Slaughter, Shanelle Smith, Gus Speth, Chuck Spinney, Frank Starkey, Pete Steen, Al Stokes, Jake Sullivan, Phaedra Svec, Kevin Sweeney, Jon Taplin, Hildy Teegan, Sherman Teichman, Carol Thaler, Alison Thomas, Alex Toma, Scott Truex, Tom Tyrrell, Mike Ursem, Parry VanLandingham, Kurt Volker, John Warbach, Jim Waring, Cheri Warren, Arnold Weinfeld, Linton Wells, Llew Wells, Caitlin Werrell, Mitzi Wertheim, Jim Wertsch, John Whalen, John and Margie Wheeler, Allan White, Daisy Nelson White, Scott Witter, Gary Wnek, Matt Wolf, Kate Wolford and the McKnight Foundation, Steve Wrage, John Yaeger, Juan Zarate, Sue Zielinski, Andrew Zolli, and Kim Zucker.

MARK MYKLEBY WISHES TO THANK:

My life in the Marine Corps delivered me to the place of this book. It would take an entire book to list all the Marines who deserve recognition and thanks. So, at the risk of seeming unappreciative to any single individual, I hope it is enough to say how proud and thankful I am to our nation and our Marine Corps for giving me the opportunity to serve "in every clime and place"; and to my fellow Marines for leading me, serving with me, and taking care of me. You all know who you are. Thank you and Semper Fi.

I also wish to thank the many leaders, mentors, and friends I served with while at the U.S. Special Operations Command (USSOCOM). Given that my work on national strategy began in earnest at USSOCOM, I would like to offer specific thanks to a few individuals. First, to COL George Thiebes, USA, for being my USSOCOM sponsor and introducing me to the SOF community. To ADM Eric Olson, USN (ret.) for the guidance he gave to the fledgling USSOCOM J56 strategy team as they set out in 2007 to develop the first ever comprehensive USSOCOM strategy: "Figure out how to get out in front of the guns." This very simple yet profound guidance opened my mind to view the world with more than military eyes and to elevate opportunity beyond threat and risk as a strategic driving force. Thanks to LTG David Fridovich, USA (ret.), former Director, Center for Special Operation (DCSO), for the guidance he offered, the intellectual freedom he extended, and the lofty standards he demanded that drove the Strategy Division's groundbreaking work. To SES and COL Joe Miller, USA (ret.), USSOCOM J5 Director, Strategy, Plans, and Policy, thanks for his energetic leadership and support, not to mention introducing the Systemic Operational Design theories of Israeli Defense Force BG (ret.) Shimon Naveh (and thanks to Shimon and his team for the mentorship and friendship). Also, thanks to Joe Miller for releasing me to the Pentagon when I was called upon to work on grand strategy. (Sorry it lasted two years rather than two months.)

Most importantly, thanks to the J56 strategy team during my time at USSOCOM: CAPT Joe Rogers, USN (ret.); Col Mike Malachowsky, USMC (ret.); LTC Gary Ramsdell, USA (ret.); Lt.Col. Sid Atwater, USMC (ret.); CDR Joel Royal, USN (ret.); COL Bob Jones, USA (ret.); LTC Hoot Gibson, USAF (ret.); CDR Disco Dittbenner, USN (ret.); MAJ Jeremy Kotkin, USA; LTC Scott Roxburgh, USAF; LTC Sweaty St. Onge, USAF (ret.); and COL Ken Hurst, USA (ret.). It was an unbelievable experience to watch this incredible team at work. I am thankful to them all for letting me be part of the team.

As for my time in the Pentagon, I must recognize CAPT Wayne Porter, USN (ret.) above all others. I will never be able to adequately thank my friend and running mate for dreaming up the grand strategy effort in the Pentagon and making me part of it. The written word fails to capture the scope of Wayne's brilliance, patriotism, tenacity, and friendship. Next to commanding a fighter squadron, the time I spent with Wayne creating *A National Strategic Narrative* was the most challenging and rewarding experience of my military career. It is with great pride and gratitude that I had the opportunity to serve with Wayne and can now call him and his wife, Kate, friends.

I would also like to thank former Chairman of the Joint Chiefs of Staff ADM Mike Mullen, USN (ret.), not only for the opportunity to work on grand strategy and for his support for *A National Strategic Narrative*, but also for his leadership, stewardship, integrity, and never-ending patience. It was a distinct honor to serve on his staff for two years. Thanks to all the members of ADM Mullen's personal staff for their never-ending support, notably: RADM Mike Gilday, USN; Dr. Lani Kass; and RADM John Kirby, USN (ret.). And thanks to the following additional supporters in the Pentagon: General Jim "Tamer" Amos, USMC (ret.); Kate Brandt, Rosa Brooks; Sharon Burke; CAPT Shoshana Chatfield, USN; Marian Cherry; LTG Mike Flynn, USA (ret.); ADM Bill Gortney, USN; GEN Charles Jacoby, USA (ret.); Richard Kidd; Gen John Paxton, USMC; VADM Ann Rondeau, USN (ret.); Gerry Roncolato; GEN Paul Selva, USAF; and James Swartout.

I would also like to give my heartfelt thanks to a few key people who provided critical support around Washington, D.C., during my time in the Pentagon. First, I am very thankful for the late Dr. David Abshire for taking me under his wing and affording me the opportunity to learn from one of America's great public servants. I would like to extend a special thanks to Tom Friedman of the

New York Times for his advice, mentorship, friendship, and support that began in 2010 and continues to this day. To the Honorable Bijan Kian, a true American patriot, thanks for the commitment, generosity, and friendship he has extended to both Wayne Porter and me over the years. To Air Vice Marshal Michael Harwood, RAF (ret.) (and to Group Captain Rob "Bed" Adlam, RAF (ret.) who introduced me to Harwood), a special thanks for both supporting and intellectually challenging the *Narrative* work. Having a U.K. perspective only made it better. To Dr. Janne Nolan, many thanks for guiding me through the murky waters of Washington, D.C. I would have been lost without the help. To former Congresswoman Jane Harman and the Woodrow Wilson International Center for Scholars, thanks for releasing the *Narrative* to the public domain and starting a new conversation about an American grand strategy for the twenty-first century. Finally, to Anne-Marie Slaughter, deepest thanks for the collaboration and the bureaucratic blocking and tackling she provided on our behalf while she was the Director of Policy and Plans at the State Department. Even more so, thanks for being the mouthpiece of the *Narrative* after it went public and for the continued support for the grand strategy work as it has developed to this day.

Moreover, there have been many friends who have provided constant and unwavering support. I am humbled by and grateful for their devotion and friendship. Owen Casas, who, on his own dime, printed copies of *A National Strategic Narrative* and delivered them to members of Congress. Betty Sproule and the National Strategic Narrative community who, as a collection of citizens acting on their own volition, established a website dedicated to spreading the concepts of the *Narrative* across the country and throughout the world. To Jeremy Kalin, thanks for the ongoing friendship and the never-ending education in financing (the flow of capital, after all, is what makes stuff real). To CAPT Kathy Harger, USN (ret.), thanks for the connections, ideas, and great friendship.

A special thanks to Col Ross "Migs" Roberts, USMC (ret.) for the lifelong camaraderie, for always thinking big, and for always being up for a few beers. Thanks as well to Bob Turner for the great friendship and for introducing me to the whole sustainability thing. None of this would have been possible without that burst of insight.

Finally, to my family (my mother and father, Nancy and Chuck; my brother Col. Scott Mykleby, USMC (ret.), sister-in-law Janice, nephew Paul, and niece Keaghlan; my sister Lisa Stockstad, brother-in-law Jim, nephew Tyler, and niece Anna; my father-in-law COL Dave Jenney, USAF (ret.) and mother-in-law Mary-Ellen; my sister-in-law Pam Jenney Irvine, nephew Harper, and niece Alice): thanks for the lifelong support and love you have always shown. Most important of all, thanks to my wife, Lisa, and son, Keaton, for all the love, support, patience, and humor. You keep my heart full and my hope for the future bright. You are what is best in my life. And for that, I am truly blessed and eternally grateful.

PATRICK DOHERTY WISHES TO THANK:

General Jack Galvin, USA, who passed away during the editing of this book, who introduced me to the concept of grand strategy in 1999. Cardinal Theodore McCarrick, for convincing me in 2003 that some initial musings written while in Belgrade had enough promise to warrant my coming back to Washington and for all the encouragement since. Tim Roemer and Steve Clemons, for a master's course in the ways and means of Washington. Steve Coll and Peter Bergen for giving me the platform to explore grand strategy and for inspiring me to write in long form. Larry Wilkerson, whose wisdom and experience provided the adult supervision I relied on so often. Tom Rautenberg, who sacrificed everything. And David Cooperrider for embracing and enhancing the vision and bringing us to his green city on a blue lake.

To my daughter Cecilia, this book is about ensuring that you get your American dream, and my beloved wife Anne, without your love and support none of this would be possible.

JOEL MAKOWER WISHES TO THANK:

A debt of gratitude to my associates at GreenBiz Group, in particular my two partners, Pete May and Eric Faurot, whose commitment to and support for this project cannot be overstated. I am blessed with a terrific and talented team of colleagues, whose individual and collective support have been instrumental in enabling me to engage in this worthy project.

Grateful appreciation is due an extraordinary corps of colleagues whose support, encouragement, and inspiration have been influential in my work and this book, including Andrew Beebe, Janine Benyus, Libby Bernick, Peter Byck, Aimée Christensen, Aron Cramer, John Davies, John Elkington, Rick Fedrizzi, Lisa Gansky, Alisa Gravitz, Chris Guenther, Marc Gunther, Paul Hawken, Denis Hayes, Van Jones, Greg Kats, Anne Kelly, Beth Lowery, Bob Langert, Sue Lebeck, Mindy Lubber, Richard Mattison, Liz Maw, Bill McDonough, Angela Nahikian, John Picard, Marty Pickett, Glenn Prickett, Will Rosenzweig, Will Sarni, Peter Schwartz, Rob Shelton, Galen Silvestri, Greg Staple, Alex Steffen, Elizabeth Sturcken, Mark Tercek, Bill Weihl, and Brandy Wilson.

To my family, including Diana and Beni Warshawsky and Lorraine and Norman Rosenberg and, especially, Randy Jayne Rosenberg, whose love and laughter are the foundation upon which all else stands. Finally, this book is dedicated to my mother, Frances Makower, who passed during our final days of writing, and whose support of my life and career are incalculable.

BIBLIOGRAPHY

GRAND STRATEGY

Abshire, David. "U.S. Global Policy: Toward an Agile Strategy." *Washington Quarterly* 19, no. 2 (June 1996): 41–61.

Ambrose, Stephen E. *Eisenhower: Soldier and President*. New York: Touchstone, 1990.

Art, Robert J. *A Grand Strategy for America*. Ithaca, NY: Cornell University Press, 2003.

Churchill, Winston. *Triumph and Tragedy*. Boston: Houghton Mifflin, 1953.

Doherty, Patrick C. "A New U.S. Grand Strategy." January 2013, ForeignPolicy .com. http://foreignpolicy.com/2013/01/09/a-new-u-s-grand-strategy.

Egan, Timothy. *The Worst Hard Time: The Untold Story of Those Who Survived the Great American Dust Bowl*. New York: Houghton Mifflin, 2006.

Flournoy, Michele, Vikram J. Singh, and Shawn Brimley. "Making America Grand Again: Toward a New Grand Strategy." Report for Center for a New American Security, 2008. http://www.cnas.org/publications/reports/making -america-grand-again-toward-a-new-grand-strategy.

Freedman, Lawrence. *Strategy: A History*. New York: Oxford University Press, 2013.

Gaddis, John Lewis. "What Is Grand Strategy?," speech, Woodrow Wilson School, Princeton University, Princeton, N.J., June 1, 2009. https://www.you tube.com/watch?v=5mTNH2Pe9IQ.

Haas, Richard N. *Foreign Policy Begins at Home: The Case for Putting America's House in Order*. New York: Basic Books, 2013

Hart, Gary. *The Fourth Power: A Grand Strategy for the United States in the Twenty-First Century*. Oxford: Oxford University Press, 2004.

Herman, Arthur. *Freedom's Forge: How American Business Produced Victory in World War II*. New York: Random House, 2012.

Ikenberry, G. John, and Anne-Marie Slaughter, codirectors. "Forging a World of Liberty Under Law: U.S. National Security in the Twenty-First Century," Final Report of the Princeton Project on National Security. Princeton, N.J.: Woodrow Wilson School of International Affairs, September 26, 2006. https://www.princeton.edu/~ppns/report/FinalReport.pdf.

Kennan, George F. *Memoirs: 1925–1950*. Boston: Atlantic Monthly Press, 1967.

Kennedy, Paul. "Grand Strategy in War and Peace: Toward a Broader Definition." In *Grand Strategies in War and Peace,* ed. Paul Kennedy, 1–7. New Haven, CT: Yale University Press, 1991.

"Memorandum to the National Security Council by the Executive Secretary (Lay). Subject: Project Solarium." July 22, 1953. *Foreign Relations of the United States,* 1952–1954, vol. 2, pt. 1, National Security Affairs, Document 79, U.S. Department of State, Office of the Historian, Washington, D.C. https://history.state.gov/historicaldocuments/frus1952-54v02p1/d79.

Mykleby, Mark, and Wayne Porter. *A National Strategic Narrative.* Woodrow Wilson International Center for Scholars, Washington, D.C., April 2011. https://www.wilsoncenter.org/sites/default/files/A%20National%20Strategic%20Narrative.pdf.

"NSC-68: A Report to the National Security Council by the Executive Secretary on United States Objectives and Programs for National Security." April 14, 1950. Washington, D.C. https://history.state.gov/historicaldocuments/frus1952-54v02p1/comp1.

"NSC-162/2: A Report to the National Security Council by the Executive Secretary on Basic National Security Policy." October 30, 1953. Washington, D.C. https://fas.org/irp/offdocs/nsc-hst/nsc-162-2.pdf.

Paine, Thomas. *Common Sense.* London: Penguin Books, 1976.

Perry, Mark. *Partners in Command: George Marshall and Dwight Eisenhower in War and Peace.* New York: Penguin Press, 2007.

Schlesinger, Arthur M., Jr. *The Coming of the New Deal.* Boston: Houghton Mifflin, 1959.

Truman, Harry S. "Memorandum and Statement of Policy on the Need for Industrial Dispersion." August 10, 1951. Harry S. Truman Public Papers, Harry S. Truman Library and Museum, Independence, Mo. https://trumanlibrary.org/publicpapers/index.php?pid=404.

GLOBAL TRENDS & SYSTEMS

Brown, Lester R. *World on the Edge: How to Prevent Environmental and Economic Collapse.* New York: W. W. Norton, 2011.

Brynjolfsson, Erik, and Andrew McAfee. *Race Against the Machine: How the Digital Revolution Is Accelerating Innovation, Driving Productivity, and Irreversibly Transforming Employment and the Economy.* Lexington, Mass.: Digital Frontier Press, 2011.

Burrows, Mathew, et al. "Global Trends 2030." National Intelligence Council, 2013. http://www.dni.gov/files/documents/GlobalTrends_2030.pdf.

Calthorpe, Peter. *Urbanism in the Age of Climate Change.* Washington, D.C.: Island Press, 2011.

Charles, Prince of Wales. *The Prince's Speech: On the Future of Food.* New York: Rodale Books, 2012.

Clifton, Jim. *The Coming Jobs War.* New York: Gallup Press, 2011.

Collier, Paul. *The Bottom Billion: Why the Poorest Countries Are Failing and What Can Be Done About It.* Oxford: Oxford University Press, 2007.

Costanza, Robert, et al. "Changes in the Global Value of Ecosystem Services." *Global Environmental Change* 26 (2014): 152–58. http://www.sciencedirect.com/science/article/pii/S0959378014000685.

Dalio, Ray. "How the Economic Machine Works." Bridgewater Associates, 2015. http://www.virginiacec.org/manual/how-the-economic-machine-works-bridgewater-associates.html.

Doerr, John, and Jeff Immelt. "U.S. Needs to Lead in Clean Energy Future." *Washington Post,* August 3, 2009. http://www.washingtonpost.com/wp-dyn/content/article/2009/08/02/AR2009080201563.html.

Ellen MacArthur Foundation. "Towards the Circular Economy: Opportunities for the Consumer Goods Sector." Ellen MacArthur Foundation, 2013. http://www.ellenmacarthurfoundation.org/publications.

Friedman, Thomas. *Hot, Flat and Crowded: Why We Need a Green Revolution—And How It Can Renew America.* New York: Picador, 2008.

Generation Foundation. "Allocating Capital for Long-Term Returns." Generation Foundation, May 2015. https://www.genfound.org/media/pdf-genfound-wp2015-final.pdf.

International Energy Agency. "World Energy Outlook 2012." International Energy Agency, 2012. http://www.worldenergyoutlook.org/weo2012/.

Intergovernmental Panel on Climate Change, 2014. *Climate Change 2014: Synthesis Report.* Contribution of Working Groups I, II and III to the Fifth Assessment Report of the Intergovernmental Panel on Climate Change [Core Writing Team, R. K. Pachauri and L. A. Meyer (eds.)]. IPCC, Geneva, Switzerland, 151 pp. http://www.ipcc.ch/report/ar5/syr/.

Jacobsen, Mark Z., and Mark A. Delucchi. "A Path to Sustainable Energy by 2030." *Scientific American,* November 2009. https://web.stanford.edu/group/efmh/jacobson/Articles/I/sad1109Jaco5p.indd.pdf.

Lovins, Amory, and Rocky Mountain Institute. *Reinventing Fire: Bold Business Solutions for the New Energy Era.* White River Junction, Vt.: Chelsea Green, 2011.

Lovins, Amory, et al. *Winning the Oil Endgame: Innovation for Profits, Jobs, and Security.* Snowmass, Colo.: Rocky Mountain Institute, 2005.

Lynn, Barry C. *End of the Line: The Rise and Coming Fall of the Global Corporation.* New York: Doubleday, 2005.

Millennium Ecosystem Assessment. *Ecosystems and Human Well-being: Synthesis.* Washington, D.C.: Island Press, 2005.

Mitchell, Joshua. *Tocqueville in Arabia: Dilemmas in a Democratic Age.* Chicago: University of Chicago Press, 2013.

Morris, Ian. *Why the West Rules—For Now: The Patterns of History, and What They Reveal About the Future.* New York: Farrar, Strauss and Giroux, 2010.

Nidumolu, Ram, C. K. Prahalad, and M. R. Rangaswami. "Why Sustainability Is Now the Key Driver of Innovation." *Harvard Business Review,* October 2012.

Organization for Economic Cooperation and Development/Food and Agriculture Organization of the United Nations. *OECD-FAO Agricultural Outlook 2015.* Paris: OECD Publishing, 2015. http://dx.doi.org/10.1787/agr_outlook-2015-en.

Paskal, Cleo. *Global Warring: How Environmental, Economic, and Political Crises Will Redraw the World Map.* New York: Palgrave Macmillan, 2010.

Piketty, Thomas. *Capital in the Twenty-First Century.* Cambridge, Mass.: Harvard University Press, 2014.

Schwenninger, Sherle R., and Samuel Sherraden. "The U.S. Economy After the Great Recession: America's Deleveraging and Recovery Experience." Economic Growth Program, New America. March 2014. https://www.newamerica.org/economic-growth/the-us-economy-after-the-great-recession/.

Sen, Amartya. *Development as Freedom*. New York: Alfred A. Knopf, 1999.

Wolf, Martin. *Fixing Global Finance*. Baltimore, Md.: Johns Hopkins University Press, 2008.

Wolf, Martin. *The Shifts and Shocks: What We've Learned—and Have Still to Learn—from the Financial Crisis*. New York: Penguin Press, 2014.

World Economic Forum. "Global Risks 2014: Ninth Edition." World Economic Forum, 2014. www.weforum.org/risks.

Yergin, Daniel. *The Prize: The Epic Quest for Oil, Money, and Power*. New York: Touchstone, 1991.

DOMESTIC POLICY

Calthorpe, Peter. *The Next American Metropolis: Ecology, Community, and the American Dream*. Princeton, N.J.: Princeton Architectural Press, 1993.

Columbia University Mailman School of Public Health. "Obesity Kills More Americans Than Previously Thought." August 12, 2013. https://www.mailman.columbia.edu/public-health-now/news/obesity-kills-more-americans-previously-thought.

Conant, Jennet. *Tuxedo Park: A Wall Street Tycoon and the Secret Palace of Science That Changed the Course of World War II*. New York: Simon & Schuster, 2003.

Duany, A., E. Plater-Zyberk, and J. Speck. *Suburban Nation: The Rise of Sprawl and the Decline of the American Dream*. New York: North Point Press, 2000.

Dunham-Jones, Ellen. "Retrofitting Suburbia," TEDxAtlanta, January 2010. https://www.ted.com/talks/ellen_dunham_jones_retrofitting_suburbia.

Howard, Ebenezer. *Garden Cities of Tomorrow*. London: S. Sonnenschein, 1902.

Johnson, Steven. *Where Good Ideas Come From: The Natural History of Innovation*. New York: Penguin Group, 2010.

Kincaid, Ellie. "California Isn't the Only State with Water Problems." *Business Insider,* April 21, 2015. http://www.businessinsider.com/americas-about-to-hit-a-water-crisis-2015-4.

Likosky, Michael. *Obama's Bank: Financing a Durable New Deal*. Cambridge: Cambridge University Press, 2010.

Mackey, John, and Ragendra Sisodia. *Conscious Capitalism: Liberating the Heroic Spirit of Business*. Cambridge, Mass.: Harvard Business Review Press, 2013.

Moskowitz, Peter. "Emission Statement: A Carbon Tax Won't Happen Anytime Soon. Chevrolet Just Proved It Should." *Slate,* November 19, 2014. http://www.slate.com/articles/business/moneybox/2014/11/chevrolet_buying_carbon_credits_how_the_carmaker_just_showed_a_carbon_tax.html.

Nelson, Arthur C. *Reshaping Metropolitan America: Development Trends and Opportunities to 2030*. Washington, D.C.: Island Press, 2013.

Orr, David W. *Hope Is an Imperative: The Essential David Orr*. Washington, D.C.: Island Press, 2011.

Plumer, Brad. "Eight Facts About Terrorism in the United States." *Washington Post,* April 16, 2013. http://www.washingtonpost.com/news/wonkblog/wp/2013/04/16/eight-facts-about-terrorism-in-the-united-states/.

Rodale Institute. "The Farming Systems Trial." Fall 2011. http://66.147.244.123/~rodalein/wp-content/uploads/2012/12/FSTbookletFINAL.pdf.

Samuelson, Robert. "Three Myths About the Highway Trust Fund." *Washington Post,* July 9, 2014. https://www.washingtonpost.com/opinions/robert-samuel

son-three-myths-about-the-highway-trust-fund/2014/07/09/edb7c758
-0770-11e4-a0dd-f2b22a257353_story.html.

Spence, Roy M. *It's Not What You Sell, It's What You Stand For.* New York: Portfolio, 2009.

Zelizer, Julian. *Arsenal of Democracy: The Politics of National Security—From World War II to the War on Terrorism.* New York: Basic Books, 2008.

FOREIGN POLICY

Barnett, Thomas P. M. *The Pentagon's New Map: War and Peace in the Twenty-First Century.* New York: Berkley Books, 2004.

Brzezinski, Zbigniew. *Second Chance: Three Presidents and the Crisis of American Superpower.* New York: Basic Books, 2007.

Brzezinski, Zbigniew, and Brent Scowcroft. *America and the World: Conversations on the Future of American Foreign Policy.* New York: Basic Books, 2008.

Chua, Amy. *World on Fire: How Exporting Free Market Democracy Breeds Ethnic Hatred and Global Instability.* New York: Doubleday, 2003.

Foley, Jonathan A. "Can We Feed the World and Sustain the Planet? A Five-Step Plan Could Double Food Production by 2050 While Greatly Reducing Environmental Damage." Science of Food Special Collector's Edition, *Scientific American* (summer 2015): 84–89.

Hachigian, Nina, and Mona Sutphen. *The Next American Century: How the U.S. Can Thrive as Other Powers Rise.* New York: Doubleday, 2008.

Kennan, George F. *American Diplomacy.* Chicago: University of Chicago Press, 2012.

Kennan, George F. *Realities of American Foreign Policy.* Princeton, N.J.: Princeton University Press, 1954.

Klare, Michael. *The Race for What's Left: The Global Scramble for the World's Last Resources.* New York: Metropolitan Books, 2012.

Koenig, Peter. "Russia and China: The Dawning of a New Monetary System?" Global Research, January 9, 2015. http://www.globalresearch.ca/russia-and -china-the-dawning-of-a-new-monetary-system/5423637.

Lehane, Sinead. "China's Water-Energy Nexus Challenge." Future Directions International, May 6, 2014. http://www.futuredirections.org.au/publications /food-and-water-crises/1668-china-s-water-energy-nexus-challenge.html.

Schmidt, Eric, and Jared Cohen. *The New Digital Age.* New York: Alfred A. Knopf, 2013.

Slaughter, Anne-Marie, and Thomas Hale. *The Idea That Is America: Keeping Faith with Our Values in a Dangerous World.* New York: Basic Books, 2007.

United Nations Department of Economic and Social Affairs. "2014 Revision of the World Urbanization Prospects." July 10, 2014. https://www.un.org/devel opment/desa/publications/2014-revision-world-urbanization-prospects.html.

"Where China's Future Will Happen." *Economist,* April 19, 2014. http://www .economist.com/news/leaders/21601027-worlds-sake-and-its-own-china -needs-change-way-it-builds-and-runs-its.

GOVERNING INSTITUTIONS

Fukuyama, Francis. *The Origins of Political Order.* New York: Farrar, Straus and Giroux, 2011.

GovTrack. "U.S. Congress List of Committees." July 21, 2015. https://www
.govtrack.us/congress/committees/.

Hanauer, Nick, and Eric Liu. *The Gardens of Democracy: A New American Story of Citizenship, the Economy, and the Role of Government.* Seattle: Sasquatch Books, 2011.

Project on National Security Reform. *Forging a New Shield.* Arlington, Va.: Project on National Security Reform, 2008.

Rousseau, Jean-Jacques. *The Social Contract.* New York: Penguin Group, 2006.

Tocqueville, Alexis de. *Democracy in America.* New York: New American Library, 2001.

WALKABLE COMMUNITIES

BCC Research. "Smart Cities: Growing New Markets for Information Technology." June 2015. http://www.bccresearch.com/market-research/information -technology/smart-cities-growing-new-markets-information-technology -report-ift115a.html.

CEOs for Cities. "Walking the Walk: How Walkability Raises Home Values in U.S. Cities." August 2009. http://www.reconnectingamerica.org/assets/Uplo ads/2009WalkingTheWalkCEOsforCities.pdf.

Doherty, Patrick C., and Christopher B. Leinberger. "The Next Real Estate Boom: How Housing (Yes, Housing) Can Turn the Economy Around." *Washington Monthly,* November/December 2010. http://www.washingtonmonthly.com /features/2010/1011.doherty-leinberger.html.

Labrador, David, and Rocky Mountain Institute. "A Small Iowa Town Embraces Energy Independence." *GreenBiz,* June 2015. http://www.greenbiz.com/art icle/small-iowa-town-embraces-energy-independence.

Leinberger, Christopher B. "Now Coveted: A Walkable, Convenient Place." *New York Times,* May 25, 2012. http://www.nytimes.com/2012/05/27/opinion /sunday/now-coveted-a-walkable-convenient-place.html.

Leinberger, Christopher B. *The Option of Urbanism: Investing in a New American Dream.* Washington, D.C.: Island Press, 2009.

Leinberger, Christopher B., and Mariela Alfonzo. "Walk This Way: The Economic Promise of Walkable Places in Metropolitan Washington, D.C." Brookings Institution, Metropolitan Policy Program, May 2012. http://www.brookings .edu/research/papers/2012/05/25-walkable-places-leinberger.

Leinberger, Christopher B. *The WalkUP Wake-Up Call.* The Center for Real Estate and Urban Analysis, George Washington University, September 2012. http:// www.smartgrowthamerica.org/documents/walkup-wake-up-atlanta.pdf.

McKinsey Global Institute. "Urban World: Mapping the Economic Power of Cities." McKinsey Global Institute, March 2011. http://www.mckinsey.com /insights/urbanization/urban_world.

Orr, David W. "Systems Thinking and the Future of Cities." *Solutions* 5, no. 1 (2014). http://www.resilience.org/stories/2014-05-30/systems-thinking-and -the-future-of-cities.

National Association of Realtors. "National Community Preference: Frequencies, September 18–24, 2013." http://www.realtor.org/sites/default/files/reports /2013/2013-community-preference-topline-results.pdf.

PwC and Urban Land Institute. "Emerging Trends in Real Estate 2015." October 2014. https://www.pwc.com/us/en/asset-management/real-estate/assets /pwc-emerging-trends-in-real-estate-2015.pdf.

Siemens, PwC, and Berwin Leighton Paisner. "Investor Ready Cities: How Cities Can Create and Deliver Infrastructure Value." 2014. http://www.pwc.com /gx/en/industries/government-public-services/public-sector-research-centre /publications/investor-ready-cities-how-cities-can-create-and-deliver-infra structure-value.html.

Smart Growth America and Cushman & Wakefield Center for Real Estate and Urban Analysis. "Core Values: Why American Companies Are Moving Downtown." 2015. http://www.smartgrowthamerica.org/documents/core-va lues.pdf.

Stephenson, Bruce. "The Roots of the New Urbanism: John Nolen's Garden City Ethic." *Journal of Planning History* 1, no. 2 (May 2002): 99–123. http://www .livingnewurbanism.com/#!publications/c1m0m.

SustainAbility. "The Case for Corporate Leadership in Urban Sustainability." May 2015. http://www.sustainability.com/library/citystates-II.

Urban Land Institute. "Americans' Views on Their Communities, Housing, and Transportation." March 2013. http://uli.org/wp-content/uploads/ULI-Doc uments/America-in-2013-Final-Report.pdf.

REGENERATIVE AGRICULTURE

Bittman, Mark, Michael Pollan, Ricardo Salvador, and Olivier De Schutter. "How a National Food Policy Could Save Millions of American Lives." *Washington Post,* November 7, 2014. https://www.washingtonpost.com/opinions/how-a -national-food-policy-could-save-millions-of-american-lives/2014/11/07/89 c55e16-637f-11e4-836c-83bc4f26eb67_story.html.

Byck, Peter. "Soil Carbon Cowboys." Video, May 2014. https://vimeo.com/805 18559.

Center for Food Safety. "Food & Climate: Connecting the Dots, Choosing the Way Forward." March 2014. http://www.centerforfoodsafety.org/reports/2947 /food-and-climate-connecting-the-dots-choosing-the-way-forward.

Cook, Christopher D. "Seed Libraries Fight for the Right to Share." *Shareable,* February 11, 2015. http://www.shareable.net/blog/seed-libraries-fight-for-the -right-to-share.

Cox, Craig, Andrew Hug, and Nils Bruzelius. "Losing Ground." Environmental Working Group, April 2011. http://www.panna.org/sites/default/files /losingground_EWG%20report%204_11.pdf.

Grey, Clark, Shih and Associates. "Farming the Mailbox: U.S. Federal and State Subsidies to Agriculture," November 2010. http://www.greyclark.com/wp -content/uploads/2014/05/DFC_Study_on_US_Expenditures_2010_FI NAL-rvsd-Nov-14_w-footer-added.pdf.

Food & Water Watch. "The Economic Cost of Food Monopolies," November 2012. http://www.foodandwaterwatch.org/insight/economic-cost-food-mon opolies.

Gewin, Virginia. "Crop Gene Banks Are Preserving the Future of Agriculture. But Who's Preserving Them?" *Ensia,* May 21, 2015. http://ensia.com/fea tures/crop-gene-banks-are-preserving-the-future-of-agriculture-but-whos -preserving-them.

Goode, Erica. "Farmers Put Down the Plow for More Productive Soil." *New York Times,* March 9, 2015. http://www.nytimes.com/2015/03/10/science/farm ers-put-down-the-plow-for-more-productive-soil.html.

Kelley, Emily C. "NMSU Researcher's Carbon Sequestration Work Highlighted in 'The Soil Will Save Us.'" New Mexico State University science blog, July 8, 2014. http://nmsu.scienceblog.com/2014/08/21/nmsu-researchers-carbon-sequestration-work-highlighted-in-the-soil-will-save-us/.

Marin Carbon Project. http://www.marincarbonproject.org/.

Rushing, James, and Jens Ruehle. "Buying into the Local Food Movement," A.T. Kearney, July 2012. https://www.atkearney.com/documents/10192/709903/Buying+into+the+Local+Food+Movement.pdf.

Salatin, Joel. *Folks, This Ain't Normal: A Farmer's Advice for Happier Healthier People, and a Better World.* New York: Center Street, 2011.

United Nations Conference on Trade and Development. "Trade and Environment Review 2013." September 2013. http://unctad.org/en/PublicationsLibrary/ditcted2012d3_en.pdf.

World Bank. "Carbon Sequestration in Agricultural Soils." May 2012. http://documents.worldbank.org/curated/en/2012/05/16274087/carbon-sequestration-agricultural-soils.

RESOURCE PRODUCTIVITY

D'Aveni, Richard. "The 3-D Printing Revolution." *Harvard Business Review,* May 2015. https://hbr.org/2015/05/the-3-d-printing-revolution.

Dobbs, Richard, Jeremy Oppenheim, Fraser Thompson, Marcel Brinkman, and Marc Zornes. "Resource Revolution: Meeting the World's Energy, Materials, Food, and Water Needs." McKinsey Global Institute, November 2011. http://www.mckinsey.com/insights/energy_resources_materials/resource_revolution.

Economic Development Research Group. "Economic Impacts of Intelligent Infrastructure." May 2015. http://www.edrgroup.com/library/economic-impact-analysis/economic-impacts-of-intelligent-infrastructure-2015.html.

General Electric. "Digital Resource Productivity: Ecomagination, the Industrial Internet, and the Global Resource Challenge." October 2014. https://www.ge.com/sites/default/files/ge_digital_resource_productivity_whitepaper.pdf.

Heck, Stefan, Matt Rogers, and Paul Carroll. *Resource Revolution: How to Capture the Biggest Business Opportunity in a Century.* New York: New Harvest, 2014.

McDonough, William, and Michael Braungart. *Cradle to Cradle: Remaking the Way We Make Things.* New York: North Point Press, 2002.

McKinsey Global Institute. "The Internet of Things: Mapping the Value Beyond the Hype." McKinsey Global Institute, June 2015. http://www.mckinsey.com/~/media/McKinsey/dotcom/Insights/Business%20Technology/Unlocking%20the%20potential%20of%20the%20Internet%20of%20Things/Unlocking_the_potential_of_the_Internet_of_Things_Full_report.ashx.

Muro, Mark, Jonathan Rothwell, Scott Andes, Kenan Fikri, and Siddharth Kulkarni. "America's Advanced Industries: What They Are, Where They Are, and Why They Matter." Brookings Advanced Industry Project, February 2015. http://www.brookings.edu/research/reports2/2015/02/03-advanced-industries.

PWC. "3D Printing and the New Shape of Industrial Manufacturing." June 2014. http://www.pwc.com/us/en/industrial-products/3d-printing.html.

INDEX

ABOUT THE AUTHORS

Mark Mykleby is a founder and codirector of the Strategic Innovation Lab at Case Western Reserve University. He was commissioned as a second lieutenant in the Marine Corps following his graduation from the U.S. Naval Academy in 1987. Designated as a qualified F/A-18 pilot in December 1990, he served in five fleet fighter squadrons from 1991 to 2006, executing numerous land-based and ship-borne deployments to the European, Pacific, and Southwest Asian theaters in support of Operations Provide Promise, Deny Flight, Southern Watch, Enduring Freedom, and Iraqi Freedom.

In 2007, Mykleby was assigned to the U.S. Special Operations Command, where he developed strategy for the Special Operations Forces. From 2009 until 2011, he served as a special strategic assistant to the Chairman of the Joint Chiefs of Staff. In that capacity, he coauthored with Navy Captain Wayne Porter *A National Strategic Narrative,* a concept and vision for a twenty-first-century grand strategy for the nation. Mykleby retired from the Marine Corps in 2011. From 2011 until 2014, he served as a senior fellow at the New America Foundation, working alongside Patrick Doherty to develop the framework for a new U.S. grand strategy.

Patrick Doherty is a founder and codirector of the Strategic Innovation Lab at Case Western Reserve University. He is a strategist focused on the intersection of macroeconomics, sustainability, and national security. Previously, Doherty was deputy director of the National Security Studies Program at the New America Foundation in Washington, D.C., where he worked with Puck Mykleby to develop a coherent approach to grand strategy in the twenty-first century.

Before joining New America, Doherty was director of communications at the Center for National Policy, a senior editor at TomPaine.com, and spent more than ten years in the Middle East, Africa, the Balkans, and the Caucasus, working at the intersection of conflict and development. He was a research associate at the Harvard Negotiation Project and holds a master's degree in security studies from the Fletcher School of Law and Diplomacy at Tufts University and a bachelor's degree from the School of International Service at American University.

Joel Makower is chairman and executive editor of GreenBiz Group, Inc., a media and events company focusing on the intersection of sustainable business and clean technology. Makower hosts the annual GreenBiz forums as well as the VERGE conferences produced around the world by his company, and he is principal author of GreenBiz's annual "State of Green Business" report. He also serves as a senior fellow at the Strategic Innovation Lab at Case Western Reserve University.

A former nationally syndicated columnist, Makower is author of more than a dozen other books, including *Strategies for the Green Economy* (2008), *The E-Factor* (1993), and *Beyond the Bottom Line* (1994), among the earliest books on corporate environmental responsibility and corporate social responsibility. In 2012, he was awarded the Hutchens Medal by the American Society for Quality, which cited "his ability to tell compelling stories that both inform and inspire business leaders toward profitable action." In 2014, he was inducted into the Hall of Fame of the International Institute of Sustainability Professionals. The Associated Press has called him "the guru of green business practices."

ABOUT THE STRATEGIC INNOVATION LAB

The mission of the Strategic Innovation Lab (SIL) is to catalyze and support a new American grand strategy for the twenty-first century. Based at Case Western Reserve University in Cleveland, Ohio, SIL is implementing a top-down, bottom-up grand strategic framework that places the economic and security logic of sustainability at the center of a new national strategy.

As a starting point, SIL has launched the Economic Strategy Task Force—a process to bring together more than 100 national business leaders from ten major economic sectors along with 30 civil society leaders and subject matter experts—to develop a new "Business Plan for America," a business-led macro-economic path to a new era of American prosperity and security. At the same time, SIL is working from the bottom up, developing and launching regional-level economic development initiatives across the United States that capture, leverage, and amplify the economic opportunities that sustainability offers to Main Street USA.

Taken together, this top-down, bottom-up approach is designed to show that American citizens at all levels can shape the future of their country—and they don't need to wait on Washington, D.C., to get started.

For more information, visit www.strategicinnovationlab.org.